Indian Media
in a Globalised World

Indian Media
in a Globalised World

Maya Ranganathan
Usha M. Rodrigues

⑤SAGE www.sagepublications.com
Los Angeles • London • New Delhi • Singapore • Washington DC

First published in 2010 by

SAGE Publications India Pvt Ltd
B1/I-1 Mohan Cooperative Industrial Area
Mathura Road, New Delhi 110 044, India
www.sagepub.in

SAGE Publications Inc
2455 Teller Road
Thousand Oaks, California 91320, USA

SAGE Publications Ltd
1 Oliver's Yard, 55 City Road
London EC1Y 1SP, United Kingdom

SAGE Publications Asia-Pacific Pte Ltd
33 Pekin Street
#02-01 Far East Square
Singapore 048763

Published by Vivek Mehra for SAGE Publications India Pvt Ltd, Typeset in 10.5/12.5 pt Adobe Garamond Pro by Tantla Composition Pvt Ltd, Chandigarh and printed at Chaman Enterprises, New Delhi.

Library of Congress Cataloging-in-Publication Data

Ranganathan, Maya.
　　Indian media in a globalised world/Maya Ranganathan, Usha M. Rodrigues.
　　　　p. cm.
　　Includes index.
　　1. Mass media—India.　2. Mass media—Social aspects—India.　3. Mass media—Economic aspects—India.　4. Globalisation—Social aspects—India.
I. Rodrigues, Usha M.　II. Title.

P92.I7R38　　　　　302.230954—dc22　　　　2010　　　　2010015417

ISBN: 978-81-321-0401-8 (HB)

The SAGE Team: Elina Majumdar, Swati Sengupta, Anju Saxena
and Trinankur Banerjee

For my parents Janaki and (late) J. Ranganathan.
–Maya Ranganathan

For my children Isaac and Rishika.
–Usha M. Rodrigues

Contents

Acknowledgements

The idea for this book germinated a couple of years ago. However, it required one of the authors to move to Australia from India in 2007 for the idea to take further shape. Since then it has meant more shifts, lots of juggling and heaps of hard work, all of which was possible, thanks to the guidance, support and encouragement of a number of people.

Maya Ranganathan thanks the generous help extended by Monash University in the form of a grant to travel to India for data collection in 2008. She is appreciative of the support extended by the School of Humanities, Communication and Social Sciences (HUMCASS), especially its research director Professor Jenny Hocking. She acknowledges the insightful comments on various issues covered in the book by her Indian friends—columnist Gnani, Observer Research Foundation Chennai director N. Sathiya Moorthy, *Business Line* correspondent Mony K. Mathew, *Frontline* correspondent T.S. Subramaniam, Loyola College Professor S. Rajanayakam and Advocate T. Venugopal. She thanks author Vamanan nee' N. Krishnaswamy, Radio One station director in Chennai Navaneet and Dr James Gomez of School of Humanities, Communication and Social Sciences, Monash University, Victoria, Australia—for the time and effort they dedicated to commenting on initial drafts of some of the chapters. The painstaking references have been made possible by the quick and most efficient response from Manipal Institute of Communication librarian Rathi Nair. Three chapters in the book were written with the help of the excellent research of three students of Manipal Institute of Communication—Judhajit Bagchi, Bernadette Lobo and Shiva Roy-Chowdhury—who dealt with the issues in their post-graduate dissertations. Special thanks are also due to Ragamallika Karthikeyan for recording episodes of 'mega serials'. Seline Augustine was there from the beginning, working as an informal research assistant in Chennai, and so also Jerry, who helped in many ways to help the project proceed smoothly.

Usha M. Rodrigues is grateful to her husband Sunitho Rodrigues for his unflinching support in undertaking yet another research project. She is also humbled by her children's patience and love to allow Mom to work on the chapters. Usha would also like to thank her sister Poonam and brother Raj for their constant support. Some of these chapters stem from her PhD research, for which she is thankful to her supervisors: Dr Chris Lawe Davies and Dr Levi Obijiofor at the University of Queensland. The writing of the two chapters on citizen journalism and print media in India were supported by a grant provided by the Public Memory Research Centre at the University of Southern Queensland.

Introduction

In November 2006, an exhibition on Bollywood was organised 9,802 km from the place where it originated. In the Immigration Museum in Melbourne, Australia, a small theatre showed clips from Bollywood films, while in the room next door, life behind the celluloid was documented in photographs. In the days that followed, the city played host to an academic seminar, 'Transnational Dialogues on Bollywood: Australian Perspectives'. Bollywood dance schools and regular Hindi film screenings ensured that Australians were no strangers to the largest film industry in the world. The global Indian brand, Bollywood, had won over yet another country. The time-tested formula of heroism, romance and tradition could be packaged more sophisticatedly to draw audiences from cultures across the world.

Since the liberalisation of the 1990s, the Indian media has been growing phenomenally. In May 2009, the World Association of Newspapers (WAN) said that India was one of the developing markets where newspaper readership figures were constantly increasing. At the time of independence in 1947, the Indian population was around 345 million (Srinivasan 2004), with the literacy rate averaging around 18 per cent (Rao 2002). There were 214 newspapers including 44 English newspapers published in India (Shrivastava 2008), and there were six All India Radio (AIR) stations and no television network (All India Radio 2006). The Indian print media, which had played a significant role in the freedom movement, has since then multiplied to 62,483 registered newspapers (Registrar of Newspapers for India 2008), and according to National Readership Survey, Indian newspapers and magazines are being read by 222 million readers (Shrivastava 2008). Meanwhile, there are more than 500 radio stations and nearly 450 television channels broadcasting news, entertainment and other programmes in India (Indiantelevision.com 2009a, 2009b). The media—print, radio, television and online—at present, caters to a huge market by any standards with 1.1 billion people, of which more than 65 per cent are literate. The phenomenal growth of media in India, along with potential audience numbers, has today made Indian media and entertainment industry one of the most vibrant sectors in the world.

The globalisation era, which has reached the Indian economy via competition and investment from overseas in the media industry, seems to have transformed the media industry in India, which is going through one of its most exciting phases in post-independence times. When the Government of India reversed its protectionist economic policies in the 1990s to allow foreign investment and goods to flow into the country to increase the domestic industrial sector's efficacy, it also opened the country to foreign ownership. Television was the first to experience the *de facto* regulation, and as a result of the entry of foreign and private channels, the industry was transformed from a government-owned single network to a multi-channel industry. The opening of Indian doors to satellite television from overseas was not confined to its television industry alone. Technological advances and the introduction of entrepreneurial media management strategies also changed the traditional print media industry in India. As a result, newspaper circulation has continued to grow in India, particularly in non-English languages where print media adopted a strategy of 'localisation' of news to reach smaller towns and rural India.

This volume addresses the various issues that have impacted or failed to impact on Indian media in the era of globalisation. It contains empirical details of how the Indian media has evolved in the age of globalisation as theoretical considerations of the potential of Indian media to transform, construct and nurture particular identities in response to globalisation. The study of the transformation of Indian media at a macro level is significant not only because globalisation has allowed access to a host of things hitherto represented as 'foreign' to Indian culture by the media, but has also opened the floodgates for foreign media. This has, in recent times, necessitated subtle and drastic changes in political and economic ideologies advocated by the founding fathers of the nation and reflected in the media, leading to quantitative and qualitative changes.

Introduction

The volume deals exhaustively with the way in which the Indian media is coping with challenges of globalisation, its role and content.

Considering that the Indian media still functions as a powerful tool of hegemony, newspaper writings, contemporary literature, films and television soaps, indicate how the people are made to see the world in national terms in general, and to think in patriotic terms about the nation in particular. A study of the media brings to light current definitions of 'we' and 'they', the 'other' and indeed, how the 'other' is sought to be perceived in contemporary India. The political and economic turnaround in the last couple of decades has necessitated changes in ways through which the media has to portray the nation and the 'other'. First, globalisation has called for a redefinition of citizenship and national identity as reflected in the Dual Citizenship Act of 2003. Second, globalisation has given an impetus to nationalistic rhetoric in the country so much so that *swadeshi*, a term associated with the freedom movement, has regained currency and multi-national corporations (MNCs) are resorting to the use of nationalist ideologies in their advertisements. Third, in a country which despite two decades of liberalisation treats foreign entry into the country with fears of 'cultural imperialism', the media is caught between portraying a changing society that is adapting itself to the changing needs and Indian cultural values that have formed the backbone of the country's identity. Viewed in this context, a study of the Indian media and its transformation is essential to understand the changes taking place in the country.

Straddling disciplines of media studies, journalism, political science and sociology, the book places changes in Indian media in the context of economic, political and cultural spheres and draws from studies on the 'nation' as an imagined or abstract community. It is divided into four sections that cover the gamut of media transformation and its influence in India. Section 1 is devoted to tracing the economic influences of globalisation on the Indian media and highlights the subtle and not-so-subtle changes in media content and management practices that have been necessitated by globalisation. In Chapter 1, Usha M. Rodrigues uses television as a case study to take a theoretical look at whether the inception of foreign and private television in India has been a threat to local culture; whether it has led to 'cultural imperialism' or an improvement in the quantity and quality of television programmes available to Indian audiences; or whether the entry of commercial television and competition vis-à-vis foreign and private channels has further skewed developmental goals of Indian broadcasting as envisaged in the 1950s? The historical growth of the television industry in India in the past 15–20 years has raised the question whether Indian audiences have benefited from this transformation from one public television monopolistic market to a global market consisting of multiple networks, owned in various degrees by foreign and private entrepreneurs vying for viewers all across the Indian society. The chapter engages with theories of 'modernity', 'cultural imperialism' and 'globalisation' advanced by various scholars over the past five decades to analyse the growth of television as an institution of capitalist modernity (Barker 1997: 13).

In Chapter 2, Maya Ranganathan traces the use of nationalism as a marketing tool by MNCs. The empirical study is significant in the context of two antithetical developments—the resurgence of nationalism post 9/11 and the economic globalisation that necessitates economic interdependence, which in turn leads to political interdependence making flagging of national identities difficult. While the MNCs are able to bulk-produce their goods ignoring national boundaries, their marketing strategies have taken into account the national, local or 'glocal'. India offers a good case study considering the changes in its economic policies since the 1990s that have influenced the political and cultural scenario as well. The invocation of the national symbols, cultural elements and tradition has made it possible for the MNCs not only to place their products in the Indian milieu, but also to mask their 'foreignness'. Considered in the light of the fact that India is just 62 years out of colonial rule and is still fearful of cultural imperialism, the identification and employment of nationalist images and ideologies provide the MNCs an effective tool to woo the Indian consumer.

Economic liberalisation in India has, in turn, led to changes in the Indian national identity. The technological developments have made physical location insignificant and mass migrations have made a reconstitution of difference necessary. Whereas earlier, an Indian citizen was defined solely by the Indian Constitution, the era of globalisation, in which foreign remittances of the non-resident Indians have become important for the economic development of the nation, has necessitated rethinking the ideal 'Indian citizen'. In Chapter 3, Rodrigues takes a critical look at contemporary print media in India and at the current trends and strategies adopted by its owners to maintain and expand their market share in a country, which is seeing exponential increase in television and radio audience numbers. The author analyses reasons for this expansion in recent years, at a time when online media seems to be threatening the survival of newspapers in more advanced economies. The chapter also raises questions about the quality of journalism, and whether it is being compromised in these times of boom in print media, in a rush to profit from this 'sunrise industry'. The era of globalisation has also marked the revival of one of the older forms of communication—the radio—although in the new *avatar* of Frequency Modulation radio (FM radio). Even as community radio proved effective in development communication, FM radio took the Indian cities by storm. In Chapter 4, Ranganathan looks at the intensity of local medium in the age of globalisation. The popularity of FM radio in cities is interesting in the context of the fact that since the 1990s, television upstaged almost all other forms of entertainment in India. The chapter traces the evolution of FM radio and contentious issues related to it including the process of licensing and curbs on broadcasting news and news-based programmes.

Section 2 deals with political identities and elaborates the ways in which particularly contentious and conflicting political identities are being portrayed in the Indian media, in television, print and online.

In Chapter 5, Ranganathan focuses on the identities purveyed by regional media. Taking into account the coverage of the ethnic conflict in Sri Lanka both by English-language newspapers and popular magazines in Tamil in Tamil Nadu, she points out that not only was regional media more sympathetic to the Tamil cause, but it also seemed to attempt the creation of a pan-Tamil identity. In its coverage, the regional media equated all Tamils with the Liberation Tigers of Tamil Eelam (LTTE), despite the fact that the organisation was treated as a terrorist organisation in India. It also relied more on the sources which were supportive of the LTTE, consequently contradicting reports of events in Sri Lanka published in mainstream English media. The author argues that the carefully articulated pro-LTTE slant of the Tamil popular press may be prompted by economics when technological advancements have made the magazines accessible to the Tamil diaspora abroad, which comprises mostly of Sri Lankan Tamils. The issue becomes especially significant when viewed through the prism of 'media studies', as it, first, reveals the dynamics of regional media in Tamil Nadu; second, brings to light the issue of objectivity, and; third, explores the concept of 'audience as market'.

Chapter 6 is an exploratory study of the recent expansion of citizen journalism in the world, and manifestation of this trend of community participation in the production of media in India. It deliberates on audience dissatisfaction with mainstream media, despite its increasing take up to outline the Indian version of citizen journalism, its adaption by mainstream media, and ponder upon its purpose in a land with thousands of publications, hundreds of television channels and radio stations. In this chapter, Rodrigues explores whether the current momentum in community participation in the media is sufficient to consider it to be an alternative form of media in India.

Chapter 7 explores the success of online media as an alternate media in the politically-sensitive north-east regions of India. It highlights the process of construction and perpetuation of Naga nationhood online, which runs counter to the official nationalism propagated by the dominant media in India. In the context of political turmoil in the region and the role of dominant media, political websites have emerged as powerful tools of information and for mobilisation of the people. The Naga websites, by being registered outside the boundaries of India, where the writ of the Indian government does not run, exploit the features of online media to propagate Naga nationalism. A study of three websites dealing with the Naga nation has been done to delineate ways in which political agenda is furthered. Of particular interest is the way in which technological features of the medium are employed and how they contribute at the same time to the creation and curtailing of the Habermasian public sphere.

Section 3 analyses mediated culture in the era of globalisation, with particular reference to popular culture. The opening up of the skies in 1991 brought into Indian homes a plethora of television channels—foreign and privately-owned—called 'satellite television'. Indian television audiences, who were fed on the public service broadcaster Doordarshan's fare, were now exposed to programmes that were clearly influenced by the foreign channels, both in format and content. A most significant consequence was the soap opera termed 'mega serial' in

Indian television parlance. Running between a period of six months to seven years, the mega serial dealt with women's lives—women who had moved out of their hearths and homes to make a mark in the male-dominated world, in the era of globalisation. Chapter 8 looks at the 'new' Indian identity in context of the passing of the Dual Citizenship Bill in 2003. Ranganathan argues that this 'new' identity, however, is not entirely 'new', but draws heavily from the 'inherited culture' of the nation. This is done through a case study of the Bollywood film *Swades* released in 2004. The study explores how the hitherto 'other', that is, non-resident Indians who have left the country for greener pastures are now sought to be brought back into the fold of 'we, the Indians' by the mass media. It is argued that through a careful invocation of tradition and employment of symbolism, domicile in India, which is how the Constitution of India defines Indian citizenship, is stressed as an important factor for inclusion.

Chapter 9 explores the role of public service broadcasting, using Doordarshan as a case study, in a developing nation, particularly following the advent and exponential burgeoning of foreign and private television channels in India. It examines the changing role of Doordarshan from being a tool for 'development communication' to becoming a 'mouth-piece' of the ruling party; from being a monopoly to being one of the many networks in a 400-plus television channels market. The chapter argues that Doordarshan still has a significant role in India's development goals, in providing choice to Indian audiences, and in 'raising the taste' and quality of programming in a competitive environment where private media remains focused on profit margins.

In Chapter 10, Ranganathan argues that Indian satellite television, while seeming to portray women of the 'new age', confines neo-liberalism to the demeanour and occupation of women. Women who are engaged in challenging jobs outside the private space of home are shown to be still preoccupied with emotions that sway home-bound women. By focussing on three Tamil mega serials, the author demonstrates that neo-liberalism does not permeate and the women protagonists are archetypes of mythological or historical characters such as Sita, Kaikeyi and Kannagi. Adhering to the traditional values of a 'good' Indian woman is touted as the solution to the problems that women face in the era of globalisation.

This leads to the subject of media policy in India to which Section 4 is devoted. Media laws in India do not always take into account the changes in media technology and when they do, they become draconian in the name of national security. In the light of some of the recent cases where bloggers in India have had to close down owing to threat of legal action, Chapter 11 argues that it is time for law makers to take into account the specific features of the technology, which make computer-aided media technologies ideal for free expression. Media laws in India do not seem to distinguish between online newspapers, which are sources of information and blogs, and which are often used as a platform for a personalised means of communication. It is argued that treating both forms as mass communication works to the detriment of the users as has been seen lately.

With the multiplication of television channels and their content in the past two decades, it has become significant to note the dual role, which television plays in disseminating information to all segments of Indian population—the poor and disadvantaged, and the middle and upper classes. Although the expansion of private and foreign television in India is seen as increasing choice for the individual vis-à-vis 'glocalisation' of Indian media content, questions remain whether the government is doing enough to guide this popular industry, including public service broadcasting, to meet the developmental goals envisaged for television in 1959 when it was launched in India. In Chapter 12, Rodrigues claims that the Indian government continues to make ad hoc decisions, without providing a clear legal framework in which this potentially 'catalytic' media can grow, and meet the education and entertainment needs of the various segments of the Indian population.

References

All India Radio. 2006. 'About us'. Available online at http://allindiaradio.org/about1.html (downloaded on 16.01.2006).

Barker, Chris. 1997. *Global television: An introduction*. Oxford: Blackwell Publishers.

Indiantelevision.com. 2009a. '180 TV channels await government clearance', 26 February. Available online at http://www.indiantelevision.com/headlines/y2k9/feb/feb245.php (downloaded on 28.05.2009).

———. 2009b. '110 pay channels are on cable networks in India: Trai', 2 April. Available online at http://www.indiantelevision.com/headlines/y2k9/apr/apr18.php (downloaded on 28.05.2009).

Introduction

Rao, I.V. Subba. 2002. 'Indian case study', Discussion paper for ILI/UNESCO Lap 2nd Experts' Meeting, Paris, 7–8 March. Available online at http://www.literacy.org/pdfs/LAPIndiaCase_total.pdf (downloaded on 21.06.2009).

Registrar of newspapers for India. 2008. 'General review'. Available online at https://rni.nic.in/pii.asp (downloaded on 21.06.2009).

Srinivasan, K. 2004. 'Population and development in India since independence: An overview', *The journal of family welfare*, Special issue, 50: 5–12. Available online at http://www.midiind.nic.in/jah/t04/s1/jaht04s1p5g.pdf (downloaded on 21.06.2009).

Shrivastava, K.M. 2008. 'Information technology and print media', in National Documentation Centre on Mass Communication (ed.), *Mass media in India*, pp. 37–64. New Delhi: Ministry of Information and Broadcasting.

The Economic
Aspect

Chapter 1

Glocalisation of Indian Television

Usha M. Rodrigues

Introduction

It is well-documented that television in India and other Asian countries changed dramatically in the early 1990s with the use of satellite technology by commercial media. The Indian television was transformed from a single government-owned player to a multi-channel global media market. Until 1991, Indian audiences received a controlled, sometimes development-oriented, and at other times, propaganda-induced television programming (NAMEDIA 1986; Singhal and Rogers 2001; Verghese 1978). Since 2009 audiences are being subjected to a cacophony of nearly 450 commercially driven broadcasts[1], which caters to around 500 million[2] viewers in India compared to 30 million in 1984–85 (Doordarshan 1997; Indiantelevision.com 2008a). The number of cable and satellite homes in India is around 67 per cent[3] of the total number of homes with access to television (Indiantelevision.com 2008b), whereas the Indian television software industry is estimated to be worth Rs 30 billion (AUS$ 1 billion) in 2009–10 (Indiantelevision. com 2008c). Doordarshan, the public service broadcaster launched in 1959, is no longer a monopoly in the Indian television market, albeit it remains a significant player with an extensive network of channels and more than 90 per cent reach. This growth raises the question of whether Indian audiences have benefited from this transformation from a monopolistic public television market to a global market consisting of multiple networks, owned in various degrees by private and foreign entrepreneurs, all vying for viewers across Indian society. This chapter takes a theoretical look at whether the inception of foreign or satellite television in India has been a threat to local culture, whether it has led to cultural imperialism or an improvement in the quality and quantity of television programming, and whether the entry of commercial television channels and competition has further skewed developmental goals of Indian broadcasting as envisaged by the Indian government leaders in the 1960s. The chapter engages with theories of development and modernity advanced by many scholars over the past five decades to analyse the growth of television as an institution of capitalist modernity (Barker 1997: 13).

Development and modernity

In 1959, when television was launched in India, two contrary views were expressed: first, if television was allowed to degenerate into an entertainment medium, it would waste the country's precious resources; second, that television could be used as an effective education tool to enlighten the masses and change people's attitudes, thereby leading to social and economic development (Ninan 1995; Singhal and Rogers 1989).

> For India, the entertainment component, though essential for recreational purposes, and for mitigating the rigours of everyday life, was secondary to instruction, education and information, and the tackling of larger issues like unity, integrity, integration, socio-economic and secular justice and an enlightened citizenry which were very vital—indeed a question of survival and progress. (NAMEDIA 1986: 12)

Over the next three decades (1960–90), the two opposing views of the way television had developed in the country persisted. First, that Doordarshan was a government channel and thus, had no credibility, particularly in news programming, and that its programmes in general were 'dull' and 'boring' (Gupta 1998). The other view was that television had degenerated into an entertainment medium and was not meeting its social objectives of informing and educating the masses, particularly those living in rural India (NAMEDIA 1986; Verghese 1978). Now that the Indian television industry with nearly 450 channels has become part of the global television industry, it needs to be understood in the wider context of the globalising Indian economy and capitalist modernity. Broad terms used in this chapter are: development and modernity; cultural imperialism and globalisation. In the 1950s and 1960s, academics generally defined 'development' as economic growth. The goal was that all newly-created nations would and should evolve to a common point of being a modern society by a 'transfer of capital, ideology, technology and know-how' (Servaes and Malikhao 2003: 7). Based on earlier studies, communication scholars believed that mass media had a 'magic multiplier' effect in increasing the level of development in less developed nations (Rogers 1976).

Linking the concept of modernity with communication, Lerner described it as 'primarily a state of mind—expectation of progress, propensity of growth, readiness to change' (in Singh 2003: 193). He argued that the Western model (including the population's state of mind) could be reproduced anywhere in the world by mass media dissemination of modern ideas, images and values. Indian political leaders including the then Prime Minister Jawaharlal Nehru were greatly influenced by writings about the role of mass media in national development. Schramm (1964) saw information play an important role as an agent of change and modernisation. He argued that mass media could be used to impart information by playing three important roles: the watchman's role, the policy's role and the teacher's role. Schramm contended that as national development got underway, information would need to be available on-demand so that expert knowledge was available where needed, raising the population's aspirations and providing 'a forum for discussion, leadership, and decision making' (1964: 43).

> It is generally the increasing flow of information that plants the seed of change. It is also the widened background of information that furnishes the climate for 'nation-ness' itself. By making one part of a country aware of other parts, their people, arts, customs, and politics; by permitting the national leaders to talk to the people, and the people to the leaders and to each other; by keeping the national goals and the national accomplishments always before the public—thus modern communication, widely used, can help to weld together isolated communities, disparate subcultures, self-centered individuals and groups, and separate developments into a truly national development. (Schramm 1964: 44)

The existence of traditional beliefs and practices was seen as an impediment to modernisation, which was considered a pre-requisite for economic growth. However, modernisation theory was criticised for generating inequality and underdevelopment by accelerating the westernisation and urbanisation of traditional societies (Servaes and

Malikhao 2003: 7). Rogers (1976) criticised the paradigm of development and broadened the definition from one that centred on materialistic economic growth to other social values such as social advancement, equality and freedom. The concept of development in the 1970s was expanded as 'a widely participatory process of social change in a society, intended to bring about both social and material advancement, including greater equality, freedom, and other valued qualities, for the majority of the people by giving them greater control over their environment' (Rogers 1976: 133). Similarly, the new concept of 'development communication' dealt with the promotion of social change leading to improvement in people's quality of living, by encouraging better health, higher literacy and higher production of goods through more effective communication. Rogers and Hart (2003: 266) define the core elements of the 'development communication' paradigm as: *(i)* the notion that mass media can deliver 'informative and motivational' messages to large audiences in developing countries and *(ii)* the research-based evidence that exposure to these messages can alter people's attitude, knowledge and behaviour toward economic growth and social betterment. Rogers also emphasised the role of interpersonal communication in his thesis on Diffusion of Innovations. According to him, 'mass-media channels are primarily knowledge creators, whereas interpersonal networks are more important at persuading individuals to adopt or reject' (Rogers 1962 in Singh 2003: 194).

Cultural imperialism and globalisation

However, the transfer of technology, know-how, institutional frameworks and western lifestyle in the 1960s and 1970s caused some anxiety among western theorists and those in developing countries alike. In the 1970s, the discourse moved on to 'cultural imperialism' caused by the 'transfer' of western values to traditional local cultures. Many government officials and politicians in developing countries saw this dependence on the developed world as a sign of 'imperialism', which may be defined as economic or political domination and dependency, but without the political form of 'colonialism'. More worrying was the trend of 'cultural imperialism' where 'authentic, traditional and local

6

culture in many parts of the world was being battered out of existence by the indiscriminate dumping of large quantities of slick commercial and media products, mainly from the United States' (Tunstall 1977: 57). Schiller's description of the concept of 'cultural imperialism' is useful here as:

> ... the sum of the processes by which a society is brought into the modern world system and how its dominating structure is attracted, pressured, forced and sometimes bribed into shaping social institutions to correspond to, or even promote, the values and structures of the dominating centre of the system. (Schiller 1976: 9)

Schiller also says that the system of colonialism has been replaced by domination of certain power centres, their organisations and control over the modern world system. Fejes links the discussion of 'media imperialism' to the dependency model vis-à-vis the relationship between developed and developing countries, and the developmental goals of developing nations: 'It's (the dependency model's) major conclusion that the Third World countries occupy a subordinate position in the international economic and political systems which are seen as being structured primarily according to the needs of the developed countries' (1981: 283). Golding says 'cultural imperialism', which is a more inclusive term than 'media imperialism', includes the effects of international media, educational and cultural systems (Golding 1983: 291). This dependency of the developing world on the developed nations led to a call for a new economic order and New World Information and Communication Order (NWICO). The International Commission for the Study of Communication Problems in its report (MacBride 1980) recommends that developing countries should establish national cultural policies to foster cultural identity and creativity. At a global level, it recommends that the promotion of 'the cultural identity of every society' is necessary to enable it to enjoy a harmonious and creative inter-relationship with other cultures (MacBride 1980: 259).

In the 1990s, with the collapse of the communist Soviet Union and the expansion of the market economy paradigm, a much broader term 'globalisation' replaced 'imperialism'. Tomlinson (1991) points out that the idea of 'cultural imperialism' is connected to the critical discourse

7

of 'modernity'. He argues that the critiques of cultural imperialism are protests against the spread of (capitalist) modernity 'for capitalism, the nation-state and mass communications are all distinctive features of modern societies and determinants of the cultural condition of modernity' (Tomlinson 1991: 173). The idea of 'imperialism' contains the notion of a purposeful project with the intention of spreading a social system from one centre of power across the globe. 'The idea of "globalisation" suggests interconnection and interdependency of all global areas which happens in a less purposeful way. It happens as a result of economic and cultural practices which do not, of themselves, aim at global integration, but which nonetheless produce it' (Tomlinson 1991: 175). Tomlinson also says that although people's everyday experiences are 'local', these experiences are increasingly shaped by global processes particularly through mass media. Tomlinson further notes the link between the processes of globalisation with cultural demands for localisation.

It is significant to note that in this discussion, television is seen as being 'bound up with capitalist modernity, both as a set of economic activities and as a cultural force constituted by and constitutive of modernity' (Barker 1997: 21). Barker says that if the expansion of television across transnational boundaries in the late 1980s and 1990s is a function of satellite technology and the spread of capitalist modernity across the globe, then:

> ... television constitutes, and is a consequence of, the inherently globalising nature of the institutions of modernity. Television is globalised because it is an institution of capitalist modernity while at the same time contributing to the globalisation of modernity through the worldwide circulation of images and discourses. (Barker 1997: 13)

Barker argues that 'television programmes are not simple reflections of the world but specific constructions of it and thus represent forms of knowledge about the world' (Barker 1997: 12). The nature of television programmes is significant because if most of the programmes broadcast in the developing world are imported from overseas, it raises issues of cultural imperialism where the knowledge of the local population is then framed by these imported programmes.

8

Globalisation, localisation and regionalism

Summarising various views about globalisation among theorists and socio-political thinkers, Held (2000) says some equate the modern trend of world integration to the expansion of 'cultural imperialism' on a broader scale where the world is increasingly becoming homogenised and westernised, while others believe that the impact of globalisation is mixed. Held identifies four different views about globalisation. First, globalisation is characterised by homogenisation of economy and culture; second, there is the significance of increased connectedness and sharing of cultures; third, the view denies the existence of globalisation and emphasises continuation of unregulated capitalism; and fourth, the consequences of contemporary global interactions as complex, diverse and unpredictable. French and Richards note that some perceive 'globalisation as an opportunity for change, while others see it as having fractious effect on local cultures by creating new global communities with common interests' (French and Richards in Held 2000: 18). Giddens (2002) notes that the sceptics of globalisation theory say globalisation is not real, but just an extension of the old system where countries continue to do business with their neighbouring partners. Considering the level of economic turnover in the world market, Giddens (2002: 10) says that globalisation is not only new, but also 'revolutionary'. Globalisation, which could be said to be driven by advances in communication technologies, 'is political, technological and cultural, as well as economic', and media is but a sub-set in this process (Giddens 2002: 10).

Many authors such as Giddens (2002), Nederveen Pieterse (1995), Robertson (1995) and Straubhaar (1997) discuss the various possible definitions and meanings of the process of globalisation as it is manifested in many developing countries via this technological, commercial and cultural import from Western nations, particularly the United States of America (USA). The attempt is to modify the general view that the world is becoming 'more uniform and standardised, through a technological, commercial and cultural synchronisation emanating from the West, and that globalisation is tied up with modernity' (Nederveen Pieterse 1995: 45).

According to Giddens (2002), the process of globalisation has been influenced by the developments in systems of communication, dating

9

back to the late 1960s. He says the advent of satellite communications has made a dramatic impact on breaking away from the past and modernising the world. 'Instantaneous electronic communication isn't just a way in which news or information is conveyed more quickly. Its existence alters the very texture of our lives, rich and poor alike' (Giddens 2002: 11). Globalisation is a complex set of processes: it pulls away power from local communities, it revives local cultural aspirations and it creates new economic and cultural zones within and across nations. Giddens does not agree with those who say that nation-states lose power as the world becomes more globalised, stating that nation-states are still powerful, and political leaders still have a large role to play in the world. However, he believes that the nation, the family, work and tradition, have changed. 'They are institutions that have become inadequate to the tasks they are called upon to perform' (Ibid.: 19). To Giddens, globalisation is not 'a global order driven by collective human will. Instead, it is emerging in an anarchic, haphazard, fashion, carried along by a mixture of influences' (Ibid.). He states that 'globalisation is not incidental to our lives today. It is a shift in our very life circumstances. It is the way we now live' (Ibid.).

Nederveen Pieterse argues that because of the pervasiveness of this process across many spheres, 'globalisation may be understood in terms of an open-ended synthesis of several disciplinary approaches', extending from social science to technology, agriculture or business sectors (Nederveen Pieterse 1995: 45). Two points of relevance emerge—one is that globalisation can be a 'tandem operation of local/global dynamics, global localisation or globalisation' (Ibid.), and, the second being that the world cultural experiences are not moving in one direction of uniformity and standardisation, but are a two-way process, including the impact of non-western cultures on the West. He says that 'for some time now we have entered a period of accelerated globalisation and cultural mixing' (Ibid.: 62). Nederveen Pieterse describes the process of globalisation as the process of 'hybridisation', where introvert cultures are gradually receding, and translocal cultures made up of diverse elements are coming to the foreground. As a result, there is a nostalgic upsurge of ethnicity and religious revivalism in some parts of the world. His view is that the world is a place for a global 'mélange' of cultures.

Robertson (1995) talks about the concept of 'glocalisation', which is defined in terms of the co-presence of both 'universalising' and 'particularising' tendencies. He says that, contrary to common belief, the concept of glocalisation has its origins in Japan and not in the USA. According to him, the agricultural principle of adapting the farming technique to the local situation was adopted in Japanese business for global localisation, 'a global outlook adapted to local conditions' (Robertson 1995: 28). Glocalisation also manifested itself as the 1990s business mantra of tailoring a company's services to local market needs. For example, in 1996, Coca-Cola engaged the services of '30 advertising agencies to bring a creative local flavour to the global message' (Rodwell 1996: 16). Robertson describes this process of corporations producing products for the global markets by adapting to local and other particular conditions as 'universalisation' and 'particularisation'. 'To considerable extent micromarketing—or, in the more comprehensive phrase, glocalisation—involves the construction of increasingly differentiated consumers, the "invention" of "consumer traditions" (of which tourism, arguably the biggest "industry" of the contemporary world is undoubtedly the most clear-cut example)' (Robertson 1995: 29).

Similarly, television corporations seek global markets by employing strategies of glocalisation that is tailoring their products (programmes) to suit local tastes and needs by employing local producers or using local language or local-language titles at the minimum. In 2002, Hong Kong-based Blaise D'Sylva, CEO, Greater China and North Asia for Starcom Media Vest, said the American and European media owners would increasingly have to publish more editions or sections in local languages when marketing their publications in Asia. He said 'they [media owners] realised in order to grow their audience and revenues they have to deliver what's important—language and culture—to local consumers' (Madden 2002: 20).

Straubhaar extends the 'glocalisation' theorisation by Robertson and Nederveen Pieterse to argue that in the area of television production, 'there is good evidence that regional or geo-linguistic area productions of major genres are influenced by global developments in those genres, such as the global evolution of the soap opera, in which global, regional and national experiences interplay' (Straubhaar 1997: 295). According to him, the impact of globalisation in homogenising world culture is overstated. Straubhaar quotes Ferguson to argue that the world is not becoming one homogeneous culture, largely fed by the USA's cultural industries. 'The media imperialism and cultural synchronisation theories assumed an epochal change in the power of media to affect culture' (Straubhaar 1997: 296). Straubhaar argues that television's flow and impact need to be looked at not only at the global level, but also at regional or geo-linguistic, national, sub-national or even local levels. At the global level, some television channels take the same content to worldwide audiences such as the CNN, whereas others are creating more regionally or locally adapted versions of the CNN programmes. There are minimalist approaches such as the cartoon channel dubbing its programmes in Hindi for the Indian audience, and STAR TV broadcasting Hindi programmes.

The geo-linguistic focus on the impact of global media is significant because 'many local audiences would like to see programming in their own languages, addressing their own cultures' (Ibid.). If the local language is shared by a larger geo-linguistic group, the programming may be imported to the other region, adding to the regionalisation of television programme that flows along language boundaries. Straubhaar says there is 'a subtle interplay between the global and local in television form and content' (Ibid.: 288). The television programmes on one hand are spreading the message of materialism, of comfort, of enhanced consumerism, but are doing so in local language, moderating its message to local needs and cultures. In a sense Straubhaar and others argue that globalisation is not equal to global homogenisation. So, how does the growth in the television industry in India fit into this overall debate on globalisation?

Economic reforms and satellite television in India

After attaining freedom from British colonial rule in 1947, Indian leaders favoured the 'communication for development' approach, by not allowing the new mass communication media (radio and television) to become private businesses, which they believed would encourage advertising and consumerism, in turn leading to cultural imperialism by raising people's needs for foreign products, both cultural and material

(Mitra 1986). Subsequent Indian governments maintained monopolistic arrangement for the two public service broadcasters—All India Radio and Doordarshan. At the time, television was considered a powerful means of nation-building and national integration (Ninan 1995) because it was envisaged that the audio-visual medium would be effective as the promoter of economic and social development through education and attitude change in a country where some traditional beliefs and practices based on caste system and mass illiteracy were considered a hindrance to people's participation in development activities (Kothari 1988a, 1988b). However, over the next three decades, though a world leader in experimenting with television and satellite technology, India failed to capitalise on the lessons learnt from earlier communication development projects such as The Satellite Instructional Television Experiment (SITE) and Kheda.[4] Singhal and Rogers (2001) outline a number of failures in utilising television as an education and development tool: a misplaced focus on hardware expansion, and too little attention to developing local software; an inability to grant autonomy to the two public service broadcasters, instead using them as partisan political tools; Hindi-centric programming on the national broadcasters and, urban, particularly Delhi, focused policy and programming decisions (Singhal and Rogers 2001: 97–98). However, it was lack of competition on the software front (in all areas—educational, entertainment and information-oriented programmes) that led to Indian television viewers being bored with Doordarshan's programming (Gupta 1998: 42). As a result, no one was satisfied—neither the intellectuals (due to insufficient quality and quantity of informational and educational programming for all Indians, including the large segment of poor and illiterate population), nor the urban middle class (due to insufficient quality and quantity of informational and entertainment programmes for all Indians).

In 1991, India faced a serious economic crisis when the country's foreign exchange reserve went down to less than one month's import bill. The country was already faced with serious problems of high inflation, high interest rates and high government budget deficit. In this scenario, the Congress party government launched a drive to restructure the country's economic system through a process of liberalisation. The government used the fiscal crisis as a catalyst to change the economic policy—it took a massive loan from the International Monetary Fund

(IMF) to avert the danger of defaulting on its debt payment, agreeing to IMF's condition to open Indian markets to foreign competition and investment. 'The cornerstone of the Government's new economic policy was globalisation' (Sinha 1998: 26). This meant lowering and simplifying import tariffs and quotas imposed to protect the domestic industry, getting rid of the licencing raj (regime), and providing incentives for exports and foreign investment (Ghosh 1998; Rodrigues 1994). And, to convince foreign investors that it was serious about economic reforms and liberalisation policies, the Indian government ignored the unsanctioned revolution in the broadcasting industry: the receiving and illegal re-distribution of satellite signals of foreign and private channels from foreign soil into Indian homes. It also overlooked the mushrooming of cable operators, and the illegal and ugly proliferation of dish antennas and cables in urban streets. Sinha (1998: 27) states that the government's attitude toward the new satellite television was a barometer of its commitment to (economic) reforms: '[G]overnment clearly recognised that television is a highly visible cultural product that functions as the best marketing tool for the liberalisation of the Indian economy.' Whether it was the mindset of the Indian government at the time or a compulsion of liberalisation policy vis-à-vis the IMF loan condition of economic reforms, the globalisation process in effect resulted in de-regulation of the television market in India. Since then Indian viewers have not looked back—the choice of programming and channels has become massive. This process of globalisation and de-regulation of television has been part of the general condition of economic liberalisation and privatisation prevailing in India (McDowell 1997: 217). McDowell says that a technical determinist explanation of the importance of satellite services for communication development and communication policy is not sufficient to explain the expansion of cable and satellite television in India. According to him, the technical version does not take into account strategies adopted by private and foreign television networks to expand their market in India (localising programming by building alliances with local producers), nor does it account for the Indian government's response to invasion from the skies of expanding Doordarshan's reach via satellite distribution and adding a number of national and regional channels to compete with the international players.

Competition and glocalisation
of television programming

However, the entry of private and foreign television media meant that television channels not only had to compete in a crowded market, but that it also needed to deliver audiences to their advertisers. The new entrants had to compete with other private channels as well as the established monopoly of the public service broadcaster, which was (as a result of the competition) already in the process of launching multiple regional channels and offering more privately produced and sponsored local entertainment programmes. Doordarshan became but one player (albeit a strong established network) in the market. As a result, all television networks began looking for niche markets and producing programmes that would interest local audiences. As discussed earlier in the chapter, globalisation goes hand-in-hand with the counter force of the need to localise products. For television media, this means producing local programmes in local languages by local talent, particularly in a multilingual country like India. This is a common trend in many of the Asian media markets, depending on the size of the local market along with each national government's ability and willingness to control this 'invasion from the skies' (i.e., satellite television). As French and Richards say, 'recent evidence from national and local television practices in many Asian countries points to the importance of local programming, ethnic and cultural differentiation, and the use of local language and dialect in influencing program preferences' (2000: 17). In the case of Greater China and India—the two largest markets in the world:

> ... the providers of new 'global', satellite relayed television have been forced to recognise the need to 'localise' their services in recognition of the reality of local market conditions. Often, but not always, this takes the form of adapting genres to meet specific requirements of language or other cultural circumstance. (French and Richards 2000: 19)

So in the mid-1990s, the 'cross-border' channels began changing their strategy to reach audiences beyond a small urban elite population which watched their foreign-originated English programmes. STAR was the first to start adding Hindi sub-titles to Hollywood films (Thussu 2000). In 1996, STAR Plus began telecasting locally-produced programmes in English and Hindi. Thussu notes that the STAR TV network boasted a policy of localisation, but he also argues that 'this change of heart was not because of any respect for Indian languages or culture on the part of the media conglomerates but the sheer logic of market pressure— localising the product to reach a wider consumer base and increase advertising revenues' (Thussu 2000: 297). This change in strategy, to cater to a wider audience, also indicates a realisation that the way to get into the hearts and minds (i.e., living rooms) of a mass audience was through localising their programmes.

Needs of a diverse society

India, which is a multi-class, multi-religious and multi-lingual country, has 22 scheduled languages and several hundred dialects (Census of India 2001a). Hindi is spoken by about 41 per cent of the population (Census of India 2001b). At the same time, English, which is a foreign language, is spoken and understood by about 2.2 per cent of the population (Census of India 2001c). However, English, because of India's colonial past, carries a degree of prestige and, many times, is used as a substitute common language in metropolitan India. Many people in southern and north-eastern parts of India either do not speak Hindi or resent the imposition of Hindi as the national language (Gupta 1998: 43). As a result, channels such as Zee began using the hybrid language 'Hinglish' (a mix of Hindi and English) to reach as many people as possible, thereby increasing the number of viewers they could deliver to advertisers.

India also has two large segments of population: the growing middle class and the huge underbelly of poverty-stricken people. Some would contend that the numerical strength of the Indian middle classes is about 650 million of the total one billion population (Asian Development Bank 2002), while others put the statistics at 300 million (Perry 2004; Sridharan 2004). However, there is a consensus that the number of people living below the poverty line is about 300–350 million (Asian Development Bank 2002). In fact, some political scientists such as Rajni Kothari argue that it was the model of development that India imported from overseas which has led to the creation of 'two-Indias:'[5] 'with one India cornering resources and institutions and, the other India left to fend for itself' (Kothari 1988a: 2227). As a result, the government's broadcast policy needs to focus on uplifting the lives of millions of illiterate and poor people by resourcing 'public service' programming on television.

Meanwhile, the process of liberalisation or deregulation in the 1990s for another segment of society went beyond the official unchaining of the government's control over businesses. Those often exposed to a western lifestyle or aspiring to enjoy the comforts of a western lifestyle had already moved on to a different time and space of life and work in a globalised world. Indian society, which was going through a transformation after more than four decades of development and economic growth, also had to accept the cultural impact of modernisation, where the upper middle and middle class started breaking away from some of the Indian traditions, including being told by the government what to watch on television. The economic reforms expressed themselves in terms of rising literacy and aspirations, economic prosperity, exposure to western culture and a new generation breaking away from joint-family ideals, leading to the rise of the nuclear family and a need for accessibility to entertainment and information at home. These changes in turn also led to significant numbers of middle-class people embracing cable and satellite television (Ninan 1995). With Doordarshan unable to meet the growing number of people's entertainment and information needs, coupled with falling costs of new hardware (television, video recorders and, later, digital video players), multinationals were well placed to tap the huge Asian markets, with satellite technology making it possible to telecast programmes from the skies. It is ironic that the expansion and privatisation of the broadcasting industry is seen as a positive move toward democracy and choice for the individual rather than an abandonment of public service broadcasting in India (Pendakur and Kapur 1997: 196).

Globalisation to development

Anthropologist Rico Lie links the concept of development communication to globalisation via the localisation of media messages. Localisation, which is mostly accepted as an integral part of the globalisation process, is an inward process of articulation of local identities and local cultural practices. Localisation reinforces cultural identities at the local level by contrasting it with other cultures (Lie 2001). Globalisation is the 'tandem operation of local/global dynamics' leading to a cultural mixing or global mélange of cultures (Nederveen Pieterse 1995) or a complex set of processes, which not only pulls away power from local communities, but also revives local cultural aspirations by creating new economic and cultural zones within and across nations (Giddens 2002). Thus, the revival of local aspirations and cultures is synonymous with development as it puts emphasis on 'the articulation of local cultural identities and local community characteristics' (Lie 2001: 19). Lie argues that the link between globalisation and development can only be established by taking the concept of localisation seriously. Lie (2001) says that thinking about cultural globalisation is not new, but builds on existing theories and ideas of dependency theory, Westernisation, cultural imperialism, cultural synchronisation and 'the global village'. 'Globalisation and localisation, as far as they refer to culture, are interpretative processes. This means they are not objective processes, but are defined differently by different subjects, belonging to different communities, in different times and different spaces' (Ibid.: 20).

It is not a global structure that plays a role in people's lives, but it is the local context that shapes people's everyday lives. By the act of interpretation, global messages emerge in a local context, and thereby 'localise the exogenous, and make them relevant for their daily lives' (Ibid.: 20). The other parallel process to this localising of global messages is the articulation of local cultures in a global environment, leading to an invigoration of local cultures. For example, the revival of some Indian folk music and dance rituals after being remixed as pop or rap music. The classical version of folk music from the northern states of Punjab and Rajasthan seemed to have gone past their heyday of popularity. However, the adoption of these traditional, local songs and dance rituals as upbeat pop music presentation in Indian movies and on MTV has revived the local artists' fortunes. Some critics feel the mixing of local folk music with western styles of presentation has destroyed the local music and culture, while others see it as a revival of folk music and dance.

Appadurai contends that modernity has become more practical and experimental as a result of globalisation, which has 'shrunk the distance between producers and consumers, broken many links between labour and family life, obscured the lines between temporary locales and imaginary national attachments' (Appadurai 1996: 10). He states that this process of modernisation in the 1980s and 1990s with its experimental characteristics has seen greater working-class engagement with modernity, resulting in electronic mass mediation and a high degree of transnational mobility. This has in turn broken the monopoly of nation-states over the modernisation process. In case of India, television, as an important tool for modernising the masses, is no longer the state's monopoly. In fact, since the *de facto* deregulation of the Indian television industry in 1991, it is the state which has been floundering on the media policy front and has embraced the mantra of self-sufficiency and commercialisation for its public service broadcaster.

Impact of the *de facto* deregulation

The sea-change in the Indian television market has meant a significant amount of choice of programming for the Indian audience—from one channel to nearly 450 channels for cable subscribers. It needs to be acknowledged that all households do not receive 450-plus channels on their television sets due to lack of capacity of either the set itself, or the hardware used by the cable service provider, and/or the package a household may subscribe to. However, there is no denying that Indian households have more choice of programmes than before 1991. If one looked at just news and information programmes, Doordarshan's national channel in 2009 typically broadcasted four newscasts of about 15–20 minutes each in Hindi and English, and one-to-two news programmes on its regional channel/s depending on what feed a viewer could receive. However, a cable subscriber could watch news on a number of 24-hour news and other entertainment channels such as DD News, STAR News, Zee News, CNN, CNBC India, BBC, CNN, and daily newscasts on several regional channels, such as Sahara Samay, Udaya TV, Raj TV and Gemini TV. Before 1991, there were many stories which remained untold on television because the time slots available on one Doordarshan channel were limited. In 2009, with the increase in the number of television channels (both within the Doordarshan network and the launching of numerous private and foreign networks in India), theoretically, the story of development and modernisation can be told by many and not just one public service broadcaster.

Before 1991, the monopolistic Doordarshan was expected to 'promote national integration' (Doordarshan 1997: 23) by creating 'mutual awareness' (NAMEDIA 1986: 13). However, the public service broadcaster failed as the multi-lingual and multi-religious personality of the nation, struggling against being fitted into one straightjacket (Gupta 1998; Mitra 1986). As Kothari notes, the challenge India faced at the time of independence was to produce a nation out of a vast heterogeneity of social and regional entities without destroying them (Kothari 1993). A similar strategy of incorporating many regional cultures needed to be reflected on Indian television, in this case, on Doordarshan, but, instead, there was a monolithic image of Delhi-centric India being portrayed on television (Verghese 1978). The stifling control by the Information and Broadcasting Ministry, the bureaucratic managerial structure and lack of competition made Doordarshan programming 'dull' and 'boring' (Gupta 1998). At the same time, commercialisation pushed Doordarshan to schedule the unadventurous and less popular education and development programmes to unpopular hours.

Early 21st century India seems divided not only along caste, religious and gender lines, but also class. The 'two Indias', made up of the privileged and impoverished sections of Indian society, have different needs and expectations from the broadcast media. The constant dissatisfaction with Doordarshan's performance as a tool for development and as a source of mass entertainment, stemmed from its position as the sole television network. The expectation that as a public service broadcaster, Doordarshan could meet the needs of middle classes and underprivileged groups (women, children, the poor, those living in rural areas and other minority religious and lower caste groups) was unattainable from the beginning, particularly when one took into consideration the size of the population and diverse needs of the multi-lingual, multi-religious and multi-class nature of the nation. Using the arguments presented by political scientist Kothari, one could say the model of television, where there was only one public service broadcaster catering to the needs of all, was flawed from the beginning. Although the public network continued to expand its reach across India's population rapidly, it lacked a coherent policy and any significant competition (Ohm 1999). In these circumstances, the entry and establishment of private and foreign television networks was welcomed by the general population (Pendukar and Kapur 1997; Rahim 1994; Rodrigues 1998; Thussu 1999). The foreign media also changed its programming to suit local taste and local demand by localising their programmes—producing and broadcasting programmes made by Indians for Indians (Thapar 1998). This prompted the government to allow Doordarshan to expand its reach further and modify its content, by launching a number of regional channels to meet different geographic and linguistic needs (Doordarshan 1997). Doordarshan remains a serious competitor in a crowded market, but the audience has greater choice today—to watch Doordarshan or switch to one of the other cable channels. The production of television software too has been a boon for local actors and crews (Indiantelevision.com 2002).

In a way, we have completed a full circle, where television, which was envisaged as a catalyst for social change, is finally reaching more and more people in the country. Many more stories of local interest are now being told with the help of this powerful audio-visual medium. Reiterating anthropologist Lie's (2001) argument, the revival of local aspirations and cultures is synonymous with development as it puts emphasis on the articulation of local identities and local characteristics. However, the need still remains to maintain a healthy competition in the industry in such a way as to not overlook the other half of India, which is yet to benefit from the globalisation process. Television, which can be a powerful agent of change has to meet the needs of these two distinct constituencies in the country—the 'haves' and 'have-nots'. And, it is in this context that Doordarshan as a public service broadcaster can find a permanent place in a competitive market without imitating its commercial counterparts where profitability for the network is the most important imperative. This is where the government needs to regulate television content in the interests of all sections of the 'public' without making the public service broadcasters 'an organ of the government' as referred to by late Indira Gandhi in 1976 (Kothari in Ohm 1999: 84).

Endnotes

1. According to Minister of State Information and Broadcasting, Anand Sharma, in February 2009, there were a total of 215 news and current affairs television channels received by Indian viewers, while there were 233 non-news including general entertainment and niche channels (Indiantelevision.com 2009).
2. According to the Indian Readership Survey report released in November 2008, about 352.83 million viewers catch television at home, while 105.786 million watch television at their friends and neighbours' houses, and 49 million watch on community sets (Indiantelevision.com 2008b).
3. According to the Indian Readership Survey report released in November 2008, there are about 100.38 million homes with televisions, of these 66.54 subscribe to one or more cable and satellite services (Indiantelevision.com 2008c).
4. See details in Chapter 9.
5. According to Kothari, the two Indias are: one that comprises the urban and rural elite, the big farmers, the industrialists, the bureaucrats, the executives and professionals and the intelligentsia; and the other, which comprises the impoverished, the malnourished, the poor, the untouchables, the backward classes, the lower castes and a large section of the religious minorities and women (Kothari 1988a, 1988b, 1993).

References

Appadurai, A. 1996. *Modernity at large: Cultural dimensions of globalisation.* Minneapolis: University of Minnesota Press.

Asian Development Bank. 2002. 'Monthly reports, March 2002'. Available online at http://www.abdindia.org/janeco-02.htm (downloaded on 18.01.2005).

Barker, Chris. 1997. *Global television: An introduction.* Oxford: Oxford Blackwell Publishers.

Census of India. 2001a. 'India at a glance'. Available online at http://www.census india.gov.in/Census_Data_2001/India_at_glance/popu1.aspx (downloaded on 14.08.2009).

———. 2001b. 'Scheduled languages in descending order of speakers' strength'. Available online at http://www.censusindia.gov.in/Census_Data_2001/Census_ Data_Online/Language/Statement4.htm (downloaded on 14.08.2009).

———. 2001c. 'Distribution of the 100 non-scheduled languages-India/states/union territories—2001 Census'. Available online at http://www.censusindia.gov.in/ Census_Data_2001/Census_Data_Online/Language/partb.htm (downloaded on 14.08.2009).

Doordarshan. 1997. 'Doordarshan handbook', *Doordarshan 1997 Annual Report.* New Delhi: Audience Research Unit, Doordarshan.

Fejes, F. 1981. 'Media imperialism: An assessment', *Media, Culture and Society*, 3 (3): 281–89.

French, D. and M. Richards. 2000. *Television in contemporary Asia*. New Delhi: Sage Publications.

Ghosh, J. 1998. 'Liberalisation debates', in T.J. Byres (ed.), *The Indian economy: Major debates since independence*, pp. 295–334. New Delhi: Oxford University Press.

Giddens, A. 2002. *Runaway world*. London: Profile Books.

Golding, P. 1983. 'Media professionalism in the third world: The transfer of an ideology', in J. Curran and J. Woollacott (eds), *Mass communication and society*, pp. 291–313. Hong Kong: Edward Arnold with The Open University Press.

Gupta, N. 1998. *Switching channels: Ideologies of television in India*. Delhi: Oxford University Press.

Held, D. (ed.). 2000. *A globalising world?: Culture, economics, politics*. London: Routledge.

Indiantelevision.com. 2002. 'EnterMedia 2001 moots broadcaster-MSO promoted regulatory body', Special Report, 21 February. Available online at www.indian televison.com/special/y2k2/spenter.htm (downloaded on 04.04.2006).

———. 2008a. 'IRS 2008 R2: The lowdown on TV viewership', 5 November. Available online at http://www.indiantelevision.com/headlines/y2k8/nov/nov63.php (downloaded on 15.12.2008).

———. 2008b. '66.54 million C&S homes in India: IRS', 8 November. Available online at http://www.indiantelevision.com/headlines/y2k8/nov/nov94.php (downloaded on 15.12.2008).

———. 2008c. 'Going global is a key part of our TV content scale up plan', 8 September. Available online at http://www.indiantelevision.com/interviews/y2k8/executives/ajit_thakur.php (downloaded on 15.12.2008).

———. 2009. '180 TV channels await government clearance', 26 February. Available online at http://www.indiantelevision.com/headlines/y2k9/feb/feb245.php (downloaded on 28.05.2009).

Kothari, R. 1988a. 'Integration and exclusion in Indian politics', *Economic and Political Weekly*, 23 (43): 2223–27.

———. 1988b. 'Class and communalism in India', *Economic and Political Weekly*, 23 (49): 2589–92.

———. 1993. *Human consciousness and the amnesia of development*. London: Zed Books.

Lie, R. 2001. 'Globalisation, development and "communication for localisation"', *The Journal of International Communication*, 7 (2): 14–24.

MacBride, S. 1980. *Many voices, one world: Communication and society, today and tomorrow*. New York: UNESCO.

Madden, N. 2002. 'Local vs. global: English-language titles fight for their spot in the locally-driven Asian media market', *AdAgeGlobal*, 2 (10): 20.

McDowell, S.D. 1997. *Globalisation, liberalisation and policy change.* London: Macmillan Press.

Mitra, A. 1986. 'For a new kind of software', *A vision for Indian television, Seminar Series,* pp. 92–95. New Delhi: Media Foundation of the Non-aligned.

NAMEDIA. 1986. *A vision for Indian television.* New Delhi: Media Foundation of the Non-aligned.

Nederveen Pieterse, Jan. 1995. 'Globalisation as hybridisation', in M. Featherstone, S. Lash and R. Robertson (eds), *Global modernities,* pp. 45–68. Thousand Oaks, CA: Sage Publications.

Ninan, S. 1995. *Through the magic window: Television and change in India.* New Delhi: Penguin Books India (P) Ltd.

Ohm, B. 1999. 'Doordarshan: Representing the nation's state', in C. Brosius and M. Butcher (eds), *Image Journeys: Audio-visual media & cultural change in India,* pp. 69–98. New Delhi: Sage Publications.

Pendakur, M. and J. Kapur. 1997. 'Think globally, program locally: Privatisation of Indian national television', in M. Bailie and D. Winsech (eds), *Democratising communication?,* pp. 195–218. New Jersey: Hampton Press.

Perry, A. 2004. 'A tale of two Indias', 6 December, *Time Asia* 164 (23). Available online at http://www.time.com/time/asia/magazine/article/0,13673,501040223-591347,00 (downloaded on 17.04.2005).

Rahim, A. 1994. 'Impact of cable TV on television and video viewing in Hyderabad: A survey', *Media Asia,* 21 (1): 15–20.

Robertson, R. 1995. 'Globalisation: Time-space and homogeneity-heterogeneity', in M. Featherstone, S. Lash and R. Robertson (eds), *Global modernities,* pp. 25–44. Thousand Oaks: Sage Publications.

(Rodrigues) Manchanda, U. 1994. 'Economic reforms in India', *Eyewitness,* Doordardshan, 5 September. India: Hindustan Times Vision Ltd.

———. 1998. 'Invasion from the skies', *Australian Studies in Journalism,* 7: 136–63.

Rodwell, T. 1996. 'Local flavour for a global message is common sense', *Marketing, Advertising Policy,* December, 19: 16.

Rogers, E.M. 1976. 'Communication and development: The passing of the dominant paradigm', in E.M. Rogers (ed.), *Communication and development: Critical perspectives,* pp. 121–48. London: Sage Publications.

Rogers, E.M. and W.B. Hart. 2003. 'Looking back, looking forward', in B. Mody (ed.), *International and development communication,* pp. 261–74. London: Sage Publications.

Schiller, H.I. 1976. *Communication and cultural domination.* New York: International Arts and Sciences Press Inc.

Schramm, W. 1964. *Mass media and national development.* Stanford: Standford University Press.

Servaes, J. and P. Malikhao. 2003. 'Development communication approaches in an international perspective', in J. Servaes (ed.), *Approaches to development: Studies on communication for development*, pp. 1–38. Paris: UNESCO.

Singh, J.P. 2003. 'Communication technology and development', in B. Mody (ed.), *International and development communication*, pp. 189–207. London: Sage Publications.

Singhal, A. and E.M. Rogers. 1989. *India's information revolution*. New Delhi: Sage Publications.

———. 2001. *India's Communication revolution: From bullock carts to cyber marts*. London: Sage Publications.

Sinha, Nikhil. 1998. 'Doordarshan, public service broadcasting and the impact of globalisation: A short history', in M.E. Price and S.G. Verhulst (eds), *Broadcasting reform in India—Media law from a global perspective*, pp. 22–40. New Delhi: Oxford University Press.

Sridharan, E. 2004. 'The growth and sectoral composition of India: Its impact on the politics of economic liberalisation', *India Review*, 3 (4): 405–28.

Straubhaar, J. 1997. 'Distinguishing the global, regional and national levels of world television', in A. Sreberny-Mohammadi (ed.), *Media in global context—A reader*, pp. 284–98, New York: Oxford University Press.

Thussu, D.K. 1999. 'Privatising the airwaves: The impact of globalisation on broadcasting in India', *Media, Culture and Society*, 21 (1): 125–31.

———. 2000. 'The Hinglish hegemony: The impact of western television on broadcasting in India', in D. French and M. Richards (eds), *Television in contemporary Asia*, pp. 293–312. New Delhi: Sage Publications.

Tomlinson, J. 1991. *Cultural imperialism*. Baltimore: The Johns Hopkins University Press.

Tunstall, J. 1977. *Media are American: Anglo-American media in the world*. London: Constable and Company Ltd.

Verghese, B.G. 1978. 'Excerpts from "major recommendations" of the working group on autonomy for Akashwani and Doordarshan', Indiantelevision. com, Legal Resources. Available online at http://www.indiantelevision.com/ indianbrodcast/legalreso/verghesereport (downloaded on 14.11.2004).

Interview

Thapar, K. 1998. Host, BBC. Interviewed by author, 12 January, New Delhi.

Chapter 2

Nationalism as a Marketing Tool by MNC Advertisements*

Maya Ranganathan

Introduction

Post 9/11, the news media is dominated by 'nationalist movements, ethnic conflicts and secessionist struggles' (Motyl 2001: xi) leading one to perceive perhaps a resurgence of nationalism. At the same time it is also marked by the integration of the world's political, economic and media structures where the nations are 'interdependent and interconnected through links, visible, invisible, intended and accidental' (Lilleker 2006: 86). The media's role, both in the resurgence of national identities and the simultaneous interdependence for largely economic needs, has been significant. The media has been employed to 'flag' the nation at all times, reiterating the self-identity made by a people over and against other peoples or states and to declare their right to maintain and further their own identity in the global context. In the world of diversities, rendered more so thanks to advancements in communication technologies and mass migrations, communities when transforming/transformed into nation-states, define themselves in national terms by adopting the dominant identity (Motyl 2001: 360). Such an identity, though difficult to generalise, includes claim to a common culture, language, traditions, values and common symbols, among others. The media plays an important role in hegemonising people, by bestowing the dominant identity and constantly reiterating it

*This article is drawn out of the Master's dissertation submitted by Bernadette Lobo under the supervision of Maya Ranganathan, to Manipal Institute of Communication, Manipal University, Karnataka, India, in 2006. An earlier version of this paper was published in *Nationalism and Ethnic Politics*, Vol. 14, No. 1, Winter 2008, pp. 117–42.

among the people.[1] This leads to a consciousness of nationhood among its people.

However, the process seems to hinder economic globalisation, which by necessitating economic interdependence and by extension, a certain degree of political interdependence among countries, makes flagging of distinct national identities difficult.[2] Economic globalisation has given rise to multi-national corporations (MNCs) whose markets seem to have little respect for national boundaries.[3] Although MNCs can bulk produce their goods and services and sell them across national boundaries, it is seen that the process of marketing can little ignore the national boundaries. Forced to take note of 'the continuous stream of discourse produced by a local society' which experiences events 'differently from those happening elsewhere in the world', MNCs grapple with the challenge of introducing 'fresh concepts about the outside world' that more often represent a 'reversal of archetypes' (Dijking 1996: 1, 2). It is this process that this chapter explores in the context of MNCs' advertisements in India. India offers an interesting case study for two reasons: the basis on which her national identity has been crystallised and the turn around in her economic policies in the last couple of decades. The chapter analyses how the introduction of fresh concepts draws on concepts that have been naturalised over years.

Changes in the rubric of Indian national identity

One aspect that underlies the vast literature on Indian national identity formation is the conscious construction of India as an essentially cultural nation. Hansen traces the rise of cultural nationalism in India to the late-19th century 'public stirrings', consequent to the Indian elites' perception of the differences between the East and West (Hansen 2004: 43). Chatterjee cites Plamenatz to argue that 'Eastern' nationalism arose out of the realisation that Eastern culture did not provide the 'adaptive leverage' that could lead to Western standards of progress (1986: 2). Consequently, it was accompanied by a need to 're-equip' the nation culturally, to transform it. This could not be achieved by blindly aping Western culture because then the nation would lose its distinct identity. The nation had to retain its distinct culture, but at the same time adapt it to suit the requirements of progress by Western standards, which is what dictated the nationalism project in the eastern nations. It is in this context that Indian nationalism should be viewed. The construction of the Indian national ideology indicates an inversion of the orientalist epistemology of the 'other' (Hansen 2004: 3–290). Europe saw India as spiritual as opposed to the materialist Western world. This distinction was taken forward in the Indian nationalism project by Jawaharlal Nehru, Bankim Chandra Chatterjee and Swami Vivekananda. The distinction between the British ruler, and the ruled Indians, was based on the creation of 'an "inner" spiritual, culturally sovereign realm closed off from the colonial state while competing in the "outer" realm of politics and economy' (Chatterjee cited in Hansen 2004: 43).[4] The distinctive identity of the contemporary Indian nation-state lies in the fact that while 'resolutely pursuing modernity, (it) does claim a certain moral-cultural or cultural-political continuity with tradition' (Pantham 2004: 426).[5] To this day, the Indian nationalism discourse is marked by a negotiation of, and oscillation across, the realm of 'sublime culture' and 'profane politics' (Chatterjee cited in Hansen 2004: 12; Sen 2005: 334–55). Indian nation-building straddles the two worlds of culture and science—'to bring the learning of the modern world to the educated, but console by tradition those already regretting mechanised living and fearing the dangers of an atomic age' (Vatsyayan 1998).

Thus, Gandhi's concept of *Swadeshi*, which implied a boycott of foreign goods questioning and threatening the economic supremacy of the British, formed the bulwark of the Indian freedom movement.[6] During the Independence struggle, the future Indian nation-state was 'imagined' to be one 'which would sustain and be sustained by, a complex conception of pluralist, civic-communitarian nationalism, rather than by any simple ethnic, religious or linguistic nationalism' (Pantham 2004: 438). In the years after Independence, Jawaharlal Nehru's 5-year plans were aimed at achieving self-sufficiency within India. His aim was to create a self-reliant nation because he believed that independence depended on resisting economic and political domination (Chandra et al. 1999: 180). During Indira Gandhi's prime ministership in the 1970s, banks, the insurance and coal industries and enterprises in the textile industry were nationalised. Restrictions were placed on foreign investments apparently to 'defend national sovereignty' (Khilnani 1997: 92). Located within such an economic history, the Indian citizen was told to patronise Indian products and services. This created a strong national fervour and 'Be Indian, Buy Indian' was a popular slogan in the 1970s which was actively propagated by the Central Government.

However, the country had to change its economic ideologies when the massive foreign exchange borrowing by the Rajiv Gandhi government in the years 1984–89 led to a fiscal crisis leading to the economic reforms in 1991. Since the early 1990s, the nation has moved away from the protectionist economic regime following a 'shift in the state's developmental ideology from socialism to the idea of a liberalising state' (Pantham 2004: 439).[7] To tide over the economic crisis, the finance minister, Manmohan Singh, in 1991, instituted path-breaking economic reforms. Among the reforms were attempts to reduce government spending, to devalue the rupee, to ease the controls placed on the private sector and to bring in foreign competition by opening the Indian market to foreign investment (Vohra 2000: 277). These reforms were initiated with the aim of increasing the foreign exchange reserves and expanding exports, and marked a turn around in the country's economic policies. This liberalisation marked the advent of MNCs in India. Liberalisation also led to an onslaught of foreign television channels into Indian homes (Singhal and Rogers 2001). The process began with CNN in 1991, leading to Star TV and other foreign services that introduced a range of entertainment programmes as opposed to Doordarshan's educational programmes and mythological dramas. By 1996, there were more than fifty channels operating in India (Indiantelevision.com: online).[8] One can now find on Indian television a host of 'Star TV' channels, CNN, BBC, FTV and AXN among a number of other foreign channels. The popularity of entertainment programmes has led to a situation where a 1-hour programme is punctuated by at least 4 advertising breaks that promote a range of products and services, causing fears of promoting materialism in the Indian viewer's life. Perhaps, the fear of Westernisation, particularly Americanisation, which is still cited as the dangerous fall-out of liberalisation in India the entry of foreign channels and products in fact, has given an impetus to nationalist rhetoric in the country.[9] This led to the term *Swadeshi*, associated with the freedom movement, gaining currency yet again in public debates.[10] Thus economic globalisation, which called for opening the Indian markets to foreign players, was accompanied by a resurgence of nationalist sentiments which was marked not only by a routine, banal flagging of the nation in other spheres (Billig 1995: 116) but also by a harking back to the older nationalist idiom of *Swadeshi*, advocating a conscious choosing of goods and services that were identifiably Indian.

The Indian advertising industry has always been quick to take advantage of the resurgence of nationalism by borrowing the themes, sounds and personalities associated with it. After all, nationalistic rhetoric is popular among Indian politicians, particularly during election times. Although not so apparent in post-independent India, politicians have never failed to use phrases like 'our country' and 'this nation' constantly, thereby reinforcing a sense of national belonging, simultaneously creating a concept of the foreign as the 'other' (Smith and West 2001: 94). The 2004 national elections brought nationalism to the forefront in two major ways. First was through the BJP's campaign of 'India Shining',[11] which sought to create a pride among the people of India on their economic achievements. Second, when nationalistic feelings were appealed to, against the election of Italian-born Sonia Gandhi as prime minister of the country, by the Congress party that emerged victorious in the elections. In the years that followed, an innocuous remark by the Prime Minister, Manmohan Singh, on his visit to Oxford, that Mahatma Gandhi had recognised that many of the British practices in India were fair and that India had benefited in many ways from Britain, set off a furore in India (Singh 2005: 10). The language of nationalism is thus current and popular among Indians.

Even before the dawn of the era of globalisation, nationalism has been the favoured tool of advertisers. For instance, a study in the year 2000 cites an advertisement for Ambassador cars that shows two policemen standing with guns above a road where 8 white Ambassador cars are parked. The police here symbolise the state's power and security, while the cars are used by politicians. One caption reads: 'Congratulating the enduring success of India's democracy', while another says 'HM Ambassador—It's Always There'. These two captions link the commodity with the power of the Indian nation-state and to its political ideology of democracy (Fernandes 2000: 618). This use of identity connects with the ideologies of the nation. In the era of globalisation, Indian advertisers were quick to realise that the 'local' and 'global' were not diametrically opposite, but were 'mutually constitutive imaginary moments in every attempt to make sense of the world' (Ibid.: 14). Advertisements in the 1990s gave the Indian soul an international feel linking the global with the local (Fowles 1996: 5). This was attempted through the invocation of Indian cultural elements 'already extant in popular culture' related to Indian 'nationalist ideologies'—values related to nationalism, national identity and national consciousness (Ibid.).

Although codification does not exist, Indian nationalist ideologies have come to include ancient Indian traditions, culture and beliefs that are common to people in a large part of the nation-state.[12] Indian companies have adopted one of the many aspects that govern the nationalist ideologies to sell their products or promote their services. The Indian youth between the ages of 20 and 35 years, who form the greatest section of the country (Gahlaut 2005: 18), and are also the greatest spenders, prefer the 'outward trappings of Western culture', but are still very traditional (Bobb 2005: 98). A typical Indian youth may wear *Nike* shoes and a *Lacoste* T-shirt, but he/she will still remove those shoes before entering a place of worship, will live with his/her family and shows signs of respect to parents (de Mooij 2004: 9). People define themselves through the differences of their self, family and nation (Ibid.: 16). When the 'local' is the nation-state, advertisers can draw on popular nationalist songs, commercial film actors or sporting events that have national support to create what Lèvi-Strauss calls a *bricolage*, underlining this identity (Fernandes 2000: 615).[13]

MNCs in India[14]

Viewed in the above context, it is not surprising that nationalist ideologies make good marketing tools. Studies have dealt with the effective use of nationalist ideologies to sell Indian products.[15] However, what is interesting is that MNCs peddling global products and services, often at loggerheads with Indian cultural values and beliefs, invoke traditional Indian values to peddle their products and services. This is especially significant in the case of India, as the country understands the implications of imperialism, having been colonised for hundreds of years, and is still wary of any form of imperialism, as can be seen from the fear of a foreign-born Indian, viz. Sonia Gandhi, leading the country. Moreover, media reports have time and again pointed out that in the face of globalisation, Indian nationalist sentiments have grown stronger.[16] According to a study conducted on Indian youth, they are anti-American and anti-globalisation (Bobb 2005: 96). According to de Mooij, 'the notion of Western imperialism in particular has linked negative connotations to the word globalisation. Critics of globalisation tend to protest against an emerging global monoculture consisting of McDonald's, Nikes, Levi's, Barbie dolls and American television' (2004: 3).

Although there is an understanding amongst a section of the population that economic globalisation is here to stay, benefits of liberalisation are still debated on the grounds that the poor are exploited by the MNCs who engage Indian labour to produce products at cheaper rates for private profit.[17]

To briefly look at the MNCs' presence in India: MNCs, as mentioned earlier, entered the Indian economy in 1991 when an earlier law, which limited foreign ownership in industries to between 41 to 50 per cent was altered to allow them to own between 51 to 100 per cent of a company in an industry (Varma: online). Some of the MNCs entered India as joint ventures, while many opted for fully-owned subsidiaries. The latter option enabled most of the earnings from the Indian markets to go to the parent company (Nathan: online). Even some of those companies that had entered India as joint ventures and explored the Indian market later set up wholly-owned subsidiaries, thereby acting as competitors for their own joint ventures (Mahalingam: online). Among the 63,000 MNCs in the world (Progressive Policy Institute), there were 871 of them in India in 1998 in various sectors, including the services sector (Mohan 2003: 130). In a country where to 'Be Indian and Buy Indian' defined nationalism in the 1960s and the 1970s, the MNCs have been forced to Indianise themselves to find favour with the Indian consumer. They have done it, on one level, by peddling tandoori pizzas and zari-embroidered denims and on another level, by disguising their foreignness in Indian nationalism. In this article I focus attention on two kinds of MNCs in India—those whose parent companies own 100 per cent of the subsidiary and those that function in the country through agents. The rationale for this choice is that such companies are not legally bound to reinvest their profits in India. Instead, they are allowed to completely repatriate their earnings to their home country, justifying the criticism that their contribution to the country's economy is limited. Although both Indian companies and MNCs can be criticised for promoting consumerism, by creating a culture of materialism, MNCs come under fire, because of their 'foreign origins' and as they are not bound to reinvest their profits in India. They have earned ire for creating a desire for their products and services masking their 'foreignness' and then transferring their earnings to their home country, in the process leading to fears of cultural imperialism.

The MNCs seem to have found a way to face the criticisms levelled against them by first, placing their products within the environment of the Indian lifestyle, and second, countering charges of spreading cultural homogenisation or imperialism by invoking cultural and traditional values.[18] Using such a vehicle also seems appropriate given the appeal of nationalism in India. Kevin Roberts, CEO worldwide of the advertising agency Saatchi & Saatchi, believes that a company which wants to become global has to first understand 'their own local and the locals of all their customers.' Thus the MNCs have come to speak the same language to promote the global as the local. Consequently, 'foreign' products go through a process of naturalisation to become Indian. Even as the Indian service sector is growing steadily, the foreign services, by Indianising themselves, have come to play a role in the Indian economy.

In the following sections I look at the negotiation of 'Indianness' by multi-national organisations (MNCs) to sell products and services that are not always part of the Indian cultural milieu in a purposive sample of advertisements on Indian television aired between August and October 2005. The economic relationships being embedded within the social fabric, a semiotic and rhetoric analysis is made of the data to identify the use of Indian nationalist ideologies to understand the manner in which the MNCs position themselves within the Indian context, using the ideologies in order to sell their products (Vidal 2004: 389). It is to be noted that at least 3 advertisements taken for study, barring the scooters and motorcycles, deal with products and services not essentially Indian. The predominant ideology conveyed in the advertisements is distilled by identifying the beliefs, values, and other cultural and political symbols that are embedded in the advertisements.

Persuading the unsuspecting consumers

Advertisers try to delude people and dull their powers of perception making people buy products that are unnecessary and perhaps harmful. What is significant to this study is that advertisers create this desire by using the culture, values, rituals and symbols that relate to the consumer. Given that a consumer, while paying for any product or service, pays also for the cost of advertising, the Indian consumer is, in effect, paying for all the advertisements that he/she sees. Thus the Indian consumer, swayed by the nationalist images, willingly contributes to the MNCs' coffers, perhaps unaware that neither the producer nor the product is Indian. The success of television advertisements in this context is bound to owe more to the medium's efficacy in combining various stimuli and in appearing more 'real' to the viewer. In the context of individuals seeing something of themselves in the characters used in advertisements (Griffiths: online), widespread accessibility to television (TV) programmes in India and the central role that TV plays in most urban Indian homes,[19] advertisements on television are bound to lead to a situation where the corporate 'voice' comes to constitute the 'national symbolic environment' (Schiller 1989: 44).

The four 'compound' advertisements recorded during prime time between 9 and 12 September 2005 (See Appendix 1 for descriptions of the advertisements)[20] are those of Honda Motorcycles and Scooters India, Kellogg's Corn Flakes, Visa Card and Western Union Money Transfer. Honda and Kellogg's are wholly-owned subsidiaries and represent the manufacturing sector, while Visa and Western Union function in India through agents and represent the services sector. Honda Motorcycles and Scooters India Private Limited (HMSI) began producing scooters in 2001 and motorcycles in 2004. Kellogg's entered the Indian market in 1994 with a wholly-owned subsidiary and in course of time created a market for convenience foods, at least in urban areas in the country. Visa is an electronics payment network that works as an association of financial institutions. The Visa Asia Pacific's headquarters of this non-traditional MNC, set up in 1973, is in Singapore and 700 financial institutions are connected in this region. Western Union Financial Services, which began as a telegraph service, is a wholly-owned subsidiary of the First Data Corporation and has its headquarters in America. It has more than 225,000 agent locations in more than 195 countries and its services include sending money and telegrams and payment of bills (Western Union: online).

Invoking Indian beliefs

According to a study conducted on Indians by Shunglu and Sarkar in 1995, Indians prefer not to wear clothes that are considered disrespectful in society. They consider it important to obey elders and to have meals with the family. They prefer to stay in joint families and they believe that lives are determined by what is written in the stars (de Mooij 1998: 107). Members of the Indian society are able to identify with these values, images, festivals, customs, rituals and other symbols due to the learnt patterns of associations or codes. These codes are mental structures that affect the manners in which the audience interpret the signs they find in the media (Berger 2005: 30).

In India, besides traditional social arrangements, sociological enquiry has to address traditional norms and values (Bèteille 2004: 48). Ritual and beliefs contribute to the unity and identity of communities at different levels, as has been revealed in Srinivas' study of the Coorgs (1952). Moreover, modernity coexists comfortably with traditional and religious beliefs as 'discrete sectors' (Srinivas 1971: 54–55).[21] Thus Indians are still superstitious people and adopt rituals to either ward off bad luck or to bring good luck. The Hindu calendar specifies auspicious days on which marriages and other celebrations can be held. Even certain times of the day are marked as auspicious. Though all the rituals are not followed throughout the country, the very belief in luck, and belief in rituals to attain it or keep bad luck away, is common among Indians.[22]

The advertisement for Visa credit card revolves around an old Rajasthani ritual where caged birds are released for good luck. The more birds released from cages, the more good luck the person for whom it is done can be expected to beget, explains an Indian guide to Hollywood actor Richard Gere as he walks through a colourful and crowded market-place in the backdrop of palaces. Here, Visa, essentially a foreign service provider, represented by Gere, is shown not only interested in

Indian rituals but also ready to adopt them. If the little girl who wants to release five birds for her brother can be taken to represent Indians, then she realises her desire thanks to the benevolence of an understanding white man. When Gere turns away towards the end of the advertisement, Visa tells the Indian viewers that the company will unobtrusively help Indians realise their desires in their own ways. The Visa advertisement reviving an ancient Indian custom bringing luck is created so as to not only position the product and service in the Indian milieu, but show it as a part of the Indian cultural ethos. Though its choice of ritual is not common throughout the country, the concept behind the ritual—of wanting to bring luck—is definitely pan-Indian.

The Honda Motorcycles advertisement is similar to the Visa advertisement in that it uses an Indian market-place as the scene of action but differs in that it employs *mehendi* or *henna* to symbolise an Indian tradition.[23] During weddings, though many of the women apply *mehendi*, it is considered especially auspicious for the bride. *Mehendi* is believed to be pure, as it is a plant derivative, and symbolises the prosperity a bride is expected to bring to her new family (About.com: online). Today, Indian women sport *mehendi* even outside the tradition of marriage or festivals. Honda Motorcycles by using the *mehendi* ritual, connect to the Indian viewer immediately. The *mela* (fair) situation in the rural context, signified through the roads and buildings and the model who is dressed and made up like a city girl, reveals the company's attempts to appeal to both the rural and the urban Indian. While in the Visa advertisement it was the white man paying homage to an Indian ritual, in the Honda Scooters advertisement it is a Japanese man drawing intricate *mehendi* patterns on the palm of the Indian woman. By drawing the Honda symbol right in the middle of the woman's palm, the company represented by the smiling Japanese man is symbolically embedding itself in the lives of the Indian viewer/potential customer. Just like a typical Indian *mehendi* design, the design drawn by the Japanese man contains a number of peacocks (Mehendiworld.com). The use of *mehendi* can even be taken to signify the bringing together or the 'wedding' of cultures. This is compounded by the narrator's statements at the end of the advertisement—that Indians would be surprised at how much a part of their lives Honda is. In contrast, Western Union Financial Services uses *karva chauth*,[24] a ritual that is now part of the 'public culture' to placate the Indian viewer (Appadurai 2004: 257–72). Much like Visa and Honda Scooters, Western Union positions its services as a means to continue Indian traditions. The major difference lies in the fact that the advertisement features no non-Indians, making Western Union seem very much like an Indian company. All three advertisements 'recondition' public symbols in order to 'supply agreeable meanings to the new creation' (Fowles 1996: 9).

Indicating a flow of tradition

Indian society has been characterised by a flow of tradition providing for some identities to be influenced, threatened or extinguished even while ensuring that others remain unaffected or unchanged (Vatsyayan 1996: 39–49). Thus, Indian values are relationships between two things that can be concepts of right and have wrong, desirable and undesirable, that endured the test of time. Although in the first two decades of Independence, focus was not on the revival of tradition, disenchantment with modernity set in soon after (Bèteille 2004: 47). Thus, for Indians, life is to be lived at two levels: in the realm of the intellect and in the realm of the emotions (Vatsyayan 1996: 41). Among other things, the ideal of the joint family has come to uniquely express and represent the valued aspects of Indian culture and tradition (Bèteille 1991: 3–28; Kapadia 1955; Karve 1953). Joint family, according to Veena Das, is not so much a specific type of household formation, as an ideology and code of conduct, which is what the Western Union advertisement focuses on (1976: 1–30). The young Indian male who calls home on the phone from abroad and immediately sends money back home to help his aging father buy a hearing aid so the father can hear his son's voice more clearly, appeals to Indian values of family and kinship. The 'patriarchal family system' where the senior-most male member is revered and the 'brotherhood of relatives' that distinguishes the Indian family system, is clearly apparent in the advertisement (Maine 1972). Into this theme is woven the present trend of migrations, particularly to the West, for economic gains. By showing the young male as employed abroad and looking after his family's needs in India at the same time missing his kin, the Western Union advertisement projects the Indian culture of kinship onto the national canvas (Uberoi 2004: 287).[25] Here, Western

Union is shown as not only recognising the importance of Indian values but also as doing its bit to help in upholding them. Similarly, the Visa Card advertisement uses the sister–brother relationship. The little girl in the advertisement wants to release 5 birds to bring good luck to her brother. Both the advertisements employ 'inherited or transmitted experience and wisdom' to shape the 'temporal existence of life' (Vatsyayan 1996: 41). The immutable Indian value system is employed to help viewers make adjustments that outer events demand.

Despite the changes in the socio-economic and political, the commitment to the 'perennial values of life at its most fundamental' remains, which again is represented in the Kellogg's advertisement (Ibid.). The emphasis on the mother–son bond in Indian families is clear in the advertisement, where the mother and son share many activities, from playing football, to watching television and shopping (Kakar 1981; Lannoy 1971: 90; Nandy 1980: 32–46). The indulgent mother would like to buy her son a toy car but then puts a question to him which he is unable to answer. The urban Indian's preoccupation with knowledge as a passport to economic prosperity is shown here. The advertisement ends at the point when the mother feels immense pride at her son winning the quiz. Kellogg's breaking into the Indian urban market has cashed in on two of the most prized aspects of Indian society—the mother–son bond and the Indian mothers' obsession with their children excelling in studies.

Drawing on a repository of cultural symbols

In the process of 'fabricating new symbols with enlivened meanings' all the advertisements draw on 'popular culture's repository of symbolic material' (Fowles 1996: 9). The advertisements employ symbols that draw from 'a composite pan-Indian moral cultural vision that accommodates religious and regional differences' (Pantham 2004: 430). Both the Honda Motorcycles and Visa advertisements use identifiable Indian music to tell their story. The Honda advertisement makes use of such instruments as the mandolin and base piano. While neither are Indian instruments, the mandolin–which is a string instrument–is used to create strains of the Indian classical music. Throughout the advertisement, this is blended with the piano. Therefore, at this level too, Western instruments are used to propagate Indian thought and culture. The advertisement begins with a melodious flute opening that inclines the viewer towards expecting Indian music. Soon after, in the background, a woman begins to sing a *nom-tom alap*. This is an improvisation of the words used while playing percussion instruments like the *tabla*. There is no *raga* being sung, it is merely a tune. This gives the music a modern touch since there is no *raga* involved, yet it is connected to Indian classical music. The words of the singer are rhythmic and continue till the Japanese man, who is applying the *mehendi*, looks up at the young woman and at the audience. At this point, the beat of the *alap* is blended into the beating of a gong. The gong is a popular instrument in Japan that is used in music (Mondaviarts.org: online). This signifies the blending of the Indian traditional music with a tradition of the Japanese. Therefore, while at the visual level, the audience is being told that the Japanese are adapting to Indian culture and are trying to blend into it, at the level of the music too, there is a fusion of styles of music and there is a clear entry of a sound from another culture.

Similarly, the Visa advertisement makes use of the *sitar*, violin, flute, guitar and piano. The *sitar* is an Indian string instrument used on auspicious occasions and the flute, though it is found in different cultures around the world, is an integral part of Hinduism, as can be seen from Lord Krishna's use of it (Deva 1973: 55). The advertisement begins with a man singing *shub prabhat bhayo*, a morning song that families around India wake up to. These are Sanskrit words that mean 'the day is dawning—may it encounter no obstacles'. The Sanskrit words immediately introduce the concept of ancient traditional India. This is followed by an ensemble that is a blend of instruments, but predominantly in the Indian style. By doing this, Visa is signifying the blending of two cultures. The tempo of the music follows the moods of the young girl as she runs through the market. In contrast to the sentiment of 'the day facing no obstacles', the girl upturns a vendor's cart, her path is blocked by a bull, she bumps into Gere and ultimately her desire to buy 5 birds is quashed. Finally, Gere, through his generosity, takes care of her final obstacle. The music that begins on a happy note and sobers down when the girl cannot attain what she wants, again picks up when Gere presents his 'special gift' to her. Also notable is the use of music in the advertisement when the Visa card appears on screen. The music, while still in the Indian style, significantly changes to create a kind of signature tune for the brand. This happens twice when Gere presents the card in the market and when the advertisement ends and the card appears on the screen. By changing the tune for the card alone, yet by using the Indian approach, Visa gives the international, an Indian feel.

Second, the clothes used in the various advertisements have specific meanings and serve to represent the changes that have been taking place in it in the national ethos. Both the Visa and Honda advertisements represent rural Rajasthan milieu. The forts and palaces of Rajasthan, along with the traditions, are of tourist interest. Apart from Richard Gere in Visa and the young woman in Honda, all the Indian models are in traditional attire. The women are in *ghagra cholis* and the men in *kurta pyjamas* and turbans. These are identifiably Indian clothes. In the Visa advertisement, Richard Gere, is dressed all in white, a signifier of purity. This stands out starkly against the colourful backdrop of the other costumes and of the market. Gere represents Visa and making him stand apart from all other elements may signify Visa's realisation that they are not yet completely a part of the Indian life and, as one realises later, they are attempting to integrate with the country and its ways. The young woman in the Honda advertisement wears a *kurta* over trousers, a blending of the traditional with the West, a popular notion with today's urban Indian youth. Thus the introduction of a modern service by Visa not only draws on traditional culture but also shows an appreciation for it. On the other hand, the Japanese man in the Honda Motorcycles advertisement is shown dressed in a *kurta pyjama* and turban, much like the other Indian men in the advertisement, a clear indication of the efforts of Honda to adapt to Indian way of life and perhaps play by the country's rules. The latter is especially significant considered in the light of the news of the labour dispute with employees demanding increased pay and permission to form a union in Honda Motorcycles in early 2005.

With Kellogg's aiming at the urban market, the advertisement is in an urban set-up with the mother, son and quiz-master being the only characters. The mother wears salwar kameez in almost all the scenes and a *sari* in the last one, representing an educated urban housewife. It is the boy's style of dressing that is interesting. His clothes are more American than Indian. In the first scene, he wears his cap backwards and he is dressed in shorts and a sleeveless, loose T-shirt. Later, he wears track pants and a sweatshirt and, in the next scene, a T-shirt. In the quiz scene, he is dressed in a T-shirt covered with an unbuttoned collared shirt, once again, a very Western if not, American, manner of dressing. These items of clothing seem common now in the urban areas, especially for children, and have come thanks to the exposure to foreign cultures. The outlook of the parents in the urban areas has also undergone changes with most of the middle and upper class children moving abroad for higher education.[26] Kellogg's, by drawing attention to all these changes, even as it reiterates the primacy of education in Indian life, also indicates the need for the change in the food habits of the new generation and places easy-to-eat nutritious Kellogg's as an ideal breakfast for school-going children.

Conclusion

MNCs have found in nationalist ideologies a marketing tool to persuade the Indian viewer through pathos, albeit in a very subtle manner, to see them as a part of the changing cultural and economic milieu. They invoke Indian beliefs, reiterate tradition and draw on a repository of cultural symbols to create myths to position themselves in the Indian life. From the diverse elements of culture that invoke nationalist images, they choose some that have become part of the public culture and use them to position themselves in the minds of the Indian viewers as an integral part of the Indian nation-state. This is done either by invoking ancient traditions and showing appreciation for the same or by laying stress on certain values which are recognisably more Indian, like stress on familial bonds and premium on education and acquisition of knowledge. While the story focuses on these themes, the narration is accompanied by typically Indian music and is dotted by liberal use of signs and symbols that invoke nationalist images. In some cases, the foreign identity of the MNC is hinted at through the presence of a non-Indian model but in most other cases, there is no indication. However, what is common in both the cases is an attempt to place the foreign product in the Indian milieu as an integral part of the country or to borrow Honda Motorcycles tag line 'you would be surprised as to how much a part of your lives we are'.

This aspect is interesting because although MNCs have come to stay in India, acceptance among the people is still not very forthcoming. In

India which is just 62 years out of colonial rule, the presence of MNCs leads to fears of cultural imperialism. Also, the country is yet to come to terms with the two-decade-old liberalisation, particularly because it marks a complete turn around in the policies of socialism and protectionism, advocated and followed till then. However, the MNCs have managed to tackle all criticisms by resorting to nationalist ideologies and indicate their willingness to adapt to the Indian socio-cultural milieu in their advertisements. The above analyses bring to light the ways in which MNCs have managed to place themselves within the nation as essentially Indian. While the traits used in the advertisements are nowhere near representative of those at work in the various ideologies, and the MNCs are not representative of all those operating in the country, analysis is indicative of a larger phenomenon. While it can be said that this phenomenon is not a new one, that any global company localises itself to appeal to consumers of various countries, what is interesting in this study is the manner in which the MNCs have identified those traits that are national in character in a country as diverse and complicated as India. Even though foreign cultures subtly influence and even change 'Indian culture', if indeed such a composite term can be applied to refer to all the diversities, even as some traditions are fighting for a space alongside newer trends, the MNCs are pandering to India's image as a nation that has deep-rooted nationalist ideologies. While a representative sample of MNC advertisements has been taken to make the argument, no assertion is made with regard to the audience perception of the advertisements. Audience reception analysis would require analysis of buying behaviour of consumers and is outside the purview of this chapter.

Appendix 1

Summary of the Advertisements

Honda

The advertisement begins with a young woman walking in Rajasthan during a fair. She goes for *mehendi* to be applied on to her hands to a turbaned man, whose face is hidden from the camera. While *mehendi* is being applied, the man's face remains hidden from the camera. He finally reveals that he is Japanese while he thanks the woman. The woman looks at her hands and sees the Honda logo drawn on her palms. The advertisement ends with the narrator saying, 'You'd be surprised at how much we are a part of your life. Honda—What you dream.'

Kellogg's Corn Flakes

A mother and son are seen spending time together, playing games and watching TV. They ask each other general knowledge questions. The son wants a toy, but cannot correctly answer a question put to him by his mother, and a visibly sad mother refuses him the toy. The narrator speaks of a mother's concern for a child and how Kellogg's contains more iron for improved concentration. The next sequence is that of the boy participating in a quiz. The 'jackpot' question is asked and the son calls for his mother, his 'lifeline'. He then answers correctly, his mother brimming with pride for her son and 'Kellogg's Corn Flakes—Iron Shakti Plus'.

Visa Card

The advertisement begins with dawn in Rajasthan while, *shubh prabhat bhayo* is sung in the background. A girl watches a young man pack his bags. She turns and runs into the market place where Hollywood actor Richard Gere is walking through the market. While she attempts to buy caged birds, a guide is shown telling Gere that releasing birds bring luck; the larger the number of birds the greater the luck it brings. The girl who wants to buy five birds for her brother is shown walking away with just one as she tells the shopkeeper that she does not have enough money for them. Gere proffers his Visa card and buys the birds for her. As she is about to release her single bird, Gere releases hundreds of them turning away innocently.

Western Union Financial Services

A young wife is shown celebrating *Karva Chauth*, while her husband is abroad. In another situation, a brother-sister conversation is shown, where the sister reminds the brother of his duty towards his father. The father with a hearing impairment is unable to hear his son properly and the son is visibly saddened by his father's disability. Both husband and the son are shown winding their way to Western Union outlets to transfer money home. The two families in India receive money with which the wife buys new clothes and the father gets a hearing aid.

Endnotes

1. I am aware of recent studies that question the hegemonic model based on the prevalence of diverse communication mediums that people have access to. While academic debates question the top down model of Marx and Gramsci, *Time* magazine named 'you' as the person of the year in December 2006 'for seizing the reins of the global media, for founding and framing the new digital democracy'. See also Martin-Barbero 1993 and *Time*, 25 December 2006/ 1 January 2007: 22–23. However, where access to the growing communication technologies is questionable, like in the Third World, the hegemonic model still prevails and media functions as a powerful tool of hegemony. See also Dijking 1996: 3. On creation of national identity and sustenance, see Greenfield L. 2001: 251 and Hroch 1995: 65–82.

2. Nation-states themselves have been forced to modify their external behaviour based on the changing political and economic equations. Dijking 1996: 5 argues that national identity is dictated by external events and foreign policies by constructed dangers. However, the process by which this is attempted is outside the purview of this study. In another chapter Ranganathan explores how economic compulsions have led to the portrayal of more inclusive national identity in India.

3. While it can be argued that nation-states still govern the entry and survival of MNCs within their borders, GATT and WTO leave little option for nation-states but to fall in line with the world economic order.

4. See Bhabha 1994 for a discussion on how the colonial power handled elements that escaped their control but was nevertheless essential for their operation.

5. The continuity is expressed, according to Pantham, in the use of the term *Bharat* to refer to India in the Constitution; the adaptation of the Sarnath lion capital of emperor Ashoka as the state emblem of India; the inscription into that emblem *Satyameva Jayate* taken from the Mundaka Upanishad, the incorporation of Ashoka's *dharmachakra* in the flag and efforts to direct panchayati raj mentioned in the Constitution.

6. *Swadeshi* meant not only use of products and services produced in the country, but according to Gandhi, 'a reliance on one's own strength'. This was the rallying cry during the freedom movement which led boycott of British-made goods. See Mazzarella 2003: 290.

7. For critical evaluation of economic liberalisation, see Byres 1988; Bhaduri and Nayyar 1996; Nayar 1989.

8. Interestingly, the proliferation of foreign-owned TV channels in India has now led to numerous studies, including on how the different channels lead to the imagination of India. See Rodrigues 2005: 171–86.

9. For instance *Kalki*, a popular magazine in Tamil published from Chennai, India, in its issue dated 31 December 2006 published a short story entitled *sudhadhira dhaagam*, (a yearning for freedom) about an elderly citizen who in contemporary India preaches against use of foreign products. See also Appadurai 1996; Breckenridge 1995; Dwyer 2000; Dwyer and Pinney 2001.

10. See Mazzarella 2003: 5–12 for a detailed discussion of the phenomenon.

11. That the campaign failed and BJP lost power has been a subject of much academic debate.

12. As Sen (2005: 135, 158) points out 'generalisations even about an individual religious community within India or about a language group can be very deeply misleading'. However, what we are drawing attention to here is that 'the internal identities of Indians draw on different parts of India's diverse traditions. The observational leanings of Western approaches have had quite a major impact—positively and negatively—on what contributes to the Indian self-image that emerged in the colonial period and survives today'. To give India one cultural identity, in view of all its cultural diversities, is idealistic. Yet there are some traits that run through the different nations that comprise the Indian state, a certain 'Indianness' that can be identified. Thus, Indian national identity is taken to refer to a certain commonness found among the different nations that make up the Indian state.

13. In India, Bollywood actors and sporting heroes are much sought after advertising models. Film actor Shahrukh Khan endorses 10 brands, including Tag Heuer, Compaq, HLL, ICICI and Hyundai while thespian Amitabh Bachchan endorses 10 others that include D'damas, Parker, and Reid and Taylor. See

'Brand success', *India Today*, 1 January 2007, Vol. XXXI, No. 52, p. 54. See also Lèvi-Strauss, 1966.

14. Various definitions of multi-national companies (MNCs) have been put out by organisations and countries; the ILO says that an MNC is one whose managerial headquarters are located in one country, while operations are carried out in a number of other countries as well. According to India's Foreign Contribution Regulation Act, 1973, a corporation operating within a foreign country or territory is a multi-national corporation, if it has a subsidiary, branch or place of business in two or more countries or territories, or it carries on business or operations in two or more countries or territories. See Mohan, 2003: 6, 7.

15. See for instance Fernandes 2000.

16. Sociologists have pointed to a correlation between economic globalisation, the pressures of structural adjustment since the early 1990s and the rise of the Hindu right. See Rajagopal 1996 and Deshpande 1995.

17. To sum up the debate, on the positive side it is said that the entry of MNCs has made the home market more competitive, breaking domestic monopolies. MNCs help build the Indian economy by investing in the infrastructure sector such as power, transport and communication, where domestic capital has been inadequate. They could also transfer their technology here and train personnel appropriately. On the whole, in India great importance has been placed on obtaining foreign investment in order to increase the speed of economic development. A wholly-owned subsidiary can attract more investments from the parent company than a joint venture can. They can therefore bring in better technology. MNCs can also contribute to the country in terms of exporting their products. In the year 2001–02, their exports were 27 per cent of India's total exports.

On the other hand, MNCs hire a small group of semi-skilled or highly skilled labour leading to limited employment opportunities. Also, MNC labour gets paid more than the employees of domestic companies, leading to inequalities in wealth. While the MNCs may make the market more competitive, local firms find it difficult to survive in a market dominated by the wealthy MNCs. For instance, in Rajasthan, cottage industry manufacturers of a snack called *Bikaneri Bhujia* claim Pepsi Foods tried taking the company over. Moreover, they claimed that the potato chips manufactured by Pepsi Foods were exorbitantly priced and the consumers in metropolitan areas bought the product since it carried an MNC name. With their use of technology and focus on quality, MNCs tend to price products higher than those in the domestic market. Sometimes, the domestic manufacturers try to match the prices, in order that they do not lose out on the market. It is said that the MNCs exploit the resources of the host country in order to maximise their profits. Coca Cola has received a lot of media attention for reducing the ground water level in Kerala. This brought anti-MNC activists to the foreground. It is not a must for an MNC to reinvest its earnings into the host country. In this case, a parent company owning 100 per cent of the business in the host country, can repatriate all the earnings to their country. Moreover, some of these companies are not listed on the stock market. They are involved in the economy, but Indian investors do not have an opportunity to participate in them. For more discussion, see Mohan 2003: 93, 112–15; India Infoline: online; Nasscom.org: online; Prasad: online; Varghese: online; Krishnakumar 2003: online; Nathan: online; and Bannock, et al. 2004: 265.

18. See also Tomlinson 1991.

19. See Yadava and Reddi 1988: 125–27; *National Readership Survey* 1997: 32 and Parameswaran 2003: 21 for percentage of TV ownership and cable subscription figures in India.

20. Fowles 1996: 11 distinguishes between two types of advertisements: 'simple', where all content pertains to the commodity or service sold and 'compound' that also includes non-commodity material, like symbolic elements that constitute the appeal.

21. In the book Srinivas recounts how a bull-dozer driver skilled enough to repair the vehicle also claims that he indulges in black magic for his own pleasure.

22. Although all these can be termed as essentially Hindu customs, an element of syncretism exists among religions in India with the result that certain cultural practices have to be viewed beyond religions.

23. *Mehendi* is a reddish dye made from the leaves of the shrub *Lawsonia Inermis*. The Mughals are said to have brought *mehendi* to India in the 12th century, AD; and from the 17th century most women are depicted with the designs on their hands and feet, regardless of social class or marital status. It is believed to have therapeutic values although it is now becoming popular as a hair dye.

24. This festival, meant for the longevity of the husband, is celebrated by Indian women who fast from morning till evening. Only after sighting the moon through a sieve and then looking at the husband's face, do they eat. References to this custom can be found in the *Mahabharata*. While the festival is very popular in the north, it can even be found under different names in various regions of the country. In the south, it is celebrated as *Karadaiyan Nonbu* whereas the *Vat-Savitri puja*, conducted for the well-being and longevity of the husband, is celebrated throughout the country. It remains popular today, with even young unmarried girls fasting for the longevity of their loved one.

25. The joint family ideology is a popular theme in Bollywood films.

26. According to the special report in *Sun TV* News dated 3 and 4 June 2006, 8 pm, Indian students constitute about 80 per cent of the foreign students in US universities and are the largest in number in the UK and the Australian universities. Their numbers are steadily increasing.

References

About.com. 'Mehendi: Dye for marriage'. Available online at http://hinduism. about.com/library/weekly/aa113000a.htm (downloaded on 3.10.2005).

Appadurai, A. 1996. *Modernity at large: cultural dimensions of globalization.* Minneapolis: University of Minnesota Press.

Appadurai. A. 2004. 'Public culture', in Veena Das (ed.), *The handbook of Indian sociology,* pp. 257–272. New Delhi: OUP.

Bannock, G., R.E. Baxter and E. Davis. 2004. *Dictionary of Economics.* London: Profile Books Ltd.

Berger, A.A. 2005. third edition. *Media Analysis Techniques.* California; London; New Delhi: Sage Publications.

Bèteille, A. 1991. 'The reproduction of inequality: occupation, caste and family', *Contributions to Indian Sociology,* 25 (1): 3–28.

———. 2004. 'Sociology concepts and institutions', in Veena Das (ed.), *The handbook of Indian sociology,* pp. 41–59. New Delhi: OUP.

Bhabha, H. 1994. *The location of culture.* NY: Routledge.

Bhaduri, A and D. Nayyar. 1996. *The Intelligent person's guide to linearization.* New Delhi: Penguin Books.

Billig, M. 1995. *Banal Nationalism.* California, London, New Delhi: Sage Publications.

Bobb, D. 2005. 'Generation Why', *India Today,* January 31, 30 (4): 98.

Breckenridge, C. 1995. *Consuming modernity: public culture in a South Asian world.* Minneapolis: Minnesota Press.

Byres, T.J. 1988. 'A Chicago view of the Indian state', *Journal of Commonwealth and Comparative Politics,* November: 246–69.

Chandra, B., M. Mukherjee and A. Mukherjee. 1999. *India after Independence.* New Delhi: Viking Penguin India.

Chatterjee, P. 1986. *Nationalist thought and a colonial world: a derivative discourse.* Delhi, Bombay, Madras, Calcutta: OUP.

Das. V. 1976. 'Masks and faces: an essay on Punjabi kinship', *Contributions to Indian Sociology,* 10 (1): 1–30.

de Mooij. M. 2004. *Consumer behaviour and culture-consequences for global marketing and advertising.* California, London, New Delhi: Sage Publications.

———. 1998. Global marketing and advertising—Understanding cultural pardoxes, p. 107. London, California and New Delhi: Sage Publications.

Deshpande, S. 1995. 'Communalising the national space: notes on spatial strategies of Hindutva', *Economic and Political Weekly,* 30 (20): 3220.

Deva, B.C. 1973. *An Introduction to Indian Music,* Ministry of Information and Broadcasting, Government of India. New Delhi: Publications Division.

Dijking, G. 1996. *National identity and geopolitical visions: maps of pride and pain.* London and New York: Routledge.

Dwyer, R. 2000. *All you want is money, all you need is love: sex and romance in modern India*, London: Cassell.

Dwyer, R. and Christopher Pinney. 2001. *Pleasure and the nation: the history, politics and consumption of public culture in India*. New Delhi: OUP.

Fernandes, L. 2000. 'Nationalizing "the global": media images, cultural politics and the middle class in India', *Media, Culture & Society*, 22 (5): 611–28.

Fowles, J. 1996. *Advertising and popular culture*. New Delhi, London: Sage Publications.

Greenfield, L. 2001. 'Etymology, Definitions, Types', in Alexander J. Motyl (ed.), *Encyclopaedia of Nationalism-Fundamental Themes, Volume I.* p. 251. California: Academic Press.

Gahlaut. K. 2005. 'The Yippie Generation', *India Today*, January 31, 30 (4): 18.

Hansen, T.B. 2004. 'The saffron wave: democracy and Hindu nationalism in modern India', in *The Hindu Nationalist Movement and Indian Politics 1925 to the 1990s*, an omnibus, pp. 3–293. New Delhi: Penguin.

Hroch, M. 1995. 'National self-determination from a historical perspective', in Sukumar Periwal (ed.), *Notions of nationalism*, pp. 65–81. New York: OUP.

Indiainfoline. 'MNCs delisting from Indian bourses'. Available online at http://www.indiainfoline.com/nevi/inde/mnde.html (downloaded on 08.10.2005).

Indiantelevision.com. 'A Snapshot of Indian Television History'. Available online at http://www.indiantelevision.com/indianbroadcast/history/historyoftele.htm (downloaded on 13.10.2005).

Kakar, S. 1981. *The inner world: A psychoanalytic study of childhood and society in India*. New Delhi: OUP.

Kapadia, K.M. 1955. *Marriage and family in India*. London: OUP.

Karve, I. 1953. *Kinship organisation in India*. Pune: Deccan College monograph series.

Khilnani, S. 1997: *The idea of India*. New York: Farrar, Straus and Giroux.

Krishnakumar, R. 2003. 'Testing times for cola firms', *Frontline*. Available online at http://www.frontlineonnet.com/fl2017/stories/20030829003803300.htm (downloaded on 26.10.2005).

Lannoy, R. 1971. *The speaking tree-A study of Indian culture and society*. London, Oxford, New York: Oxford University Press.

Lèvi-Strauss, C. 1966. *The savage mind*. London: Weidenfeld and Nicholson.

Lilleker, D.G. 2006. *Key concepts in political communication*. London, New York, New Delhi: Sage Publications.

Maine, H.S. 1972. *Ancient law*, London: Everyman edition.

Mahalingam, S. 1999. 'A Free Run for MNCs'. Available online at http://www.frontlineonnet.com/fl1613/16131080.htm (downloaded on 08.10.2005).

Martin-Barbero, J. 1993. *Communication, culture and hegemony: from the media to mediation*. London: Sage Publications.

Mazzarella, W. 2003. *Shoveling smoke: advertising and globalization in contemporary India.* New Delhi: OUP.

Mehendiworld.com. 'Mehendi wedding customs'. Available online at http://www.mehendiworld.com/mehendi-wedding-customs.htm (downloaded on 3.10.2005).

Mohan, T.K. 2003. *Multinationals and their roles,* p. 6 and 7. Sikkim-Manipal University, Sikkim.

Mondaviarts.org. 'Yamato Wadaiko Drummers of Japan'. Available online at www.mondaviarts.org/education_pdfs/yamato.pdf (downloaded on 08.10.2005).

Motyl, A.J. (ed.). 2001. *Encyclopaedia of Nationalism-Fundamental Themes, Volume I.* Academic Press, California, London.

Nandy, A. 1980. 'Women versus womanliness in India: an essay in cultural and political psychology', in Ashis Nandy (ed.), *At the edge of psychology: essays in politics and culture,* pp. 32–46. New Delhi: OUP.

Nasscom.org. 'Why India', *Nasscom.* Available online at http://www.nasscom.org/artdisplay.asp?cat_id=28 (downloaded on 08.10.2005).

Nathan, S.V. 2000. 'MNCs need to share wealth', *Business Line.* Available online at http://www.blonnet.com/iw/2000/08/27/stories/0827h101.htm (downloaded on 13.08.2005).

National Readership Survey. 1997. All India, National Readership Studies Council.

Nayar, B.R. 1989. 'The politics of economic restructuring in India: the paradox of state strength and policy weakness', *Journal of Commonwealth and comparative politics,* 30 (2): 145–71.

Pantham, T. 2004. 'The Indian nation-state', in Veena Das (ed.), *The handbook of Indian Sociology,* pp. 426–50. New Delhi: OUP.

Parameswaran, M.G. 2003. *Understanding consumers-building powerful brands using consumer research.* New Delhi: Tata McGraw-Hill.

Prasad, M. 'India: TNCs muscling into cottage industry sectors', *Third World Network.* Available online at http://www.twnside.org.sg/title/tnc-ch.htm (downloaded on 8.10.2005).

Progressive Policy Institute. 'The world has over 60,000 multinational companies', *Progressive Policy Institute.* Available online at http://www.ppionline.org/ppi_ci.cfm?knlgAreaID=108&subsecID=900003&contentID=253303 (downloaded 9.07.2005).

Rajagopal, A. 1996. 'Communism and the consuming subject', *Economic and Political Weekly,* February 10, pp. 341–48.

Rodrigues, Usha M. 2005. 'Competition and Television News in India', *Australian Journalism Review,* Journalism Education Association, 27(2): 171–86.

Schiller, H.I. 1989. *Culture, Inc: the corporate takeover of public expression.* NY: OUP.

Sen, A. 2005. *The Argumentative Indian: writings on Indian culture, history and identity.* UK: Penguin.

Singh, M. 2005. 'Of Oxford, economics, empire, and freedom', *The Hindu*, July 10, p. 10.

Singhal, A. and E. Rogers. 2001. *India's communication revolution: from bullock carts to cybermarts*. London, New Delhi: Sage Publications.

Smith, P. and B. West. 2001. 'Cultural studies', in J. Alexander (ed.), *Encyclopaedia of Nationalism-Fundamental Themes, Volume I,* pp. 81–99. California: Academic Press.

Srinivas, M.N. 1952. *Religion and Society among the Coorgs of South India*, Oxford: Clarendon Press.

Srinivas, M.N. 1971. *Social change in modern India*, Berkeley: University of California Press.

Tomlinson, J. 1991. *Cultural imperialism*, Baltimore: John Hopkins Press.

Time. 25 Dec. 2006/1 Jan. 2007, 168 (26/27): 22–23. 'Times person of the year: You'.

Uberoi, P. 2004. 'Family in India', in Veena Das (ed.), *The handbook of Indian Sociology*, pp. 275–307. New Delhi: OUP.

Varghese, A. 'Cultural Nationalism vis-à-vis Multinationals'. Available online at http://www.hvk.org/Publications/culture.html (downloaded on 14.08.2005).

Varma, J.R. 'Corporate Governance in India: Disciplining the Dominant Shareholder'. Available online at http://www.iimahd.ernet.in/~jrvarma/papers/iimbr9-4.pdf (downloaded on 13.07.2005).

Vatsyayan, K. 1996. 'From interior landscapes into cyberspace: dynamics of tradition', in Kamala Ganesh and Usha Thakkar (eds), *Culture and the making of identity in comtemporary India*, pp. 39–49. New Delhi: Sage Publications.

———. 1998. 'Culture: the crafting of institutions', in Hiranmay Karlekar (ed.), *Independent India: the first fifty years*, pp. 486–503. New Delhi: OUP and Indian Council for Cultural Relations.

Vidal, D. 2004. 'Markets', in Veena Das (ed.), *The handbook of Indian Sociology*, pp. 388–401. New Delhi: OUP.

Vohra, R. 2000. *The Making of India*, New Delhi: Vision Books Pvt. Ltd.

Western Union. 'Affiliate Programme', Available online at http://www.westernunion.com/info/aboutUsAffiliate.asp?country=U1 (downloaded on 21.10.2005).

Yadava, J.S., and U.V. Reddi. 1988. 'In the Midst of Diversity: Television in Urban Indian Homes', in James Lull (ed.), *World Families Watch Television*, pp. 125–27. California, London, New Delhi: Sage Publications.

Chapter 3

Print Media in the Era of Globalisation

Usha M. Rodrigues

Introduction

The Indian print media is the envy of many newspaper editors and owners in the developed world. At a time when circulation of newspapers in the USA and Europe is declining, newspapers in India are increasing their circulation. According to World Association of Newspapers (WAN), the number of paid-for newspapers published declined in North America by 0.56 per cent and in Europe by 2.37 per cent in 2007, as opposed to their growth by 11.22 per cent in India (WAN 2008). The WAN reported that Indian newspaper sales increased by 35.51 per cent in the five-year period between 2003 and 2007. The media and entertainment sector in India was twice as profitable as its global counterparts, according to an analysis of 37 publicly-traded Indian companies whose gross profits grew by 31 per cent between 2003 and 2007 (Press Council of India 2008). According to the Press Council, the Indian print media industry recorded a growth of 16 per cent in 2007 with an estimated worth of Rs 130 billion—a trend which is set to continue to reach Rs 281 billion by 2012. Within the print media, newspaper publishing, which constitutes more than 80 per cent, grew by 17 per cent (Ibid.). Overall, in 2008, about 100 million copies of newspapers were sold in India (WAN 2008), whereas according to the National Readership Survey, as many as 222 million readers read an Indian newspaper in 2006 (Press Council of India 2008).

In a country where 22 official (scheduled) languages and hundreds of dialects are spoken, it is not surprising that Hindi (the national language) and regional language newspapers would top the tally of dailies with maximum circulation (Census of India 2001a). The newspaper which sold the most copies was the Hindi daily *Dainik Jagran* with a total readership[1] of 56.6 million, whereas, another Hindi daily *Bhaskar* followed with a total readership of 31.9 million and *Amar Ujala* was at the third position with a readership of 29.6 million (Exchange4media. com 2008a). Other leaders among regional language newspapers were *Lokmat* (20.6 million), *Daily Thanthi* (20.6 million), *Ananda Bazar Patrika* (15.6 million), *Eenadu* (14.7 million), *Malayala Manoroma* (12.7 million), *Vijay Karnataka* (9.6 million) (Exchange4media.com 2008b). *The Times of India* tops the English daily tally with a total readership of 13.6 million for all its editions, whereas *Hindustan Times* follows with 6.3 million and *The Hindu* with 5.6 million a day, according to the Indian Readership Survey[2] for 2007 in round 1 of 2008 (Ibid.). Among the magazines too, Hindi and other non-English language publications dominated, with *India Today* being the only English magazine to make it to the top-10 list with a readership of 67 million (Exchange4-media.com 2008c). Hindi fortnightly, *Saras Salil*, led the overall magazine genre with a total readership of 98 million, followed by *Grih Shobha* with 76 million. Tamil weeklies *Kumudam* and *Kumgumam* share the third and fourth positions, respectively, with 74 million readers.

These statistics indicate the proliferation of Indian print media, at a time when the number of television viewers and radio listeners are rapidly multiplying too. This chapter takes a critical look at the reasons for this expansion in recent years, at a time when online media seems to be threatening the survival of newspapers in more advanced economies. The chapter discusses current trends and strategies employed by media proprietors to maintain and expand their market share in a competitive environment. The chapter also raises questions about the quality of journalism, and whether it is being compromised in these times of boom in a rush to make money from this 'sunrise industry'. The chapter, at first, provides a brief outline of the historical development of print media in India, which has had its own cyclical and eventful 62 years since independence. Then, it discusses current trends in print media management strategies to explore their impact on its future.

Then and now

Indian print media has a past, which is intertwined with India's freedom movement, and, therefore, has had a reputation of being the watchdog of the government in power. Although print media has had protection under the Indian constitution, as part of citizens' rights to the freedom of speech and expression, since independence, the first three decades witnessed governments exerting control over the media's reach through direct and indirect means. Tight control over newsprint because it was imported through a state-controlled corporation, high level of taxes on imported printing machinery and a wage tribunal that mandated salaries for media personnel were among the means used. Later in 1975, during the state of Emergency, the press was censored by the central government, giving birth to underground magazines. It was only after the Emergency period, in 1977, that the new government repealed most of the repressive laws and that the print media in India began 'modernising' (Kohli-Khandekar 2006). According to Jeffery (2000), three factors influenced the growth of print media between 1977 and 1999: rising literacy; increased availability of technology; and increasing influence of capitalism. In the 1980s, Indian polity was increasingly being influenced by the world phenomenon of techno-managerial structure of governance (Kothari 1988). As a result, print media too witnessed some revolutionary changes in the style of management, which became the foundation of current growth of print media in the country. New offset printing and computing technologies, introduction of colour and the entry of young entrepreneurial managers introduced the newspaper industry to shorter deadlines and risky marketing strategies of price wars and big discounts to increase circulation and under-cut competitors in the market. *The Times of India*'s Samir Jain led the pack of new blood in the industry, which was part of the new environment of free market economy in the country in the early 1990s. In fact, in recent decades, there has been a seismic shift in the newspaper arena—from being a family-owned enterprise to becoming a corporatised industry, which has also resulted in a focus on the bottom-line and profit margins. As a result, in the words of Vipul Mudgal:

> ... the trend is that the people selling newspapers are not coming from the newspaper industry anymore. They come from soft drink companies. They know how distribution of soft drinks is done in the country. How your products have to stay fresh and crisp and still have to reach everywhere. A newspaper also has a shelf life of a day. Fresh, crisp product distributed over a vast area. (Mudgal 2009)

Simultaneously, there was a new revolution taking place in the country, when foreign and private television channels via satellite technology arrived in India, hitting the bottom-line of print media by making them less useful for television audiences, and undermining their revenue stream as advertisers started shifting to the new audio-visual medium (Indiantelevision.com 2004). However, the trend was reversed in the mid-2000s and presently, print media (newspapers and magazines) shares about 48 per cent of the country's advertising revenue, while television receives 37 per cent (Indiantelevision.com 2009). In 2006–07, about 34–35 per cent of the advertising revenue went to English media, whereas about 24 per cent was spent on Hindi publications, leaving a little over 40 per cent for all other language papers (Press Council of India 2008: 19). India, unlike the United States, has had strong national and regional newspaper brands, and it is only in recent years that newspapers have started differentiating and marketing their hybrid products—a combination of national and local news pages—to local communities (Ninan 2007). Similarly, Indian newspapers have long been debating a coalition with their international counterparts to fund their expanding repertoire of offerings. However, unlike the television industry, it was only in 2002 that the Indian government decided to allow 26 per cent of foreign direct investment (FDI) into print media. The rules for foreign investment were further modified in 2005, resulting in several Indian newspaper companies raising capital in domestic and international markets (Kohli-Khandekar 2006). In 2008, the Indian government approved that foreign news and current affairs magazines can publish their local editions in India, in effect making them cheaper for the Indian consumers (Reuters 2008). Meanwhile, in the non-news category of publications, 100 per cent foreign investment is allowed, opening the floodgates to technical and specialty magazines and periodicals, such as Vogue, Rolling Stone and Marie Clare. Magazines are seen as the most suitable products for the niche market, for advertisers to reach the right demographic of savvy and upwardly mobile population. Similarly, 100 per cent foreign investment is allowed in corollary sectors such as advertising agencies, market research, public relations and media planning (Press Council of India 2008).

Structural reasons for the increasing circulation

In the past few years, the print media in India has come out on top fighting the new television era (Chapters 1 and 12 in this book). The print media management has implemented a number of strategies to cash in on the increasing literacy and purchasing power of the Indian consumer. Thakurta, a media commentator and educator, says as the economy grows, income grows, and accordingly the individual family's demand for media and entertainment grows:

> You want to read more newspapers, magazines and books. You want to listen to the radio, you want to watch television, you want to watch films, you want to surf the net more—that is a kind of a phenomenon which is true for India and the developing world. (Thakurta 2009)

Similarly, *The Pioneer*'s editor, Chandan Mitra says, apart from the increase in people's purchasing power, the idea that newspapers should be shared communally is gradually coming to an end:

> Earlier probably, in a village of 5000 people probably five copies of a paper went out and they were read out to a congregation and so on. Increasingly, people prefer to buy their own newspapers—numbers are going up in the interior areas and this reflects a substantial increase in the circulation of Indian language newspapers. (Mitra 2009)

Mitra says the third reason for the print media's growth is the people's 'urge' for more and reliable information. 'Television coverage has penetrated and cable television covers more than 60 per cent of households in India, and people recognise that television is quite sensational and not really reliable, so they cross-check and balance the information with newspapers.' Also, with an increase in literacy levels, families' aspiration levels are increasing. 'Parents want their children to be well informed and they believe that inculcating the habit of reading newspapers in children is important—I am talking particularly of smaller towns and villages' (Mitra 2009). According to the 'State of Newspaper Scene 2007':

> Four important factors could be attributed to the growth trend of newspapers. First, the spread of television particularly news channels, this unwittingly created a base for newspapers. Second, the competition: between television

channels for viewership and between newspapers for readership and, then, between new channels and newspapers. Third, economic and demographic aspects to do with literacy and lifestyles, Fourth, the wide gap in readership, between regions of the country and male–female, urban–rural, started declining although the differences are still glaring, constantly reminding the potential for growth. (Press Council of India 2008: 4)

The gap in readership between regions, male–female and urban–rural are significant barometers of India's economic growth and its impact on all segments of the population. In 2001, the overall literacy rate improved to about 65 per cent of the population of a little over one billion from about 52 per cent in 1991 (Census of India 2001b). The gap between male–female literacy rate was 75–53 per cent, whereas between urban–rural population was 80–59 per cent.

Meanwhile, Ninan (2007: 18), in her study of the expansion of Hindi newspapers, also notes that it was the revitalisation of panchayat raj (local self-government) in 1992 and its subsequent implementation, which has resulted in a considerable degree of grassroots political participation, creating awareness and hunger for news, thereby giving an impetus for regional media to expand its reach by launching a number of local editions in smaller cities and towns in each state. 'Newspapers brought increased awareness, a growing consumerism, and civic participation in their wake, and no one was left untouched. Readers, civil society, politicians, panchayats all experienced a media saturation that was as rapid as it was new' (Ibid.: 13–14). Statistics provided earlier support the assertion that it is the expansion of Hindi and regional language press in the recent decade which has continued to lead the industry's envious performance.[3] According to the 'State of Newspaper Scene 2007', both the growth and expansion of regional language print media has coincided with proliferation of news broadcasts (Press Council of India 2008). 'Although the English print media and television reach out to the more affluent sections of the population and therefore command a disproportionate share of advertising revenue, but in terms of reach and circulation, in terms of readership figures, the non-English newspapers are far bigger' (Thakurta 2009).

Strategies for maintenance of growth

The increase in circulation goes hand-in-hand with increasing competition in the print media industry. Although, as stated earlier, there are some structural reasons for the industry's growth, where individual media groups are implementing new management and marketing strategies to continue to survive and thrive in a lot more competitive market place. Media groups see an opportunity to expand their reach into new territories, particularly in rural India, and an opportunity to encroach on other groups' stronghold with aggressive marketing strategies. Whether these strategies have had an adverse impact on the quality of journalism is a moot question. 'In cities, newspapers have refashioned themselves, they've added glamour and other things which were earlier treated cursorily, which has led to a lot of young people reading newspapers.... This has also led to serious news getting underplayed and the glamour and commercial things getting precedence' (Mitra 2009). The press is moving from being elite to being a mass medium, and the Indian newspaper is evolving from being a politics-driven product for the serious-minded reader into one that is fashioning itself for the upwardly mobile, as well as for the reader who has barely begun to read, and is looking for news of his immediate universe (Ninan 2007: 18). Similarly, Vipul Mudgal, Editor (Research), *Hindustan Times*, outlines the various marketing strategies of Indian newspapers:

> Readership drivers—everybody knows that a good sports supplement or good sports coverage attracts more readers, engages them more with the paper. Everybody knows that good Bollywood coverage is interesting, people like it. It is very common for the Hindi newspaper to have a Bollywood supplement, even without advertisements, because they see it as a good readership driver. Then you have a 'niche segment' like the young people you want to attract to something like career, education—this is one way of attracting readers. Then, there are discounts, a free watch, a shiny bag. And, then you have exclusives, you have big scoops—you hope that by sheer good journalism you would attract people to your papers. (Mudgal 2009)

Ninan (2007: 276) says Hindi newspapers such as *Dainik Bhaskar, Dainik Jagran, Amar Ujala, Rajasthan Patrika* and *Hindustan* have expanded their reach over a period of 10 years (from 1995 to 2005) by creating multi-editions, adding pages, supplements, colour to their paper and by investing capital in machines and marketing, and squeezing out local stand-alone papers by initiating price wars. As a result, competition from the bigger players with deeper pockets have forced smaller players in the Hindi heartland to either come up with strategies to carve out a niche for themselves in the market by covering corruption and pollution related stories which the bigger papers do not cover, or close down. Mitra (2009) agrees that one has to make a distinction between mass circulation and niche papers, which have different strategies to compete in the market. Niche papers have to rely on newspaper subscription for their revenue, instead of advertising, which usually goes to the mass circulation papers:

> For mass circulation newspapers the target audience is very clearly, the young, children in the 12–18 years age group, who were not really newspaper readers earlier. But now children make a lot of purchasing decisions at home, they are pushing parents to subscribe to more than one newspaper, not so much for newsgathering, but all the paraphernalia that goes with it—both English newspapers as well as Hindi are aggressively targeting the youth segments with more stories on glamour, but also on employment, opportunities, career options, education prospects and so on....
>
> For niche newspapers and publications, the thrust is at the discerning reader, to get more people to buy the paper at home rather than (read it) at the workplace, which they often do, to put serious material ... to get the serious readers in universities, in business houses, government, these are areas where I think there is considerable prospect of growing. [But] there are very few niche language newspapers because the economics does not work out for them. (Mitra 2009)

The executive editor of *The Times of India*, Arindam Sengupta (2009) believes that the younger generation has always been the target of print media, but today's newspapers need to be 'less preachy', and connect with people, 'interactivity is important'. *The Times of India* has launched several verticals: education, property, life-style, *The Daily Times* in each city, 'to add greater muscle power to the main product and in times to come there will be still more verticals.'

Localisation and citizen journalism

Although the size of the cake has increased, newspapers want to in-crease their market share in lucrative metropolitan regions so they conduct consumer surveys to get an edge over the rival papers by finding out what it is that newspaper readers want and expect from their paper. Integration of the media industry with the general industry means the managers and CEOs are now coming from diverse backgrounds, and constantly looking at the bottom line.

> Also, marketing surveys have come of age. Now, you can calibrate and measure things with precision.... They do things like 'recall surveys'. They want to see what is at the back of readers' mind when they recall a story. What do they remember from last week's paper.... I must say a lot of Hindi papers are adopting these strategies more aggressively now. (Mudgal 2009)

Ninan, in her study of Hindi heartland newspapers refers to the process of localisation, where papers have launched local editions, where news—public issues and private scandals—about the local small town and village is covered. 'You now had a newsprint-enabled and advertising-supported civic square where local gentry, local governance and local crime competed for attention' (Ninan 2007: 20).

Sengupta sees this focus on 'local' as newspapers being more accountable to its readers.

> This focus on local issues arises from greater demand that a reader makes— what is there in the newspaper that is of value to me. If my street lights don't work; if I don't get water; every other day a thief breaks into my locality and I live in fear; is my plight getting at all highlighted? That's a big shift that's happened (in the newspaper coverage). (Sengupta 2009)

Since the Indian media is broadening its news market by bringing fresh, less educated audiences into the fold, there is a push towards covering community news, 'where newsmaker is the ordinary person' (Ninan 2009). The new trend in citizen journalism and community participation fits well into this trend to localise news in the expanding newspaper market. Ninan says citizen journalism makes economic sense in India, where newspapers rely on a community representative to cover their community news.

Most of the newspapers now have an online news portal, where individuals from the community are encouraged to provide feedback and news stories from their locality.

The name of the game is 'connect'. You connect with them and you have won half the race and if you get them to engage with you, then it is like an icing on the cake, and so what has happened is that lately it is a global trend, everybody wants that response.... Newspapers want to know what is in their readers' mind, and the user-generated content is a gift of the internet that is now coming into papers. (Mudgal 2009)

Thakurta says young people increasingly want to engage in a conversation, rather than being preached to by the media, '... journalism is now having to reach not only participative but also personalised readers' (Thakurta 2009). Others like Mitra (2009) see the incorporation of citizen journalism as a public relation exercise by the media.

Quality and sustainability of growth

However, the aggressive strategy of selling more copies has also had an impact on the quality of journalism and credibility of journalists in India. Media, particularly, the print media, as stated earlier, has a legacy of being part of the freedom movement in India and therefore enjoys a level of respect among its audiences which is unknown in some of the more advanced democracies, where sometimes, journalists are compared to car sales people. The increasing circulation of newspapers in India according to some commentators is under-cutting this credibility because of a fall in the quality of journalism. Some commentators are critical of the media strategy of 'dumbing down' news content to attract new readers in rural and less-educated segments of the population. Mudgal (2009), who was in-charge of the *Hindustan Times'* new editions in Lucknow, Jaipur and Dehradun, explains that as newspapers are going to smaller cities to expand their readership, they have to modify their language standards to reach the masses. In smaller towns, very few people can speak English, and the paper wants to cater to a large proportion of aspiring readers and for the 'waanabees', which results in lowering of standards, says Mudgal.

The page 3 idea—emphasis on sports coverage, the dumbing down of stories which are covered with a lot of violence, crime, rape rather than political or social stories—all of these are some of the things the papers are doing to make them more attractive and to get new readers that is those who aren't reading the papers. (Thapar 2009)

Thapar (2009) is also critical of the education level of the new crop of journalists, who are joining the booming industry with some technical skills, but 'haven't learnt to think, to question, to analyse, to understand, to judge between relevant and irrelevant and to be discriminatory.' Ninan (2009) too, believes that the print media has become too focused on its revenue base rather than quality of journalism.

> Even print media (similar to television) is heavily going into one big story mode on their front pages. There are regional newspapers which would have 10 stories on their front page, whereas English newspapers would have three–four or one dominant news story on the front page. This trend is also influenced by the revenue base of advertisement where news publications want to grab the reader and satisfy their curiosity about that one big topic of the day …
> it is rating based, it is based on what the media think its audience want.
> (Ninan 2009)

However, Sengupta (2009) thinks that journalism quality in India has 'gone up, rather than down' because newspapers today have become more responsive to the local readers' need for local news. Rather than giving them news about distant places which has little impact on their day to day lives, readers now get news about themselves and their locality. But, he agrees that the quality of English language in the newspapers has gone down:

> It's another matter that there is a tendency to sensationalise, but that is not across the board. Stories are not as well examined and filtration process is not as good as it used to be, but 25–30 years ago, those were more innocent days. Things are happening so fast these days, you need to do things at such a rapid pace that there is a bit of a problem in that sometimes a few things that ought not to go in, go in. But you get huge volume of news, that is being covered today, and from every possible sector. I think content of newspapers has gone up rather than down, what has declined is the quality of English language.
> (Sengupta 2009)

Sengupta believes the quality of language education in India has nose-dived, and as a result the newspaper desk which used to be the 'real pillar of a newspaper establishment' is under staffed and under qualified. Mitra (2009) agrees:

Sometimes when you talk of the quality going down, I would agree only to a limited extent that the presentation and the language in which the reporter has prepared is not as exact as in the past, but overall, in terms of coverage, things are pretty good right now with the print media.

However, there has been criticism of the media's coverage of trivial and sensational stories in a bid to reach the lowest common denominator, in the process breaking the Press Council of India's 'Norms of journalistic conduct' (Mitra 2009; Ninan 2009). In the recently concluded General elections, media watchers reported several cases where the press was paid to carry favourable news reports about the local political parties and candidates (Chamdia 2009; Sridhar 2009). The distinction between advertising, advertorials and news is adversely affecting the credibility of the media. It is the intensification of competition and the commercial pressures which are causing media to break the voluntary norms of journalistic conduct. Similarly, some commentators note the politicisation of media in India, particularly, in the trend towards partisan coverage (Mudgal 2009; Ninan 2009). 'There is a trend of politicizing of India. Like in pluralism, you have all kinds of lobbies jostling with each other for attention, for getting their agenda fulfilled. In the same way, their news has to be reflected in their sympathetic media' (Mudgal 2009). During the Gujarat riots, some of the regional print media's coverage was criticised for being biased and sensational, inciting riots based on religion. Subarno Chattarji (2008: 47) in his study of mass media discourses in India and Pakistan says that during the time of the Kargil war and Gujarat riots, the Indian media's coverage was inconsistent and shallow, lacking an analysis of the impact of the history of communal violence and hate speeches on Indian population, causing anxiety (among both majority and minority sections) 'frying the secular fabric of Indian polity and institutions'. Similarly, the Indian media has been criticised for ignoring the plight of the one third of the population, including farmers, women and minorities, which still lives below the poverty line. P. Sainath (in Fernandes 2008), the rural affairs editor of *The Hindu*, says that the media has neglected to analyse and report the real big issues: impediments to development, corruption and structural reasons for poverty in India. Commentators also lament the non-effectiveness of the Press Council of India, a body of representatives from print publications and nominees of the two houses of parliament, who are unable to punish the perpetrators (Mitra 2009; Thakurta 2009). Meanwhile, the 'government has no interest in uplifting the level of journalism. If they did that, good journalism will devour the government of the day' (Mudgal 2009). The only hope seems to be the audiences, who need to demand better news coverage.

The Future

When the television revolution took off in India in the 1990s, many commentators doubted the resilience of print media to thrive against the capacity of the audio-visual medium to reach the masses. After initially losing advertising revenue to television, print media has clawed back some of its share, and presently receives about 48 per cent of the advertising budget spent in India. It also has grown to reach new regions and new readers with multi-editions, while in other established markets some publications challenged others' market share by launching marketing strategies including price wars and free gifts for readers. Consequently, the Indian print media has become more and more dependent on advertising revenue than from its cover price. Advertisements account for more than 65 per cent of newspapers' revenue, and higher for most of English dailies (Press Council of India 2008). There are claims that the distinction between editorial and marketing departments is vanishing, resulting in downgrading and devaluing of news, analysis and public affairs information provided by the newspapers. 'There are tendencies of hyper-commercialisation, which tackles the newspaper and its journalism more or less like any other commodity or "product" and sees any higher ground vision as old-fashioned, sanctimonious humbug' (Ram 2007: 3). Meanwhile, it is significant to note that most of the top advertising, public relations and media planning agencies in India today are controlled by foreign owners (due to 100 FDI allowance), which raises questions about the need to restrict foreign ownership to 26 per cent in the print news media.

The commercialisation and corporatisation of print media is having an adverse impact on the quality of journalism of Indian newspapers, which have so far maintained their historical legacy of being a plural and diverse industry reflecting the vast regional, linguistic, socio-economic and cultural diversity of Indian society. However, dark clouds of concentration of media ownership are on the horizon with smaller newspapers being driven out of the market by predatory pricing by bigger counterparts. There are 13–14 media groups emerging as conglomerates in the country, which are in the news business, consolidating their position horizontally across cities and towns, and vertically across various media platforms (Press Council of India 2008). The bigger players are now becoming multimedia empires by launching or acquiring interests in television and radio stations. One such example is *Dainik Jagran* launching its own television channel, similar to *The Times of India*, which has a sister television network complete with news and entertainment channels. As noted earlier, the pressure to maximise profit and the need to maintain political influence is resulting in newspapers in some instances selling their news space to political parties, compromising the principle of demarcation between news and views content.

A Centre for Media Studies in its report 'State of Newspaper Scene 2007' (Press Council of India 2008) points out that although print media is considered to be more credible than television news channels, newspapers have lost ground as primary source of information for the readers. However, the report is critical of the fact that print media still devotes a large percentage of its space to politics, crime and international news, in the name of 'what interests people' (Press Council of India 2008: 22). There is a tendency to provide more of the same content to all markets, ignoring the trend of readers, particularly younger and more educated audience, to seek local specific and in-depth news related to social, development and environment on the internet. N. Ram, the Editor-in-Chief of *The Hindu*, says:

> Journalism need to respond better than it is doing now to the challenge and opportunity of being relevant and read. This is an era of intensifying multimedia competition, back and forth communication, when the 'always on' culture is spreading, and readers and other 'consumers' of 'media products' are asserting themselves and, along with revolutionary technologies, are setting both the terms and the pace of change. (Ram 2007)

The threat from the internet is real, and most Indian newspapers have their own online news portals. However, as internet penetration grows, people will access information online, putting pressure on newspapers. As has been witnessed in more advanced economies, the competition print media would face is not only from other mainstream media which has adapted to the online environment, but also from citizen journalism and social media websites which may seek to fill the holes left by the print media in their coverage. There is a danger that in the process of pursuing larger profits and market share, Indian journalism may lose its credibility with its audiences forcing its readers to look for quality elsewhere. As Harcup (2007: 20) says, journalism still has a role to play in a democratic society and therefore journalism standards need to be protected.

> Because journalism has an impact on society as a whole and therefore other people do have a stake in how we do our jobs as journalists. Imperfect, though it is, journalism is one of the key ways in which we can gain knowledge about the world in which we live ... knowledge is power. (Harcup 2007).

Endnotes

1. According to Press Council of India (2008), English dailies have on an average 3–4 readers per copy as against 5–7 readers for leading dailies in regional languages such as Telugu, Tamil, Kanada and Gujarati, whereas leading Hindi dailies have 5–6 readers per copy.
2. Please note, almost all the readership surveys in India are disputed by one or more media groups. Accurate surveying in India is difficult because of diversity of languages and access to rural and remote areas.
3. Readership and circulation of dailies in southern states of India have been growing, which coincides with proliferation of television channels including language television in these states (Kerela, Tamil Nadu, Andhra Pradesh and Karnataka). Similarly, in the neighbouring state of Maharashtra, Marathi newspapers have flourished (Press Council of India 2008: 5).

References

Chamdia, Anil. 2009. 'More on how the media earned from the elections', Thehoot. org, 9 June. Available online at http://www.thehoot.org/web/home/story. php?storyid=3900&mod=1&pg=1&sectionId=5&valid=true (downloaded on 09.06.2009).

Chattarji, Subarno. 2008. *Tracking the media.* London: Routledge.

Print Media in the Era of Globalisation

Census of India. 2001a. 'Scheduled languages in descending order of speakers' strength'. Available online at http://www.censusindia.gov.in/Census_Data_2001/Census_Data_Online/Language/Statement4.htm (downloaded on 14.08.2009).

———. 2001b. 'Number of literates and literacy rate.' Available online at http://www.censusindia.gov.in/Census_Data_2001/India_at_glance/literates1.aspx (downloaded on 21.05.2009).

Exchange4media.com. 2008a. 'Dainik Jagran continues the lead in Hindi dailies' and 'TOI leads English', 26 April. Available online at http://www.exchange4media.com/IRS/2008/fullstory.asp?section_id=5&news_id=30697&tag=25605&pict=1 (downloaded on 16.06.2009).

———. 2008b. 'No surprises in the language wise leaders as well', 26 April. Available online at http://www.exchange4media.com/IRS/2008/fullstory.asp?section_id=5&news_id=30698&tag=25606&pict=2 (downloaded on 16.06.2009).

———. 2008c. 'Saras Salil continues its lead in the overall magazine genre', 26 April. Available online at http://www.exchange4media.com/IRS/2008/fullstory.asp?section_id=5&news_id=30699&tag=25607&pict=3 (downloaded on 16.06.2009).

Fernandes, Naresh. 2008. 'Uncomfortable truth: P. Sainath reminds us that India is still a poor country', Second read *Columbia Journalism Review*, 5 February. Available online at: http://www.cjr.org/second_read/uncomfortable_truth.php. (downloaded on 27.10.2008).

Harcup, Tony. 2007. *The ethical journalist.* London: Sage Publications.

Indiantelevision.com. 2004. 'Media gets "media attention" in 2004', 4 February. Available online at http://www.indiantelevision.com/ye2004/atul_phadnis.htm (downloaded on 22.05.2009).

———. 2009. 'GroupM forecast grim 2009 for Indian media', 27 April. Available online at http://www.indiantelevision.com/mam/headlines/y2k9/apr/aprmam125.php (downloaded on 22.05.2009).

Jeffrey, Robin. 2000. *India's newspaper revolution—Capitalism, politics and the Indian languages press—1977–1999.* New Delhi: Oxford University Press.

Kohli-Khandekar, Vanita. 2006. *The Indian media business.* 2nd edition. New Delhi: Response Books, Sage Publications.

Kothari, R. 1988. 'Integration and exclusion in Indian politics', *Economic and Political Weekly*, 23 (43): 2223–27.

Ninan, Sevanti. 2007. *Headlines from the heartland.* New Delhi: Sage Publications.

Ram, N. 2007. 'Newspaper futures: India and the world', *The Hindu*, 15 August. Available online at http://www.hindu.com/af/india60/stories/2007081550100300.htm (downloaded on 17.06.2009).

Press Council of India. 2008. *State of newspaper scene 2007.* New Delhi: Centre for Media Studies.

Reuters. 2008. 'India allows local editions of foreign news magazines', 18 September. Available online at http://in.reuters.com/article/businessNews/idINIndia-355 44520080918 (downloaded on 05.05.2009).

Sridhar, Madabhushi. 2009. 'News for sale in general elections 2009', Thehoot. org, 27 May. Available online at http://www.thehoot.org/web/home/story. php?storyid=3863&pg=1&mod=1&sectionId=5&valid=true (downloaded on 27.05.2009).

World Association of Newspapers (WAN). 2008. 'World press trends: Newspapers are a growth business', 2 June. Available online at http://www.wan-press.org/ print.php3?id_article=17377 (downloaded on 25.05.2009).

Interviews

Mitra, Chandan. 2009. Editor, *The Pioneer*. Interviewed by author, New Delhi, 9 January 2009.

Mudgal, Vipul. 2009. Editor (Research), *Hindustan Times*. Interviewed by author, New Delhi, 10 March 2009.

Ninan, Sevanti. 2009. Editor, thehoot.org and media commentator. Interviewed by author, New Delhi, 12 January 2009.

Sengupta, Arindam. 2009. Executive Editor, *The Times of India*. Interviewed by author, New Delhi, 12 January 2009.

Thakurta, Paranjoy Guha. 2009. Media commentator and educator. Interviewed by author, New Delhi, 15 January 2009.

Thapar, Karan 2009. Host, *Devil's Advocate*, CNN-IBN. Interviewed by author, New Delhi, 12 March 2009.

Chapter 4

Commercial FM Radio
Takes Over Indian Cities
Maya Ranganathan

The 1990s are a watershed era in the history of Indian radio for at this time it made a spectacular return as a medium of development and entertainment. This is surprising and significant because, first, television seemed to have almost pushed radio into obscurity, despite the fact that given the rates of illiteracy and affordability among people, the medium was ideally suited to a developing country like India (Gopalakrishnan 2003).[1] Second, the radio comeback in a 'country besotted with television' was at a time when television technology was developing by leaps and bounds and newer models were ushering in spectacular images and colours (Ninan 2003). Third, in the era of convergence, radio did not compete for attention with any other medium, but complemented others, with Frequency Modulation (FM) radio taking over the cities by storm.

FM radio arrived in India as early as 1977 when it was introduced in Chennai. The next station came up in Jalandhar in 1982. But since 1993, it has caught the imagination of the people and become the youth medium that it is today. While the history of FM radio in India is yet to be documented, media reports indicate that the current format of FM programming can be traced to Mumbai, when on 15 August 1993 All India Radio (AIR) leased FM slots to private producers. The first entrants were 'Times FM' of the Bennet and Coleman Group, publishers of the English daily, *The Times of India*, and 'Radio Star' and 'Radio Midday'. The Supreme Court judgment in 1995 (AIR 1995 Supreme Court 1236) which ruled that broadcasting could not be treated as a monopoly by the government, organisations or individuals, led to a spurt in the leasing of air time by AIR (Noronha 2001: 72–75). In Phase II introduced by the government in July 2005, 337 channels, encompassing 91 cities, were put on bid.

Letters of Intent (LOI) were issued to 245 channels of which about 150 had become operational by the end of the year. The revenue earned by the industry had grown from Rs 350 million in 2007 to Rs 550 million in 2008 (Narasimhan 2008).

Today, while private broadcasters with investments of up to Rs 5 million are moving into smaller towns such as Siliguri and Asansol in West Bengal and Raichur in Chhattisgarh or Itanagar in Arunachal Pradesh, the government is contemplating doing away with the licensing fees that can run up to Rs 30 million for 10 years and implementing a revenue-sharing model. Some foreign broadcasters had initially formed joint ventures to bid for licences, notable among them being BBC World-wide, the commercial arm of the BBC, and India's 'Midday Multimedia' forming a joint venture to operate locally under the name of 'Radio Midday West' and run 'Go 92.5', which has now become 'Radio One FM 94.3' (Forbes.com 2006). Despite speculations that some provisions of the 'expansion policy of private FM radio' would be relaxed, the Union Cabinet in 2008, even as it approved FM broadcasters setting up subsidiaries, capped the limit at 20 per cent (Reuters 2008).

In May 2004, the Radio Broadcast Policy Committee, headed by Amit Mitra, questioned the viability of FM radio stations, pointing out that the licence fee was 'unrealistic'. Several bidders defaulted on payments with the result that few radio stations reached the operating stage (Indiatogether.com 2004). The accent on revenue also denied rural sector access to FM radio, which incidentally was overlooked by the committee. The Telecom Regulatory Authority of India (TRAI), which became the regulatory body for radio and television in 2004, in its consultation paper, argued for the expansion of coverage 'to the unserved areas, particularly north-eastern states, border region, hilly terrain …' (Venniyoor 2004). The 2006 auction of FM frequencies mostly drew media houses and corporates, besides international radio operators (AsiaMedia.com 2006).[2]

The Federation of Indian Chambers of Commerce and Industry (FICCI) and Price Waterhouse Coopers' report on the Indian Entertainment and Media Industry (2008) stated that the radio industry in 2007 recorded a growth of 24 per cent over the previous year. In fact, in the period between 2004–07, the radio industry recorded the second highest cumulative growth of 37 per cent on an overall basis after online advertising.

The local in the global

The popularity of FM stations is not hard to fathom given that they seem to, at the same time, borrow from and break every rule followed by AIR in terms of programming and content, making it a lively, casual and entertaining medium. What is significant for media analysts is that in the era of globalisation it has emerged as the most local of mediums. Covering a radius of up to 60 square kilometres, it caters to audiences comprising a few million in metropolitan cities and much fewer in smaller towns. It is this preoccupation with the local that has come as a boon to the medium, for it has become the most effective advertising medium for local and small businesses. FM advertisements account for nearly 60 per cent of the Rs 620 million that radio advertisements bring in (FICCI and Price Waterhouse Coopers 2008).[3] The figure is expected to treble in 2012. Considering that AIR charges Rs 3,000 per hour against the lease while the programme producers charge a minimum of Rs 250–300 for a 10-second advertisement, it is not surprising that FM is every advertiser's dream. The FMs also face competition from community radio stations that have been permitted to air limited advertising (Sebastian 2008).

Ironically, the FMs are still no match for the AIR commercial service, 'Vividh Bharathi', in terms of listenership, which stands at 20.26 million, mainly because of the latter's strong national penetration. However, AIR has also moved into the FM arena providing the same fare as private broadcasters, but with a slight difference in presentation. According to the 2008 Indian Readership Survey (IRS) Round 2 conducted by the Media Research Users' Council (MRUC) and Hansa Research, 'Radio Mirchi' remained the most popular station with a listenership of 16.34 million during the period of July 2007–June 2008. The second slot was occupied by AIR's FM service with 12.82 million listeners and 'Rainbow FM' with 10.32 million. The rest of the listenership cake was shared by a host of FM stations that included some recent entrants too. The FM's reach in cities and towns, however, was comparable to the press or even private television channels. In media-saturated Chennai, for instance, a quick count in 2008 revealed the presence of 10 FM stations with two of them being operated by AIR.

Interestingly, the preoccupation with the local has opened up some new employment opportunities (Dugar 2008). Small town announcers have shot to fame and this in turn has led to a feeling of brotherhood, especially in small towns. It has also emerged as a vital source of local information as is seen by the role played by small radio stations in Bihar and Orissa during times of natural calamities. For instance, during the floods in Mumbai in 2005, the FM radio stations were lauded for providing useful information to citizens who were stuck on the roads or went without electricity at home (Venniyoor 2005). In normal times, however, as one writer puts it: 'No one takes FM seriously and yet almost everyone ends up listening to it' (Mounir 2008).

FM, however, has emerged as essentially a youth medium. With the advertising revenue influencing programme content, it is the youth that are catered to the most. Of course, the definition of 'youth' varies, but it includes those with purchasing power or those who are 'decision-makers'. This has made FM a medium for those with the wherewithal to spend, leaving some categories such as the elderly or retired, out in the cold. Thus, while FM promotes film music and popular music, classical music and even old-film music hardly figures in various stations' agendas. In fact, interestingly, some of the middle-aged staff of the FM stations owned up to being World Space listeners for FMs did not cater to their 'tastes in music'.

On a staple of film music

Much like private television programming, FMs follow a time-tested formula. In 2003, it was found that 74 per cent of the listeners were unable to correctly associate FM programmes with the channels they were on (Ninan 2003). With the still-debated ban on news telecasts, their fare is confined to music and occasional interviews built around the happenings in the city that they are aired from. While each FM station caters supposedly to a niche market, for the common listener, the fare is mostly indistinguishable. Unlike in the West, where each station caters to a different genre of music, in India, almost all FM stations thrive on film music. With the current and popular being the most sought-after, it is not uncommon to hear the latest hit on almost all the stations on any given day, despite the fact that these stations are aware that there is no unduplicated audience for radio. With nothing much to differentiate between the stations, there is constant 'channel swapping' with no station or channel loyalty (Televisionpoint.com).

Explaining this, Navaneet, the programme director of Radio One in Chennai, says the differences are usually subtle. While the template for an FM station is how it can become the most local medium, the niche audience is thought of in terms of housewives, students, children, men, women or singles, he points out.[4] His radio station is more into melodies, he adds, although given the trends in Tamil film music it is difficult to slot music into clear-cut genres. The dependence on film music has reportedly led to declining sales of recorded music in the local market. Even as early as 1993, the Indian Music Industry (IMI) reported a 20 per cent slump in the sales of recorded music which was attributed to the 'non-stop airplay of popular film soundtrack hits by the FM stations' (Televisionpoint.com).[5]

Indeed, on closer analysis the FM stations seem to be categorising the youth market further. A station that attempts to appeal to the up-market youth, the 'yuppie IT crowd' seems to include a good mix of Hindi film songs and English pop as it is believed that the cosmopolitan or global Indian is more at ease with this genre of music than regional film songs. While no research in India substantiates or repudiates this claim, it is clear that the definition of 'audience as market' follows the ways in which other media define and cater to their audience, for instance, the perception of what the readers of English newspapers and regional newspapers want. However, it stands to reason that youngsters on the move would prefer FM over other media, thanks to convergence and incorporation of technology in mobile phone sets. Surprisingly, preliminary studies have revealed that listenership at home amounts to over 80 per cent and listenership on the move amounting the least (Televisionpoint.com). In the absence of an organised research body, most stations seem to rely on in-house research to assess the reach and time spent on listening. The huge numbers of callers-in for contests and interactive sessions are indicative of the stations' standing. In fact, one of the significant developments in 2007 was the introduction of Radio Audience Measurement (RAM) (FICCI and Price Waterhouse Coopers 2008: 15). But it is currently confined to a few cities. In 2008, a radio monitoring service 'AirCheck India' was launched to monitor advertisements and music on radio (Medianewsline.com 2008). Although the service can undertake custom research projects, it will, by and large, help advertisers keep track of their advertisements and help recording companies keep count of the popular charts. Another audience measurement tool is the Indian Listenership Track (ILT).

Government guidelines

Film music is to FM stations what films are to private satellite channels, providing as they do the easiest, cheapest and most popular content. They also help adhere to the guidelines laid by the Information and Broadcasting Ministry on content that FM stations can provide. Casteist, racist and sexist remarks are prohibited and FM stations are also not allowed to broadcast news programmes or political programmes. TRAI stated in September 2008, in its recommendations on the 'Third Phase of Private FM Radio Broadcasting', that broadcasters 'may be permitted to broadcast news using content from AIR, Doordarshan, authorised news channels, Press Trust of India (PTI), United News of India (UNI) and any other authorised news agency' in order to provide access to information for a large section of the population (Zubin 2008).

The issue of allowing news and current affairs programming on private radio channels, and allowing of foreign ventures, rests with the Union Cabinet. It has also been reported that the task force of the Radio Broadcast Policy is to tread the path of 'more control citing security reasons' (Indiantelevision.com 2003). Much like the community radio stations that seemed to hold a lot of promise but failed to take off in a big way due to the government regulations and restrictions, the FM stations are grappling with vague guidelines laid down by the Ministry of Information and Broadcasting. Although 'hard' news is banned, almost all FM channels carry information about the local area: events, sports and stocks throughout the day!

However, the onus of adhering to these guidelines is entirely on stations and there is no authority overseeing its implementation. The stations could suffer anything from a fine to being taken off air, for failure to adhere to the guidelines. But the action is to be initiated by self-interest groups, consumer forums or other public forums. The most celebrated case perhaps is that of the radio jockey (RJ) of Red FM, Jonathan Nitin Brady, who reportedly made offending remarks against the Indian Idol winner, Prashant Tamang, in September 2008. Tamang was referred to as a 'guard' resulting in clashes around Darjeeling leading to deployment of soldiers, which prompted the Ministry of Information and Broadcasting to term it 'racist and insulting' (*The Times of India* 2007). Tamang's fans moved the Supreme Court against the RJ (Radio Duniya News 2008). The channel also faced a week's ban which meant going off air, the first time in the history of Indian radio.

RJs: 'reckless' jockeys?

While the remarks against Tamang brought to light, the consequences of 'reckless chatter', reckless and subjective opinions have indeed become the hallmark of FM stations. If television serials have come to be known for being tear-jerkers, FM radio stations are known for their chatty and reckless programme presenters called RJs. A concept borrowed from the West, FM radio presenters do everything differently from their contemporaries in AIR. Chattier and repetitive, they command fan following and some of them move on to more 'glamorous' media like television or even feature films. The stereo format of the FM broadcast literally carries the RJ's voice to places. While some like RJ Nitin face the listeners' wrath, most of them have a fan following, if one were to go by the fan clubs formed in community forums and blogs. RJ training programmes are slowly being inducted into media institutes' curricula, but radio stations presumably look for opinionated youngsters with a sense of local geography and with great presence of mind. As a station director puts it, they must have 'an ability to laugh at themselves, even if not humorous'. A mid-range voice with a style would perhaps help. Based on audience's responses it is not difficult to deduce the essential qualities of an RJ.

The non-stop chatter that includes inanities seems to appeal to listeners, going by the popularity of some of the RJs as rated by popular magazines. For instance, Big 92.7 FM's Chennai RJ 'Big Imsai Arasi' ('the big queen of annoyance'), RJ Ophelia, was recognised as 'the best female RJ of the year 2008' by *Ananda Vikatan*, a popular Tamil weekly magazine (IndiaPRwire.com 2009). She hosts a programme between 3 p.m. and 6 p.m. on weekdays aimed at the youth, and her effort to find humour in every situation was lauded by the magazine. The popularity has even spurred RJs to win an entry in the Guinness Book of World Records with their loquaciousness.[6]

With radio disc jockeying being new to India, training is provided in-house. For instance, when Big 92 FM fanned its operations across many cities and towns in India, it launched a nation-wide search for 400 presenters and trained them (O'Connor 2007). The attrition levels are quite high at 25 percent as RJs who become household names grow bigger than the stations (Narasimhan 2008).

The future

Training almost seems superfluous going by the success of Raghav Mahato of Mansoorpur village in Vaishali district, Bihar, who enthralled 'thousands of villagers' from his make-shift FM radio station run out of his electronics shop (Tewary 2006). Illiterate and hence ignorant that one require a government licence to operate an FM station, Mahato shut operations when he became aware of the rules, only to resume on pressure from his listeners. While this indicates the ease with which FM radio can be set up and operated, in the context of McChesney's observation (2000) of pirate radio as a form of civil disobedience, Mahato's case points to the stranglehold that the state has over a medium that has the utmost potential to be employed for development, including providing the much-needed public sphere in a democracy.

Some of the concerns raised about the sector are trading of licences, management outsourcing, allotment of multiple licences/frequencies in the same city, creation of a level playing field for FMs and AIR in terms of content and music royalty. Demands range from allowing news in FM stations, formulation of credit monitoring systems and accreditation norms and listenership surveys (Sebastian 2008). But perhaps the most serious concern is that FM is treated 'as a milch cow rather than a public resource' (Ninan 2003). The issue is consequent upon the state-owned AIR usurping all functions of public broadcasting, commercial radio and community radio in India, unlike in other countries of the world.

In 2008, the Election Commission of India asked the Ministry of Information and Broadcasting to amend its laws to allow FM channels to air political advertisements. It was estimated that radio channels might corner up to 10 per cent of the parties' total advertising budget due to their reach (Donthi 2008). Indeed some of the pending issues have forced FM channels to pull down their shutters. In May 2003, Win 94.6 went off air while in June 2004, Radio Midday West India Pvt. Ltd, a subsidiary of Midday Multimedia Ltd, sent a conditional notice to the Ministry that it will surrender its licence for broadcasting in Mumbai (Indiantelevision.com 2003). In the context of studies suggesting that radio in India has a potential 98.5 per cent listenership, the evolution of broadcasting becomes significant (Gopalakrishnan 2003).

Conclusion

With the Phase III plans in place, an additional 560 radio stations can be expected to come up in the next five years, taking the total number of private FM radio stations to 800. Although, some issues like allowing news on FM stations, limits on foreign investment, reduction of licences, tradability of licences and multiple channel ownership continue to dog the industry, radio enthusiasts are hopeful that none of these issues would drastically affect the growth of the FM radio sector in India. The scope to monetise is tremendous considering that the industry could allow for anything from classical music to film. A format-based licence fee will encourage people to diversify into different genres and this specialisation and differentiation could make FM radio one of the greatest commercial successes among Indian media. As one enthusiast points out, with the distance between private FM stations and AIR shrinking, deregulation and withdrawal of licences cannot be too far away.

Endnotes

1. It is said that there are some 104 million homes with radios, twice the number of homes with television sets.
2. Radio Mirchi (Times Group), Radio City (earlier part of the Star group now held by GW capital), Red FM (once held by India Today Group), Suryan (Sun TV Group), Go FM (Midday), Win FM (Independent), besides Zee, Reliance, *India Today, Rajasthan Patrika, Dainik Bhaskar, Malayala Manorama,*

Mathrubhoomi, Dainik Jagran, Hindustan Times, Daily Thanthi, Jaya TV and *Kumudam* participated along with non-media companies like Muthoot Finance and Indigo.

3. According to the report, in 2007, the Indian radio advertising industry recorded a growth of 24 per cent over the previous year, marginally lower than the forecasted growth of 30 per cent. Over 2004–07, the Indian radio industry has grown by 37 per cent. The radio advertising industry stood at 6.2 billion in 2007, up from Rs 5 billion in 2006. The report adds that 60 per cent of the revenue of the radio advertising industry comes from private FM broadcasters and the balance from AIR.

4. Personal interviews held by the author in Chennai in July 2008 and March 2009.

5. In the era of convergence, the fall in sales of recorded music can be attributed to a number of factors, perhaps the most important being the growth of the mobile music market in India. Mobile phones with MP3 players and song capacities are becoming popular, with the mobile phone ownership exceeding 230 million at the end of 2007.

6. Chennai Big 92.7 FM RJ Dheena completed a 92 hours and 7 minutes RJ marathon in August 2007. See 'Big 92.7 FM's RJ to bid for Guinness Book', Merinews.com.

References

AsiaMedia.com. 2006. 'India: FM radio set to explode as bidding ends'. Available online at http://www.asiamedia.ucla.edu/article.asp?parentid=38464 (downloaded on 12.09.2008).

Donthi, P. 2008. 'FM radio to air political ads', *Deccan Herald*, 19 November. Available online at http://archive.deccanherald.com/Content/Nov192008/national 20081118101543.asp (downloaded on 12.01.2009).

Dugar, D. 2008. 'Reach: small towns dream big with FM radio', Radio Duniya. http://www.radioduniya.in/articles/article-details.asp?Article=Reach&fm=11&yy=2008&articleid=174&typ=Special%20Story (downloaded on 15.01.2009).

FICCI and Pricewaterhouse Coopers. 2008. 'The Indian entertainment and media industry sustaining growth report 2008'. New Delhi: FICCI and Pricewater house Coopers.

Forbes.com. 2006. 'India to invite bids for more than 300 FM radio stations', 2 April. Available online at http://www.forbes/com/markets/feeds/afx/2006/01/04/afx2427108.html (downloaded on 12.01.2009).

Gopalakrishnan, A. 2003. 'Democratising the airwaves', *Frontline*, 20 (12). Available online at http://www.hinduonnet.com/fline/fl2012/stories/20030620001608600.htm (downloaded on 08.02.2010)

IndiaPRwire.com. 2009. 'Big 92.7 FM's RJ Imsai Arasi is Chennai's most popular RJ', 5 January. Available online at http://www.indiaprwire.com/pressrelease/radio/2009010517620.htm (downloaded on 15.01.2009).

Indiantelevision.com. 2003. 'I&B slants towards news on private FM channels', 18 September. Available online at http://www.indiantelevision.com/headlines/y2k3/sep/sep176.htm (downloaded on 12.01.2009).

———. 2004. 'Commerical FM radio: Exorbitant fees, low revenues'. Available online at http://indiatogether.com/photo/2004/gov-radiofees.htm (downloaded on 12.01.2009).

McChesney, R. 2000. *Rich media, poor democracy: Communication politics in dubious times*. USA: The New Press.

Medianewsline.com. 2008. 'Aircheck launches radio monitoring service in India', 7 July. Available online at http://www.medianewsline.com/news/119/ARTICLE/2561/2008-07-07.html (downloaded on 12.01.2009).

Merinews.com. 'Big 92.7 FM's RJ to bid for Guinness Book'. Available online at http://www.merinews.com/catFull.jsp?articleID=139692 (downloaded on 15.01.2009).

Mounir, A. 2008. 'FM radio a hit in Indian cities'. Available online at http://www.itexaminer.com/fm-radio-hit-in-indian-cities.aspx (downloaded on 12.01.2009).

Narasimhan, T.E. 2008. 'FM radio making rapid strides, revenue expected to touch Rs 800 millions this year', *Business Standard*, 29 August. Available online at http://www.business-standard.com/india/printpage_sam.php?autono=332657&tp= (downloaded on 12.09.2008).

Ninan, S. 2003. 'Hijacking radio', *The Hindu*, 31 August. Available online at http://www.thehindu.com/thehindu/mag/2003/08/31/stories/2003083100190300.htm (downloaded on 12.01.2009).

Noronha, F. 2001. 'Who's afraid of radio in India?', The public domain, *Sarai Reader 2001*, pp. 72–75.

O'Connor. A. 2007. 'Indian radio hots up even as DJs undergo on-the-job training', 4 January. Available online at http://business.timesonline.co.uk/tol/business/industry_sectors/media/article1289093.ece (downloaded on 12.01.2009).

Radio Duniya News. 2008. 'Relief for RJ Nitin in Indian idol case', 11 September. Available online at http://www.radioduniya.in/news/viewincreement.asp?News=Relief-for-RJ-Nitin-in-Indian-Idol-case&newsid=14483&NewsCategeory=Radio%20Hosts (downloaded on 15.01.2009).

Reuters. 2008. 'Update 1 India approves FM radio firm setting up units', 11 September. Available online at http://in.reuters.com/articlePrint?articleId=INBOM34091720080911 (downloaded on 12.01.2008).

Sebastian, G. 2008. 'Realising radio dreams: The way forward', Radio Duniya December. Available online at http://www.radioduniya.in/articles/archive_article-details.asp?Article=Realising-RadioDreams&fm=12&yy=2008&article id=197&typ=Features (downloaded on 15.01.2009).

Televisionpoint.com. 2009. 'Media Research Reports: Indian entertainment industry focus 2010'. Available online at http://www.televisionpoint.com/research/ieif 2010_radio.html (downloaded on 12.01.2009).

Tewary, A. 2006. 'The amazing DIY village FM radio station', BBC News South Asia, 24 February. Available online at http://newsvote.bbc.co.uk/mpapps/ pagetools/print/news.bbc.co.uk/2/hi/south_asia/4735642.stm (downloaded on 12.09.2008).

The Times of India. 2007. 'Govt orders FM station to explain RJ's remark', 30 September. Available online at http://timesofindia.indiatimes.com/Govt_ to_FM_station_Explain_RJs_remark/articleshow/2416073.cms (downloaded on 15.01.2009).

Venniyoor, S. 2004. 'Frequencies of expectation', Indiatogether.com, May. Available online at http://www.indiatogether.net/2004/may/med-trairadio.htm (downloaded on 12.01.2009).

———. 2005. 'FM's hour of glory', TheHoot.org. Available online at http:// www.thehoot.org/web/home/searchdetail.php?sid=1704&bg=1 (downloaded on 12.01.2009).

Zubin, 2008. 'Govt should allow broadcast of news', *Mynews*, 6 September. Available online at http://www.mynews.in/fullstory.aspx?storyid=9730 (downloaded on 15.01.2009).

2

The Political
Aspect

2

Chapter 5

The pan-Tamil Rhetoric in Regional Media

Maya Ranganathan

Introduction

On 1 August 2008, the popular Tamil weekly *Ananda Vikatan* greeted its readers with what it termed 'amazing' results of a media poll it had conducted in the previous weeks. The 'people of Tamil Nadu' had been quizzed on their perception of the Sri Lankan Tamil issue. The weekly declared in unequivocal terms that the average Tamilian[1] supported the creation of a separate Tamil state in the neighbouring island nation at the same time demanding that the Liberation Tigers of Tamil Eelam (LTTE) supremo V. Prabhakaran[2] be arrested in connection with the assassination of former Indian Prime Minister Rajiv Gandhi in May 1991.[3]

The poll results presented at the end of a glowing introduction to the LTTE's role in the struggle for a separate state for the Sri Lankan Tamils, supported largely by die-hard supporters of the LTTE (the lone critic being political commentator Cho Ramasamy who had raised the issue of child conscription), stated that 54.25 per cent had always supported the LTTE, 55.44 per cent of the people thought that the solution to the problem lay in the creation of Eelam and 47.65 per cent people wanted the ban on the LTTE to be revoked. Although the blurb announced that Tamilians demanded the arrest of the LTTE supremo, the poll results revealed that only 43.02 per cent felt that Prabhakaran, 'who has been charged in the assassination of Rajiv Gandhi' should be arrested, 40.07 per cent had said that he 'could' be pardoned and 16.90 per cent felt that he was not guilty. In effect, the majority in Tamil Nadu wanted Prabhakaran to go scot-free. This chapter deals with the attempt to create a pan-Tamil identity by the regional media in Tamil Nadu by focusing on the coverage of the Sri Lankan Tamil issue.

The 'Tamil' issue

For those following the trajectory of media coverage on the Sri Lankan Tamil issue in India, particularly in Tamil Nadu, which comprises 6.4 crore Tamil-speaking people (Directorate of Census Operations Tamil Nadu 2001), *Ananda Vikatan*'s poll results were truly 'amazing' for various reasons. First, it stopped short of declaring that the people of Tamil Nadu backed secession in neighbouring Sri Lanka and were favourably disposed towards the LTTE supremo–both viewpoints that went against that which was held and propagated by the Government of India. Second, the methodology adopted—collating responses received online from readers worldwide and clubbing them with the responses of people within the state of Tamil Nadu—and presenting it as an unquestionable stand taken by the Tamilians, seemed to catapult ethnic identity to the forefront, blurring national identities, to make an argument that all Tamil-speaking people responded to the issue in much the same way, irrespective of the countries that they belonged to or lived in (Ranganathan 2008b).

While it is not uncommon for the media to take the ethnic angle, and instances of the language media approaching issues more emotionally and being more supportive of the regional cause elsewhere, are too many to list here,[4] the third aspect that made the poll and its publication significant was its timing. In the week that it appeared, the media, largely the English media in the state, reported that the Tigers were losing territory to the Sri Lankan Army, and that their hold over the north and east was weakening.[5] The poll also followed months of speculation on the reported turnaround of the Gandhis' attitude towards the LTTE. On 19 March 2008, Priyanka Vadra, daughter of the slain former Prime Minister Rajiv Gandhi, paid a visit to the Vellore prison to meet the first accused in the Rajiv Gandhi assassination case—Nalini—in order to come to peace with 'the violence and loss that I have experienced' (*Indian Express* 2008).

Fourth, the conduct of a poll and the publication of the results were significant in Tamil Nadu, for the state that had less than a year ago witnessed violence following a media poll prediction on the future leaders in the ruling Dravida Munnetra Kazhagam (DMK). The poll published in Kalanidhi Maran-owned Tamil daily *Dinakaran* in May

2007 attributing an insignificant support for DMK president and present Chief Minister M. Karunanidhi's eldest son M. Azhagiri who is the party's general secretary in-charge of the southern districts, had led to the transformation of the political landscape in Tamil Nadu (NDTV.com 2007).[6] This resulted in the then Union Communication Minister Dayanidhi Maran, grand nephew of Chief Minister M. Karunanidhi and younger brother of the media baron Kalanidhi Maran, resigning from the Cabinet. A rapprochement between the two was however, effected just ahead of the announcement of the 2009 Parliamentary polls. Today both Maran and Azhagiri have become ministers of cabinet rank in the Congress-led United People's Alliance (UPA).

The Tamil identity had been brought to the fore by the Tamil media earlier in November 2007 when the people of Indian origin in Malaysia were reportedly persecuted for organising meetings and protests in support of their demands. While it is not surprising that the Tamil media was quick to report on the plight of the Indo-Malaysians and express solidarity with the suffering people of Indian origin, a majority of which was Tamils, what was surprising was the attempt to look at the issue through the prism of 'Tamilness'. In the 'Web TV' section of the popular Tamil weekly *Kumudam*, available online, speaker after speaker implied that Tamils were singled out for persecution in every country in the world that they had migrated to (Ranganathan 2007d). In fact, some publications even went to the extent of placing it in the framework of the Sri Lankan Tamil problem forcing the Malaysian Indian leaders to deny it.

The August 2008 *Vikatan* poll results, combining as they did, at least at first glance, support for the LTTE's cause and yet demanding that its leader Prabhakaran be punished for his involvement in the Rajiv Gandhi assassination, is indicative of the dichotomy that exists between the English media and Tamil media, in the coverage of the Sri Lankan Tamil issue. Besides popular magazines that deal with cinema and politics, Tamil media consists of non-partisan dailies and purely political magazines like *Nakeeran* and *Tughlaq*, the latter known for its anti-LTTE stand. Yet, the *Vikatan* and *Kumudam* group of publications come in for special attention owing to their popularity and reach, with both the publications available online and being subscribed to by readers worldwide, as can be seen from the comments that follow every article. According to the Indian Readership Survey 2008 Round 2, while *Tughlaq* has a readership of 1.41 lakh, *Junior Vikatan* enjoys a readership of 5.38 lakh, *Ananda Vikatan* 15.69 lakh and *Kumudam* 17.02 lakh. These figures do not, however, include online readership.

The dichotomy

The dichotomy of the coverage of the Sri Lankan Tamil issue leads one to wonder if the Tamil media is setting an agenda—the creation of a pan-Tamil identity that will dominate all other identities, including national identities.[7] However, it must also be pointed out that some media analysts believe that the Tamil media only reflects the feeling of the Tamil masses, disseminating, as it does, ideas 'without institutional control' (McQuail 1969: 12). Also, its perceived antipathy to the Sri Lankan issue is dictated more by circumstances rather than a change in ideology.[8] Lending credence to this line of argument was the way in which the Sri Lankan Tamil issue was politicised prior to the announcement of parliamentary elections in May 2009 and in the immediate run up to the elections.

The divergent ways in which the Tamil and English media by and large treated the issue, became clearer from September–October 2008, when the war between the Tigers and Sri Lankan Army intensified.[9] While the reportage on the progress of the war depended on the sources of news that the publications had access to, the opinion pieces seemed to set the English and Tamil media apart in Tamil Nadu.[10] The English journalists seemed to rely more on official sources of the Sri Lankan government, while the Tamil media sourced information from Tamil journalists in Sri Lanka or pro-LTTE websites like *Tamilnet*.

On 14 October 2008 Malini Parthasarathy, warning of the dangers of Tamil chauvinism in an article on the leader page of *The Hindu*, wrote:

> It is ... incongruous that the political parties in Tamil Nadu, including the ruling DMK and its principal challenger the AIADMK, have decided to work themselves into a frenzy over the alleged violation of the 'human rights' of the Sri Lankan Tamils in the context of the military action against the LTTE. (Parthasarathy 2008)

Similarly, *The Times of India*, in an editorial on 18 October 2008, head-lined 'Pipe Down Please' warned the Tamil Nadu politicians against reacting emotionally to the issue (*The Times of India Editorial* 2008).

Both the *Kumudam Reporter* and *Vikatan online* however, seemed to be engaged in a concerted effort to play on the Tamil identity and whip up emotions. Most significantly, when the English media was reporting that the LTTE was losing ground, the two Tamil magazine groups were reporting to the contrary. Thus, a *Kumudam* reporter in the issue dated 23 October 2008 carried an interview with LTTE Commander Banu, who asserted that the seeming losses were a strategy adopted by the Tigers to lose the battle and win the war; while *Ananda Vikatan* in the cover story of its issue dated 29 October 2008, indicted the Sri Lankan Army for atrocities on the Tamils (2008). Even the arrest of Marumalarchi Dravida Munnetra Kazhagam (MDMK) president Vaiko and Tamil film directors Seeman and Ameer, for their passionate speeches supporting the LTTE in rallies organised to protest against the Sri Lankan army action, were reported more sympathetically by the Tamil media. In the issue dated 19 November 2008 *Junior Vikatan* published a poem by 'Tamira' defending the Tigers and implying that they only acted in self-defence (*Junior Vikatan* 2008a).[11] This trend continued well into December 2008 when the English newspapers continued to report the advances made by Sri Lankan Army forces toward Kilinocchi.

In January 2009, when it was no longer possible to deny the Sri Lankan Army's gains against the Tigers, *Junior Vikatan* in its issue dated 11 January 2009 featured Prabhakaran's family on the cover and car-ried a cover story on the Tigers' dream of a separate homeland torn asunder by Rajapakse's Sinhala Army. What is significant is that while the story clearly humanised Prabhakaran and began by recounting his anxiety over losing his military advantage, it equated the LTTE with Tamils in no uncertain terms: 'The Indian Ocean handled by the Tamils so far is now in the hands of the Sinhalese' (*Junior Vikatan* 2009a). It traced the glorious past when the Tigers recaptured Kilinocchi in the past two years when the Sinhala Army had captured it in 1996. In the issue dated 21 January 2009, *Ananda Vikatan* reproduced LTTE sym-pathiser Nedumaran's account of his travels into the Tiger heartland in 1990 and his then meeting with the LTTE supremo (2009a). The same issue carried an account of the torture of Tamil prisoners in Sinhala jails, a well-known fact which has not been dealt with at length by English publications (*Ananda Vikatan* 2009b). The Vikatan group of publications also occasionally carried statements of political leaders critical of the LTTE, causing some readers to question, in the online feedback columns, the stand of the group on the issue. However, considering that around that time the LTTE was losing in the battleground, *Junior Vikatan* announced the reproduction of the series on LTTE 'revolutionary' cadets, Thangathurai, Kuttimani and Jegan, the magazine's sympathies to the 'Tamil cause' became clear. This was reinforced by the publication of articles that humanised the LTTE leader even while well-documented articles on Sri Lankan Army's gains were being published in other magazines as the war intensified in early 2009.[12]

With the announcement of the parliamentary elections in April–May 2009, the trend became more pronounced with the regional media pitching the Sri Lankan Tamil issue as an electoral issue, forcing the leaders of almost all political parties to make known their stand on the issue. The most interesting instance was that of All India Anna Dravida Munnetra Kazhagam (AIADMK) leader J. Jayalalithaa, generally seen as the lone critic of the LTTE among Tamil Nadu politicians, who had consistently opposed the LTTE's demands for a separate nation. On 9 March 2009 at the end of a day-long fast seeking Indian intervention in the island to stop the war, the AIADMK supremo declared that she supported the setting up of a separate state for Tamils within the framework of the Sri Lankan Constitution. She also clarified that she abhorred the tactics of the LTTE, a statement that was perceived as a *volte face* by the leader, dictated by electoral compulsions (*Indian Express* 2009). In the run up to the polls she even promised voters that she would support the creation of Eelam, with the intervention of the Indian army (*The Hindu* 2009).

Historical perspective

The reasons for the differing perspectives of the Tamil and English media perhaps lie in Tamil Nadu's political and cultural history. In the state that first advocated secession from the Indian Union as early as 1962, on the grounds of a distinctly different culture and history, identity has been consistently built around the two points of Dravidianism and a fanatical love for the language of Tamil (Akbar 1985: 77–78, 83–85). Dravidianism is seen as the antithesis of Aryanism, with the term being used to refer to all things indigenous that were oppressed and suppressed by the Aryans invading from the north. Thus, the Dravidians were the dark and swarthy people who spoke Tamil—which boasted of an origin as antiquated as that of Sanskrit, with a script of 5000 years—and who practised a religion that was devoid of Sanskritised rituals and prayers of Hinduism. Interestingly, in Tamil Nadu, Ravana is seen as a south Indian prince and 'his defeat by Rama is interpreted by the Tamils as the subjugation of a nationalist, not the downfall of a demon' (Akbar 1985: 76). The Aryans were the lighter-skinned north Indians, and in Tamil Nadu belonged to the Brahmin community that spoke a Sanskritised version of Tamil, practised caste purity and adopted a Sanskritised way of worship and Hindu rituals.[13] It was hence believed that the Brahmins, because of their Aryan ancestry, owed allegiance to Sanskrit, and later to English, and treated Tamil as a lowly language.[14] The destruction of southern Brahmins was necessary as they were believed to be the agents of the northern Aryans. While the Aryan–Dravidian theory still seems to hold political currency, it must also be noted that it is not without critics, even among the non-Brahmins (Pasavaleru Perunchithanar 2005: 68–72). Also the love for the Tamil language, the hallmark of Tamil nationalism, has transcended caste, with some notable Tamil writers belonging to the Brahmin community.

The resistance to Aryanism spearheaded by E.V. Ramasamy Naicker, popularly called Periyar, took the form of opposition to the 'iniquitous caste system' and abhorrence of Brahminism in the early 1900s and was called the self-respect movement. As quoted by M.J. Akbar, Periyar believed:

> The Aryans who came to India to eke out their existence, concocted absurd stories in keeping with their barbarian status.... The blabberings of the intoxicated Brahmins in those old days are still faithfully observed in this modern world as the religious rituals, morals, stories, festivals, fasts, vows and beliefs. (Akbar 1985: 76)

Periyar's 'Justice Party' metamorphosed into Dravidar Kazhagam (DK) in 1944. The present-day Dravida Munnetra Kazhagam (DMK) started as a political outfit of the DK in 1949 and splintered into AIADMK in 1972 and later into Marumalarchi Dravida Munnetra Kazhagam (MDMK) in 1994.

The Dravidian identity was showcased strongly in yet another instance in the anti-Hindi agitation of the 1960s when DMK cadres took out processions, set fire to the effigy of the 'Hindi demon' and burnt themselves in protest against the imposition of Hindi as the national language.[15] The hallmark of a good Tamil has come to be an unconditional love for the language and a pride in Dravidianism, often translated into a hatred of anything non-Dravidian. The media in Tamil Nadu, along with theatre and films, has functioned with much success as a vehicle for carrying the Tamil identity (Velayutham 2008a) with many political players, including founder of DMK C.N. Annadurai, his successor M. Karunanidhi, founder of AIADMK M.G. Ramachandran and his successor J. Jayalalithaa, founder of Desiya Murpoku Dravida Kazhagam (DMDK) Vijayakant and founder of Akila Indiya Samathuva Makkal Katchi (AISMK) Sarath Kumar being film personalities.[16] Politicians are also known to dabble in media businesses[17] and politics and media are so interlinked in the state that the 2006 Assembly elections catapulted television centre-stage (see Ranganathan 2008a: 106–22).[18]

With the Tamil media representing Dravidianism, the English media in the state that catered to the English-educated in white collar jobs, who were traditionally the Brahmins, became a symbol of the non-Dravidian, if not Aryan, thought. In political matters concerning the state, the English and Tamil media have often taken divergent stands. It is in this context that one has to place the English media toeing the national line and Tamil media acting as a votary of the Tamil identity and interests. In the state where caste identities and political party loyalties are of paramount importance, it is not surprising that a media outlets' antipathy to the Tamil identity is often traced to the caste of its owners. *The Hindu*'s stand on the Tamil issue is attributed to the fact that its owners belong to the Brahmin community. Similarly, *Dinamalar*'s stand on the Tamil issue is perceived as being dictated by the caste of the owners of the publishing house.

Even so, the media in Tamil Nadu has also worked in unison in several instances. The main issue of significance in this context was the reportage that followed the assassination of former Prime Minister Rajiv Gandhi in Sriperumbudur near Chennai on 21 May 1991. Even as the plot unravelled and it was revealed that the LTTE was behind the assassination, the media in unison condemned the dastardly attack and the Tamil media was more virulent in its condemnation of the LTTE's suspected role in the assassination than the English media.[19] The turn around toward the LTTE could be traced to the unilateral ceasefire the organisation declared in February 2001, leading to a tenuous peace on the island and a resumption of travel to the north and east of Sri Lanka. The Sri Lankan government's curbs on information, access to the war zone and treatment of journalists since the intensification of the war in 2008–09 had lent emotional overtones to the issue with both politicians and media trying to exploit it. In such a climate of chauvinism, the few nationalist-minded, Tamil language journalists were devoid of a proper platform to air their views.

Catering to the market

The softening of the Tamil media toward the LTTE became apparent in the coverage of some events that followed the 'peace time' between 2001 and 2005. Thus, when *The Hindu* contended with just reporting the Chencholai massacre on 14 August 2006 as a hard news story, the political Tamil bi-weekly *Junior Vikatan*, sister publication of *Ananda Vikatan*, carried the picture of a computer-generated, teary-eyed Prabhakaran on the cover, with the dead children in the orphanage as an inset. The story inside reported how the Tiger supremo was traumatised by the mindless killing of innocent children, clearly highlighting the effort to humanise a leader treated as a terrorist by the Indian government (*The Hindu* 2006; *Junior Vikatan* 2006). *Junior Vikatan*'s stance was explained by an independent media commentator as having to do with the fact that the publication was born in 1983, the year of the pogrom against Tamils in Sri Lanka, when Tamil Nadu witnessed an unprecedented influx of over one lakh refugees and the Sri Lankan Tamil issue hogged media headlines. The issue has been the staple of the magazine since then, as the Tamil readers are perceived as conscious consumers of Tamil identity.[20] After all, no media would antagonise its readers; and 'sometimes media takes more than a biased attitude towards the audience and tend to appease it. Significantly, the prejudice of the journalist who is a product of the current society, adds flavour to this' (Transcurrents.com 2008).

One reason that could be attributed to placing the Sri Lankan issue within the framework of a pan-Tamil identity by the media could be the absence of any other political issue that allows for the flagging of the Tamil identity, barring, of course, the water disputes with neighbouring states. With the Hindi imposition having taken a back seat and demand for a separate Tamil country rendered non-pragmatic,[21] not to mention globalisation that has necessitated dilution of narrow regionalism, only disputes over Cauvery water and Hogenekkal dam with neighbouring Karnataka and Periyar dam with neighbouring Kerala provide opportunities for invoking the Tamil identity. Thanks to the political parties of Tamil Nadu playing a significant role in the coalition governments at the Centre since 1998, a strident anti-north Indian stand in political issues has become difficult, if not impossible.[22] The dilemma was highlighted ironically by Chief Minister M. Karunanidhi, touted as the leader of Tamils worldwide, in a statement on 6 November 2008 (*Dinamalar* 2008). Charging that attempts were made to bring down his government and defending his government's stand to refuse to pressure the union government on the Sri Lankan issue, he blamed the present situation in Sri Lanka on the LTTE. Hinting at the LTTE, he said that those who had been waging war for 40 years in Sri Lanka to secure rights for Tamils, instead of fighting the oppressor, were engaged in internecine war and in building memorials for those killed in the war, oblivious to the fact that their race was being exterminated. Just a week earlier, Ravikumar, MLA, in an opinion piece on the grant of classical language status to Telugu and Kannada in *Junior Vikatan*, had argued that the Centre, unable to stomach the distinct identity of the Tamils, was playing linguistic politics (Ravikumar 2008). What emerges is that regional media is now left with the Sri Lankan Tamil issue and the occasional problem in a neighbouring nation like Malaysia, to fit within the framework of Tamil identity, which is perceived as appealing to Tamil readers.

It must also be noted that the recent softening in stance toward Sri Lankan Tamils by Tamil media has been accompanied by an inclusive Tamil identity attempted in Tamil films.[23] While films focusing on the Rajiv Gandhi assassination and the Tigers' role in it, such as *Kuppi* (Capsule) and *Kutrapathirikai* (Charge-Sheet) bombed at the box office, films such as *Thenali* (2000), *Nandha* (2001), *Kannathil Muthamittal* (A Peck on the Cheek) (2002), *Nala Damayanthi* (2003) and *Rameswaram* (2007), skirting the political aspects of the ethnic issue, but incorporating a Sri Lankan Tamil character, have met with moderate to huge success.[24] Although such films form a negligible percentage of the approximately 200 films produced by one of the largest film industries in the country, the trend seems to continue and may well be significant (Velayutham 2008a: 1–2).

Devoid of any political compulsion to play the ethnic identity card in a major way, the Tamil media's preoccupation with Tamil identity can be attributed to the principle of constituting the 'audience as market'. The economies of film production require that the film rakes in huge returns and this in turn demands a very wide audience. Thanks to the language and a certain cultural similarity, Tamil films are watched not just by the Indian Tamil diaspora worldwide, but more by Sri Lankan Tamil diaspora. The inclusive Tamil identity attempted in some recent Tamil films should be seen as an effort toward audience maximisation. The pumping of money into the film industry by the Sri Lankan diaspora has indeed given a fresh lease of life to the Tamil film industry that has been facing a resources crunch in the past decade. This can be seen from the closing down of studios and conversion of theatres into marriage halls. Sri Lankan Tamil audiences form a significant audience of Tamil films can also be learnt from the fact that the Sri Lankan Tamil diaspora in Switzerland, Germany and Denmark announced a boycott of actor Ajit Kumar's film, *Aegan*, in October 2008, in response to the actor's announcement of his decision to stay away from the protest organised by Tamil film actors on 1 November 2008 in Chennai against the Sri Lankan government's action against Tamils in Sri Lanka (Kumudam.com 2008). While the cost of purchasing rights varies depending on the actors and film directors and the marketability of films, they are sold overseas for much higher amounts. For instance, Tamil film rights are sold in Australia for AUS$ 5,000 upwards. The significance of the Sri Lankan Tamil audience in the Tamil film industry was revealed by film director Barathirajaa at the protest organised in Rameswaram, Tamil Nadu, on 18 October 2008. In an interview to *Junior Vikatan* following the protest, the film director, castigating the two most popular Tamil film actors, Kamal Hassan and Rajnikant for their silence on the issue, pointed out that they owed their popularity and consequent earnings to the Sri Lankan Tamil diaspora worldwide.[25] 'Are you unable to issue a statement in support of the consanguineous Eelam Tamil who takes pride in elevating you to such heights,' he had asked (*Junior Vikatan* 2008b).[26]

The Tamil film industry owes more than its audience abroad to the Sri Lankan Tamils. Sri Lankan Tamil-owned Ayngaran International, headquartered in London, UK, operating in 50 countries worldwide has held overseas film distribution rights of Tamil films since 1987. Since 2007, it has forayed into Tamil film production as well. The first film was Ajit Kumar's *Billa* and Ayngaran was initially involved in co-producing Shankar's *Enthiran* starring Rajnikant and Aishwarya Rai, the 'grandest film ever to be made in India', although it pulled out of it later. The nexus between the Tamil film industry and the Sri Lankan Tamil issue was brought to light by Tamil Nadu Congress leader S.R. Balasubramaniam in an article in *Junior Vikatan* (2009c; see also *Kumudam* 2009a). It has thus become almost obligatory for the Tamil film industry at least to extend moral support to the Sri Lankan Tamils.

Interestingly, it is difficult to resist drawing a parallel between the current scenario and that which prevailed when the Cauvery water issue was raging in Tamil Nadu and Karnataka in August 2008. Rajnikant, who worked as a bus conductor in Bangalore before he became the superstar of Tamil films, had made remarks in support of Tamil Nadu in the Cauvery issue. He had to apologise for his statements when the release of his film 'Kuselan' was threatened in Karnataka. His supposed *volte face* invited acerbic comments from Sarath Kumar and film actor Satyaraj and director Barathiraaja, establishing yet again that commercial interests dictate the stand taken by the film industry and not principles per se (*The Times of India* 2008b, 2008c). Tamil film artistes also perform in 'shows' abroad where a sizeable proportion of the audience is Sri Lankan Tamils.

This has extended to the Tamil press as well. While most Tamil newspapers are still free online and at the most require a registration, efforts are on to make some of them paying sites. For instance, *Vikatan.com* is a paid site and its subscription is Rs 600 a year and USD 16.66, while *Kumudam* charges a minimum of USD 50 per year as online subscription. Although figures of overseas subscribers are hard to come by, the interaction in the feedback columns that follow every article online, clearly indicates the growing legion of online subscribers overseas. Most of them include their country of residence in their user-names or refer to their host countries in their comments, indicating just who are filling up the publications' coffers. Viewed in the light of the allegations made by some anti-LTTE politicians like Subramanian Swamy, it is also not clear if the pro-LTTE sympathy is indeed paid for.

Going by the voters' response in the 2009 Parliament elections, one is forced to conclude that the pan-Tamil identity has been a non-starter. For, the DMK-Congress combine that had been consistently criticised and held responsible for the pitiable plight of the Sri Lankan Tamils, swept the polls while those parties and candidates who spoke in no uncertain terms supporting the creation of Eelam or the Tigers, barely scraped through. However, this in no way seemed to deter these publications. On the day that the English newspapers in India and media the world over reported the annihilation of Prabhakaran by the Sri Lankan Army and displayed photographs of his dead body, some Tamil publications chose to report the assertion of pro-LTTE leaders in Tamil Nadu, like Nedumaran and Vaiko, that the LTTE leader was 'safe' and 'well'. For instance, *Vikatan.com* reported that the Sri Lankan Government 'claimed' that Prabhakaran was killed and carried a special interview with Nedumaran who asserted that the leader would live on till Eelam was realised. The 25 May 2009 report carried by English newspapers that the LTTE International Relations Head, S. Pathmanathan, had conceded that the leader was no more, found no mention in these publications on the day.[27]

Conclusion

The reasons for it may not be very clear and the success may be debatable, but it is apparent that the regional media as represented by the popular magazines, is following a pan-Tamil agenda where it attempts to push Tamil identity to the fore. Considering that first, the union government does not support secession and consequently the demand for a separate Tamil state and second, has declared the LTTE that spearheads the movement for a separate nation in Sri Lanka as a 'terrorist' organisation, the Tamil media is forced to walk the tight-rope. The articles that eulogise or humanise the LTTE are occasionally accompanied by pronouncements by political leaders or personalities opposed to it. For instance, while the 21 January 2009 issue of *Kumudam* carried an appeal by Sri Lankan Tamils to the people of Tamil Nadu to keep alive the pressure on Indian and Tamil Nadu governments to urge for a cease-fire in Sri Lanka, it also carried an interview with Congress leader S.R. Balasubramaniam in which he alleged that Tamil cinema was controlled by the LTTE (*Kumudam* 2009b). Such a ploy offers a line of defence for the publication in case of legal action and against charges that the publication is partisan. This being the case, a consistent reading of the coverage of the Sri Lankan issue, including reportage on politicians, supportive and antagonistic, becomes necessary in order to determine the agenda.

While the pan-Tamil agenda seems like an economic necessity in the age of rising newsprint prices, increasing number of publications and competition from online media and television, it cannot be concluded that the agenda will remain unchanged in the years to come. Tamil identity has mutated under the influence of politics and culture, and the current coverage of the Sri Lankan Tamil issue stands testimony to it.

Endnotes

1. The inhabitants of the state of Tamil Nadu in India who speak Tamil are generally referred to as 'Tamilians'. However, Tamil-speaking people elsewhere are 'Tamils'. Thus, there are Sri Lankan Tamils, Malaysian Tamils, Singaporean Tamils and South African Tamils. The term 'Indian Tamils' refers more to Tamil-speaking people in central Sri Lanka (otherwise known as 'Estate Tamils') who were brought by the British to work in the tea estates in the island from India.

2. On 18 May 2009 Prabhakaran was supposedly shot dead by the Sri Lankan Armed Forces while attempting to flee in an ambulance. While the Sri Lankan Army released pictures of his dead body, pro-LTTE publications, including a number of Tamil publications in India continued to assert that the LTTE leader was safe and well. This is discussed later in the chapter.

3. Former Prime Minister Rajiv Gandhi was assassinated by a human bomb on 21 May 1991 at Sriperumbudur, 30 kilometres from Chennai, when he was campaigning for Congress candidate Maragatham Chandrasekar. A protracted investigation revealed that the human bomb was a Sri Lankan Tamil called Dhanu whose name was later revealed as Thenmuli Rajarathnam or Gayathri. The LTTE was subsequently banned in India, although there is hair-splitting over whether it is a ban or a categorisation as a terrorist outfit. A designated

Terrorists and Disruptive Activities (TADA) court, after one of the longest trials, held that LTTE supremo V. Prabhakaran was responsible for the assassination and sentenced 26 people to death in January 1998. See Rediffnews (1998). The Supreme Court that heard the appeal in May 1999 sentenced four persons to death and others to jail terms. Murugan and Santhan, Sri Lankan Tamils, his wife Nalini, and Perarivalan, both Indians, are serving their sentences in the Vellore prison. Nalini's death sentence has been commuted to life on humanitarian grounds owing to her begetting a daughter in jail. Tamil Nadu politicians and literary luminaries are seeking an early release of Nalini on the grounds that she has served more than the mandatory life sentence. In June 2006, LTTE's political advisor Anton Balasingham expressed 'regret' over the assassination leading political analysts to point out that this was the closest the organisation had come to accepting responsibility for the killing. See BBC News (2006). On 10 November 2008 the Tribunal constituted under the Unlawful Activities (Prevention) Act in India upheld the ban for a further period of two years. See Venkatesan (2008).

4. For instance, in a personal interview on 25 September 2008, Mr Dinesh Kumar, who reported for the *Indian Express* and *The Times of India*, Delhi, on the Punjab problem between 1987–92 from Amritsar and Chandigarh, said, 'from my personal experience I found that the media in Punjab was divided along lingual and communal lines.'

5. Press Trust of India reported on 12 July 2008 that the LTTE had admitted that it lost a key army base in the East. See PTI (2007).

6. For the repercussions on the Tamil Nadu media scene, see Ranganathan (2007a, 2007b, 2007c).

7. Although on 12 October 2008, *The New Indian Express* published the results of a survey held in 10 cities in Tamil Nadu revealing that 51 per cent of the respondents advocated lifting the ban on LTTE and that 66 per cent of the respondents believed that the LTTE were freedom fighters or the sole and genuine voice of Tamil voice, the publication in its opinion columns, has steered away from either supporting the Tigers or garnering sympathy for the organisation. See *The New Indian Express* (2008a, 2008b).

8. Interview with freelance columnist, Gnani, in Chennai, India, July 2008.

9. I am aware that comparing English newspapers with Tamil magazines that are weekly or bi-weekly may give rise to methodological concerns. However, it must be noted that no English magazine is published from Tamil Nadu, barring *Frontline* by the Hindu Group of Publications, which has consistently taken an anti-LTTE stand. Tamil newspapers, except *Dinamani* published by the sister publication of *The New Indian Express*, do not carry editorials with the result that views have become the forte of magazines.

10. In personal interaction with journalists covering the Sri Lankan issue for popular publications in Chennai during July–August 2008, it was learnt that the

publications in Chennai, barring *The Hindu* which had posted a correspondent to Colombo, were dependent on PTI for news from Colombo and the North and East of Sri Lanka. While PTI news originating from Colombo most often carried the Sri Lankan Defence version of the happenings, the Tamil publications sourced Tamilnet, a pro-LTTE online publication, for the version of the LTTE. One researcher in a think-tank in Chennai stated that soon after momentous events such as the Sri Lankan Air Force bombing of Chencholai in the north-east where about 60 children of an orphanage were killed, pro-LTTE men made the rounds of media in Tamil Nadu to persuade publications to publish their version of events. While one senior reporter writing for one of the leading English language publications in Chennai, charged that Indian correspondents in Colombo had been bought over by the Sri Lankan Government, another pointed to the hardships of correspondents placed in a foreign land.

11. While the poem spoke about tigers in general, its reference particularly to the LTTE was in no doubt, as the accompanying picture of a snarling Tiger was superimposed on an image similar to the Eelam flag.

12. See for instance *Junior Vikatan* (2009b). The cover story on the skills of Prabhakaran's eldest son Charles Antony was based on reports of an unidentified flight spotted by the Sri Lankan Army over the north-east on 21 January 2009. On the day the magazine hit the stands, newspapers published well-documented reports of the Tigers' losses.

13. Theories Aryan invasion on abound. See Lal (2005: 50–73), Sastri (1967) and Thapar (1966: 131).

14. The feeling prevails to this day. In a private interview (in Chennai, India, in August 2008) held in another context, a Sri Lankan Tamil writer–publisher living in Chennai declared that Brahmins spoke Tamil now but clearly with the view that it was a lowly language and not on par with Sanskrit. 'It is the difference between a servant cleaning your house and you cleaning your own house,' he stated. See also Sivathamby (2006: 31).

15. For more on language agitation, see Ramaswamy (1997).

16. C.N. Annadurai was the first to realise the potential of mass media to convey political messages. He wrote 12 political plays, 86 political essays, five novels and 23 short stories. His first political play was *Chandrodayam*, written in 1943. While he also acted in his plays he was quick to realise the potential of feature films to reach out to the masses. His three plays—*Velaikari* (Servant Maid), 1949; *Nalla Thambi* (Good Young Brother), 1949 and *Oor Iravu* (One Night), 1951—were made into hugely successful films. His political successor, M. Karunanidhi, scripted *Parasakthi*, the film that launched the career of thespian 'Sivaji' Ganesan.

17. Chief Minister M. Karunanidhi continues to script films and writes a regular column in the DMK Party organ *Murasoli*; his son M.K. Azhagiri runs the

Sumangali Cable Vision in Madurai; Azhagiri's son Dayanidhi launched a film company called Cloud Nine Movies in 2008; the Sun empire which operates 14 TV channels, four FM radio stations, two daily newspapers and four magazines is owned by Kalanidhi Maran, the grand nephew of Karunanidhi and brother of former Union Minister for Communications Dayanidhi Maran and Udayanidhi, grandson of Karunanidhi produces films under the banner of Red Giant Movies.

18. In this context, it must also be noted that at least one political party in Tamil Nadu, the Patali Makkal Katchi (PMK), led by Dr S. Ramadoss continues to remain critical of Tamil cinema and often creates problems for producers and directors on grounds of safeguarding Tamil identity. However, even the PMK operates its own TV channel called Makkal TV, in which presenters speak chaste Tamil and are dressed in traditional Tamil couture. The only other political leader, Thol Thirumavalavan of *Viduthai Siruthaigal*, who charged that films and actors were posing a threat to Tamil culture, also acted in a Tamil film in 2007. For more on the intertwining of Tamil cinema and politics, see Baskaran (1981), Dickey (1993), Hardgrave (1970, 1971, 1973, 1975), Hardgrave and Neidhart (1975), Pandian (1996, 2000) and Vaasanthi (2006).

19. The LTTE has not owned up to the assassination. The closest it came to conceding that it played a role in the assassination was when its late political ideologue Anton Balasingam, announced that Mr Gandhi's killing by a suicide bomber was a 'monumental tragedy' (BBC News 2006).

20. Interview held in Chennai, India in July–August 2008. For the 'audience as market' concept, see McQuail (1997: 8–9).

21. Although C.N. Annadurai dropped the demand for a separate Tamil country following the Chinese aggression in 1962, it has been an undercurrent in Tamil Nadu politics. In 1980s, a minor militant organisation called Tamil Nadu Liberation Army revived the demand for 'Dravida Nadu', when the Indian Peacekeeping Force (IPKF) was sent to Sri Lanka. See http://en.wikipedia.org/wiki/Dravida_Nadu (downloaded on 29.10.2008). The concept was again in the news in October 2008 when M.S.S. Pandian, (2008), an academic, warned the Centre of stoking the fire of secessionism by ignoring the sentiments expressed by the people of Tamil Nadu on the Sri Lankan issue. See also Sivathamby (2006).

22. This is not to state that regional parties give up their regional ideologies. For instance, an all-party meeting chaired by Tamil Nadu chief minister on 14 October 2008 resolved that all Members of Parliament from Tamil Nadu would quit if the union government did not come forward to ensure a ceasefire in Sri Lanka in two weeks (Radhakrishnan 2008). The issue was resolved with the meeting of External Affairs Minister Pranab Mukherjee with the chief minister on 26 October 2008 (*The Times of India* 2008a). The threat and later reconciliation drew criticism that it was all a political ploy (*The Hindu* 2008).

23. Tamil films have always dealt with 'Tamilness', including the 'separatism and linguistic nationalism'. (Velayutham 2008a). Tamil films have also been shot abroad and occasionally included overseas Tamils in the narrative, as was the case with *Ninaithale Inikum* (1979), or the more *recent M Kumaran s/o Mahalakshmi* (2004). The reference here is to the recent trend of inclusion of Sri Lankan Tamils.

24. Santosh Sivan's film *The Terrorist* (1999) that dealt with a woman suicide bomber, did not refer to names or places, although it was widely believed that it focused on the Sri Lankan Tamil scenario.

25. The Tamil film actors subsequently organised a protest on 1 November 2008 in Chennai in support of the innocent Tamils dying in Sri Lanka.

26. While, as Velayutham (2008b) argues in 'The diaspora and the global circulation of Tamil cinema', Bollywood continues to dominate world over, it cannot be denied that the Tamil film industry is also becoming aware of the diasporic audiences.

27. See Reddy (2009). This chapter makes its argument in the light of the coverage of the Sri Lankan Tamil issue from the period in 2006 when hostilities between the LTTE and Sri Lankan Army heightened till the 'annihilation of the LTTE' in Sri Lanka in May 2009.

References

Akbar, M.J. 1985. *India: The siege within: Challenges to a nation's unity.* New Delhi: Penguin.

Ananda Vikatan. 2008. 'Final war: The true situation in Sri Lanka', 29 October. Available online at http://www.vikatan.com/av/2008/oct/29102008/av0202. asp (downloaded on 24.10.2008).

———. 2009a. '*Thambi irukkum idam tamizheezham*', 21 January. Available online at http://www.vikatan.com/av/2009/jan/21012009/av0303.asp# (downloaded on 15.01.2009).

———. 2009b. '*Singala chitravadhaigal kolaikara "vellai" van*'. 21 January. Available online at http://www.vikatan.com/av/2009/jan/21012009/av0204. asp# (downloaded on 15.01.2009).

BBC News. 2006. 'Tamil Tiger "regret over India"'. Available online at http://news. bbc.co.uk/2/hi/south_asia/5122032.stm (downloaded on 24.09.2008).

Baskaran, T. 1981. *The message bearers: Nationalist politics and the entertainment media in South India 1880–1945.* Madras: CRe-A.

Dickey, S. 1993. *Cinema and the urban poor in South India.* Cambridge: Cambridge University Press.

Dinamalar. 2008. '*DMK aatchiyai kavizhka sadhi: Mudhalvar Karunanidhi thidikidum thagaval*', 7 November. Available online at http://www.dinamalar.

com/fpnews.asp?news_id=2207&ncat=&archive=1&showfrom=11/07/2008 (downloaded on 10.11.2008).

Directorate of Census Operations Tamil Nadu. 2001. 'Primary Census Abstract—Census 2001'. Available online at http://www.census.tn.nic.in/pca2001.aspx (downloaded on 29.09.2008).

Hardgrave, R.L. 1970. 'Film and society in Tamil Nadu', *Monthly Public Opinion Surveys of the Indian Institute of Public Opinion*, 15 (March, April 1970), pp. 1–62.

———. 1971. 'The Celluloid God: MGR and the Tamil film', *South Asian Review*, 4 (July 1971), pp. 307–14.

———. 1973. 'Politics and the film in Tamil Nadu: The stars and the DMK', *Asian Survey* 13 (3): 288–305.

———. 1975. *When stars displace the Gods: The folk culture of cinema in Tamil Nadu.* Austin, Texas: Centre for Asia Studies, University of Texas.

Hardgrave, R.L. and A.C. Neidhart. 1975. 'Film and political consciousness in Tamil Nadu', *Economic and Political Weekly,* 10 (January 1975), pp. 27–35.

The Hindu. 2006. 'Suicide attack in Colombo', 15 August. Available online at http://www.hindu.com/2006/08/15/stories/2006081512460100.htm (downloaded on 24.10.2008).

———. 2008. 'Pranab-Karunanidhi meeting a "farcical drama"', 27 October. Available online at http://www.hindu.com/2008/10/29/stories/2008102953770400.htm (downloaded on 29.10.2008).

———. 2009. 'Tamil Eelam: Jayalalithaa cites India's role in creating Bangladesh', 30 April. Available online at http://www.hindu.com/2009/04/30/stories/2009043060430800.htm (downloaded on 21.05.2009).

Indian Express. 2008. 'Priyanka meets Nalini, says "it was my coming to peace"', 16 April. Available online at http://epaper.indianexpress.com (downloaded on 29.09.2008).

———. 2009. 'Now Jaya backs Lankans Tamils' cause', 11 March. Available online at http://www.indianexpress.com/news/now-jaya-backs-lankan-tamils-cause/432917/ (downloaded on 24.03.2009).

Junior Vikatan. 2006. *'Idhayam veditha Prabhakaran'*, 20 August. Available online at http://www.vikatan.com/jv/2006/aug/20082006/jv0601.asp (downloaded on 24.10.2008).

———. 2008a. *'Puligalin iraiaanmai'*, 19 November. Available online at http://www.vikatan.com/jv/2008/nov/19112008/jv0205.asp (downloaded on 18.11.2008).

———. 2008b. *'Valarppu Tamizhan Vijayakant'*, 26 October. Available online at http://www.vikatan.com/jv/2008/oct/26102008/jv0501.asp (downloaded on 03.11.2008).

———. 2009a. *'Piriyadha Madhivadhani, por munaiyil Charles'*, 11 January. Available online at http://www.vikatan.com/jv/2009/jan/11012009/jv0501.asp (downloaded on 08.01.2009).

Junior Vikstan. 2009 b. '*Maganodu puilithalaivarin pasa porattam*', 28 January. Available online at http://www.vikatan.com/jv/2009/jan/28012009/jv0501.asp (downloaded on 27.01.2009).

———. 2009c. '*Kodhithu kilambum SRB: Thamizh cinemavil viduthalai puligal panam*', 7 January. Available online at http://www.vikatan.com/jv/2009/jan/07012009/jv0205.asp (downloaded on 06.01.2009).

Kumudam.com. 2008. '*Ajit padathirku Eezha thamizhargal kadum edhirpu*'. Available online at http://www.kumudam.com/latest_news.php?type=latestnews&id=1114#1114 (downloaded on 30.10.2008).

Kumudam. 2009a. '*Viduthalai puligalin kattupaatil tamizh cinema*', 21 January. Available online at http://www.kumudam.com/magazine/Kumudam/2009-01-21/pg3.php (downloaded on 19.01.2009).

———. 2009b. '*Naangal vazhndhu vittu pogirome*', 21 January. Available online at http://www.kumudam.com/magazine/Kumudam/2009-01-21/pg34.php (downloaded on 19.01.2009).

Lal, B.B. 2005. 'Aryan invasion of India', in Edwin F. Bryant and Laurie L. Patton (eds), *The Indo-Aryan controversy: Evidence and inference in Indian history*, pp. 50–74. London: Routledge.

McQuail, D. 1969. *Towards a sociology of mass communications*. London: Collier-Macmillan Limited.

———. 1997. *Audience analysis*. London: Sage Publications.

NDTV.com. 2007. 'Forty people died in Dinakaran attack'. Available online at http://www.ndtv.com/convergence/ndtv/story.aspx?id=NEWEN20070011469 (downloaded on 29.09.2008).

PTI. 2007. 'LTTE admits to losing jungle base to army'. Available online at http://www.accessmylibrary.com/coms2/summary_0286-31864948_ITM (downloaded on 26.09.2008).

Pandian, M.S.S. 1996. 'Tamil cultural elites and cinema: Outline of an argument', *Economic and Political Weekly*, 13 (15): 950–55.

———. 2000. 'Parasakthi: Life and times of a DMK film', in Ravi Vasudevan (ed.), *Making meaning in Indian cinema*, pp. 65–97. New Delhi: Oxford University Press.

Pandian, M.S.S. 2008. 'Change course in Sri Lanka or face misfortune'. Available online at http://www.tamilnation.org/intframe/india/081023pandian.htm (downloaded on 29.10.2008).

Parthasarathy, M. 2008. 'The dangers of Tamil chauvinism', *The Hindu*, 14 October. Available online at http://www.hindu.com/2008/10/14/stories/2008101454490800.htm (downloaded on 24.10.2008).

Pasavaleru Perunchithanar. 2005. *Sadhi ozhippu.* Chennai: Thenmozhi pathi-pagam.

Ravikumar. 2008. '*Mozhi arasiyal ennum neruppu*', *Junior Vikatan*, 9 November. Available online at http://www.vikatan.com/jv/2008/nov/09112008/jv0503.asp (downloaded on 06.11.2008).

Radhakrishnan, R.K. 2008. 'TN MPs to quit if Centre does not ensure ceasefire', *The Hindu*, 15 October. Available online at http://www.hindu.com/2008/10/15/stories/2008101557920100.htm (downloaded on 29.10.2008).

Ramaswamy, S. 1997. *Passions of the tongue: Language devotion in Tamil India, 1891–1970*. Berkeley: University of California Press.

Ranganathan, M. 2007a. 'The Sun feels the heat', TheHoot.org. Available online at http://www.thehoot.org/web/home/searchdetail.php?sid=2560&bg=1 (downloaded on 29.09.2008).

———. 2007b. 'Making hay as the sun shines no longer', TheHoot.org. Available online at http://www.thehoot.org/web/home/searchdetail.php?sid=2567&bg=1 (downloaded on 29.09. 2008).

———. 2007c. 'Kalaignar TV makes its debut', TheHoot.org. Available on http://www.thehoot.org/web/home/searchdetail.php?sid=2679&bg=1 (downloaded on 29.09. 2008).

———. 2007d. 'The suffering "Indians" or the "Tamils" of Malaysia?' TheHoot.org. Available online at http://www.thehoot.org/web/home/searchdetail.php?sid=2846&bg=1 (downloaded on 29.09.2008).

———. 2008a. 'Give me a vote and I will give you a TV set: Television in Tamil Nadu politics', in Nalin Mehta (ed.), *Television in India*, pp. 106–23. London: Routledge.

———. 2008b. 'Ananda Vikatan's amazing poll on Eelam', TheHoot.org. Available online at http://www.thehoot.org/web/home/story.php?storyid=3255&pg=1&mod=1&sectionId=2&valid=true (downloaded on 29.09.2008).

———. 2008c. 'Taking it to the masses', TheHoot.org. Available online at http://www.thehoot.org/web/home/story.php?storyid=3391&mod=1&pg=1&section Id=21&valid=true (downloaded on 24.10.2008).

Rediffnews. 1998. '26 sentenced to death for Rajiv Gandhi assassination'. Available online at http://www.rediff.com/news/1998/jan/28rajiv.htm (downloaded on 24.09.2008).

Reddy, M.B. 2009. 'LTTE "confirms" Prabhakaran's death', *The Hindu*, 25 May, p. 1, Chennai, India.

Sastri, N.K.A. 1967. *Cultural contacts between Aryans and Dravidians*. Bombay: Manaktals.

Sivathamby, K. 2006. *Understanding Dravidian movement: Problems and perspectives*. 2nd edition. Chennai: New Century Book House.

Thapar, R. 1966. *A history of India*. New Delhi: Penguin.

The New Indian Express. 2008a. 'DMK should cut ties with UPA over Lanka', 12 October. Available online at http://www.expressbuzz.com/edition/story.aspx?Title=%E2%80%98DMK+should+cut+ties+with+UPA+over+Lanka+%E2%80%99&artid=r4TAUzFL2DY=&SectionID=vBlkz7JCFvA=&Main SectionID=vBlkz7JCFvA=&SEO=&SectionName=EL7znOtxBM3qzg MyXZKtxw== (downloaded on 24.10.2008).

The New Indian Express. 2008b. 'TNIE survey an eye opener', 13 October. Available online at http://www.expressbuzz.com/edition/story.aspx?title=TNIE+survey+an+eye-opener&artid=SCffjRDK7ZM=&SectionID=vBlkz7JCFvA=&MainSectionID=fyV9T2jIa4A=&SectionName=EL7znOtxBM3qzgMyXZKtxw==&SEO= (downloaded on 24.10.2008).

The Times of India Editorial. 2008. 'Pipe down please', 18 October. Available online at http://timesofindia.indiatimes.com/Opinion/Editorial/Pipe_Down_Please/articleshow/3610272.cms (downloaded on 24.10.2008).

The Times of India. 2008a. 'Lanka row settles as Pranab soothes DMK', 27 October. Available online at http://timesofindia.indiatimes.com/Lanka_assures_India_Tamils_will_be_protected/articleshow/3642705.cms (downloaded on 29.10.2008).

———. 2008b. 'Rajni apologises to pave film for K'taka', Chennai, 1 August, p. 1.

———. 2008c. 'Rajni fans roll out red carpet for "kuselan", ...in Coimbatore tear posters', Chennai, 2 August, p. 5.

Transcurrents.com. 2008. 'Conflicting perceptions in war reporting by Sinhala and Tamil media'. Available online at http://transcurrents.com/tamiliana/archives/560 (downloaded on 08.02.2010)

Vaasanthi. 2006. *Cut-outs, caste and cine-stars: The world of Tamil politics*. New Delhi: Viking, Penguin.

Velayutham, S. 2008a. 'Introduction', in Selvaraj Velayutham (ed.), *Tamil cinema: The cultural politics of India's other film industry*, pp. 1–14. London and New York: Routledge.

———. 2008b. 'The global circulation of Tamil cinema', in Selvaraj Velayutham (ed.), *Tamil cinema: The cultural politics of India's other film industry*, pp. 172–87. London and New York: Routledge.

Venkatesan, J. 2008. 'Tribunal confirms ban on LTTE'. Available online at http://www.hindu.com/2008/11/11/stories/2008111161251100.htm (downloaded on 12.11.2008).

Chapter 6

Citizen Journalism and the Public Sphere in India[1]

Usha M. Rodrigues

Introduction

The production and dissemination of news is undergoing significant transformation. News is now expected on demand, round the clock, and from around the world. Some consider technology to be the prime driver of these changes; however these changes in news production and consumption should not be viewed in isolation. The present news environment and new media technologies uniquely enable public participation in the news process, leading to a wide array of terms that define the phenomenon: user-generated content, citizen journalism and community media to name a few. The Indian public sphere is not immune from this trend elsewhere in the world, where citizens use technology to express their views and share news on the internet and traditional media platforms. This chapter takes an exploratory look at the manifestation of this trend of the citizen or community participating in the public discourse in India. It deliberates on the Indian version of citizen journalism and its adaptation by mainstream media to ponder its objectives and utility in a land with thousands of publications,[2] nearly 450 television channels[3] as well as 500-plus radio stations.[4] The chapter seeks to understand where the impetus for citizen participation in the media is coming from in India, and whether the current momentum is sufficient to consider it as an alternative form of media as opposed to a generally profit and ratings focused mainstream media.

The changing news media environment

A significant shift is taking place towards public involvement in media content. Historic world events are being recorded and reported by general population on the ground with the use of mobile and new media technologies. In 2005, when the London bombings took place, news agencies around the world relied on first-hand witnesses for photographs—mostly taken with mobile phones—(Sambrook 2005). In 2006, when Cyclone Larry tore through far north Queensland, the ABC's Brisbane office set up a 'You report' page and invited the public to submit photos of the disaster.[5] In 2007, when thousands of Burmese activists defied military orders to stop pro-democracy marches in Rangoon, students came armed with mobile phones to take secret pictures of the event and posted them on the internet (Holroyd and Miletic 2007). The internet and Web 2.0[6] applications have removed many barriers to independent publishing. A new wave of open source and collaborative software along with mobile technology, and a growing awareness of the 'wisdom of crowds', is changing the scope and definition of media.

In addition, the general public now, more than ever, has an opportunity to comment on issues and events taking place around them, via blogs, online feedback spaces and by participating in exclusive citizen journalism websites. This involvement, made possible by technological advancements, is also changing the nature of media consumption where consumers are proactively deciding how and when they want to receive news (Kovach 2005). The public's participation via online media in the 2009 Indian general elections, in the 2008 US presidential elections and in the 2007 Federal elections in Australia, may be perceived as a revival of the public sphere 'ideal' as outlined by Habermas in his original writing (dated 1964):

> Citizens behave as a public body when they confer in an unrestricted fashion—that is, with the guarantee of freedom of assembly and association and the freedom to express and publish their opinions—about matters of general interest. In a large public body this kind of communication requires specific means for transmitting information and influencing those who receive it. (Habermas 1974: 49)

However, the idea of citizen or participatory journalism is not new; previous phases of public-focused journalism represent a similar concern for public inclusion in news production. The dissatisfaction with the 'corporate media' (McChesney and Nichols 2002) and the one-way, homogeneous, mass-produced features of mainstream media in recent years has led to the rise of alternative media (Gans 2003; Harcup 2005; Rosen 1999). Although mainstream media has tried to include the general public's views via letters to the editor and other audience feedback mechanisms, these have generally been moderated by the editor/journalist in-charge, thereby controlled by gatekeeper/s. Saunders says media have remained inattentive to the diversity of public opinion, creating a narrow and incomplete representation of modern society (Saunders in Rodrigues and Braham 2008).

In the 1990s, journalists and non-journalists including academics began promoting journalism that was 'for the people'. Rosen, a leading figure in the development of 'public' journalism, says the movement grew out of a concern for the role of the press and ways in which the press could contribute to the public sphere (Rosen 1999: 21). Lambeth et al. (1998) say the practice of public journalism involves professional journalists reporting issues and events with particular concern for opinions and inclusion of the public. As a result, public journalism challenged the traditional journalistic benchmark for objectivity and impartiality with journalists' involvement in the stories they covered. By 2003, the movement seemed to fade away, and, presently, has evolved into citizen or participatory journalism where 'every citizen is a reporter'—a Korean citizen journalism website's (OhmyNews.com) motto.

Citizen or participatory journalism refers to the active involvement of usually untrained individuals in media (Bowman and Willis 2003). Often, these citizen journalists are part of a minority group unrepresented in traditional media or people discontented with mainstream news coverage (Shaffer 2005). More often their efforts are a product of circumstance, involving spontaneous video or camera footage of an event or disaster, which are used by traditional media to meet the demands of a 24-hour news cycle (Garrison 2005; Quinn and Quinn-Allan 2006; Sambrook 2005). This chapter uses the term 'citizen' journalism because of its pervasive use and acceptance in discourses as a representative term to describe the concept of journalistic practice by members of general public as opposed to media professionals. Here, the meaning of the word 'citizen' is accepted as a citizen of the world or humanity as opposed to a citizen of a nation-state. There is no one kind of 'citizen journalism' practice, but the concept has different layers as described by Steve Outing (2005) of PoynterOnline. The 11 layers of citizen journalism, according to Outing, range from opening up a news website to readers comments, to Wiki journalism where the readers are the editors. Other layers include traditional media recruits, add-on contributors to stories written by professional journalists or blogging either on the tradition news organisation's site or a new blogging site.[7]

Citizen journalism: revival of the public sphere discourse?

The role of the press has been an ongoing and much debated topic, underpinned by an essential awareness of the public sphere and, more broadly, by a concern for public welfare (Curran 1991; Rosen 1999). Habermas describes the concept of 'the public sphere' as 'a realm of our social life in which something approaching public opinion can be formed' (1974: 49). McKee (2004) says 'the public sphere' is a metaphor for thinking about how individuals come together to exchange ideas, information and emotions. It is useful in understanding how 'liberal' societies function, with the individual having input into the formation of general consensus as opposed to the totalitarian or Marxist model where the state/party has ultimate power in deciding what people think (Ibid.: 9). Habermas (1974: 49) describes the concept of 'the public sphere' as 'a realm of our social life in which something approaching public opinion can be formed'. McKee (2004) says the public sphere is a metaphor for thinking about how individuals come together to exchange ideas.

> The public sphere should ideally deal only with serious issues of real importance—only party politics, and not celebrity issues, sport or entertainment. It shouldn't be sensational, easily accessible or commercialized: it should refuse to dumb down to consumers, and rather demand that they work harder to improve themselves. It should only engage in rational, logical argument: not emotional or spectacular appeals. And it should be unified and homogenous, refusing the fragmentation of niche audiences and different kinds of culture. (McKee 2004:14)

However, Habermas's writing on the public sphere has been criticised for being elitist and restrictive (McKee 2004; Stevenson 2002). McKee argues that in today's post-modern era there are many public spheres:

... much of the modern writing about other forms of culture is written from a position of, what seems to me to be, ignorance. Writers condemn popular culture, Black culture, feminized culture, Queer culture or youth culture without actually being able to give examples of how it works or explain the trends in its forms of representation—because they don't know much about it. (McKee 2004: 212)

Similarly, Stevenson says Habermas wanted the 'discursive' discussions in coffee houses to be open yet closed. These discussions took place between groups of people who were predominantly 'rational', male and propertied, excluding a large number of participants, including women (2002: 49).

In the second half of the 18th century, daily political newspapers and literary journalism assumed an important role in the public sphere. Later, in the transition from literary journalism of private individuals to public services of mass media, public sphere was transformed by the entry of private interests, which became prominent in mass media (Habermas 1974: 53). Habermas initially considered the emergence of newspapers as a positive development:

The bourgeois public sphere could be understood as the sphere of private individuals assembled into a public body, which almost immediately laid claim to the officially regulated 'intellectual newspapers' for use against the public authority itself. In those newspapers, and in moralist and critical journals, they debated that public authority on the general rules of social intercourse in their fundamentally privatized yet publicly relevant sphere of labour and commodity exchange. (Habermas 1974: 52)

However, in post-modern society media has increasingly become a property of private interest. The 'ideal' public sphere has become fragmented and filled with trivia and entertainment, thus creating a population disengaged from politics and political conversations (McKee 2004: 205).

The commercialization and commodification of the popular press has undermined their ability to act as rational centres of debate and has also contributed towards a form of cultural fragmentation, where the depoliticized masses are excluded from the central debates of our political culture. (Stevenson 2002: 53)

Habermas (1989) says mass media have begun to shape, construct and limit public discourse to issues of importance to the corporate world, leading to a 'structural transformation' of the bourgeois public sphere, where private individuals came together as a public body to discuss public affairs of common concern, and opposed state power and influence of powerful interests (Kellner 2006). It is argued that the top-down model of mainstream media inherently excludes individuals from participating in public debate and political discourse (Gans 2003; Harcup 2005). McChesney (1997: 6) says: 'While democracies by definition must respect individual freedoms, these freedoms can only be exercised in a meaningful sense when the citizenry is informed, engaged and participating.' Thereby, public participation in the news process forms part of a wider discussion on the role of the press in democratic society and public sphere, where it is argued that a participatory news environment is more conducive to public engagement and facilitates the enhancement of the political process (Bowman and Willis 2003; Harcup 2005).

Citizen journalism in India

While the journalism and media industries in India have undergone massive changes in recent times, there has been no wide-scale spread of citizen journalism in the country, and the 'digital revolution' still seems a long way off. The Indian media industry is expanding rapidly. There has been a revolution in the television industry in the past two decades with the entry of hundreds of private and foreign television channels in a market which had been served by a government-funded monopoly network for nearly three decades. As a result, the Indian television industry has gone from one network, which broadcasts one or two channels depending on the location of its audience (rural or urban), to nearly 450 television channels being available to a cable subscriber for a small fee (US\$ 5–US\$ 10). Similarly, the Indian print media industry has been booming with a 35.51 per cent increase in circulation between 2003 and 2007, according to the World Association of Newspapers (2008). Although the radio industry has been lagging behind because of government control and lack of private investment, it is growing at more than 15 per cent per year, with private FM radio taking a foothold in the country (Indian Readership Survey 2007). Similarly, internet access has increased to 113 million subscribers (wire-line and wireless) in April 2009 (Indiantelevision.com 2009b), while mobile phone subscription is at 390-plus million (Prakash 2009). Within this scenario, the Indian media industry environment is diagonally different from other more mature media markets in the US, Europe and Australia, where mainstream media is in decline. One of the reasons given for the rise of citizen journalism in these mature markets is the disillusionment with the quality of journalism offered by mainstream media and the impact of commercial imperative on their media products. As a result, audiences with the aid of new technologies are moving online where they participate in news creation and blogosphere, and they tailor their news consumption by accessing news aggregating sites. However, if one is to evaluate the Indian media market, it is perhaps not a clear case of disappointment with the existing mainstream media, which is driving the trends in audience participation.

With a view to ascertaining the nature and extent of emerging trends in citizen journalism in India, and its adaptation by mainstream media, the author conducted a number of in-depth interviews in January 2009 to supplement the study of the existing media environment and literature research on the subject. Fifteen journalists, bloggers and citizen journalists were interviewed to gauge the impact of citizen journalism on the practice of journalism in India. The interviews, while semi-structured, were broad; they had mutual discussions and were conducted with an awareness of the social, political and technological context of the topic. Interviewees for the study were chosen according to their knowledge of and involvement with citizen journalism practices in India, and their position as decision-making professionals in the media (for e.g., editor, broadcasters and senior journalists). The purpose of the study was also to determine the necessary environment for the facilitation of citizen journalism, by comparing Indian media's adoption of citizen journalism with trends in other nations where citizen participation in news is more prevalent.

Independent online media in India

Although citizen journalism in India is in its infancy, there are some notable independent online media and blog websites which provide alternative voices to mainstream media in the country. A number of citizen journalism websites launched in recent years include Merinews. com, Csplash.com, WhiteDrums.com, MyNews.in and MeriKhabar. com, Purdafash.com and The Viewspaper. Some of these are easy to access, while others are not active anymore.

Merinews.com claims to be 'India's First Citizen Journalism News Portal'. Its CEO, Vipul Kant Upadhyay, is the Chief Technology Officer of an information technology firm IAP Company Limited. The portal was launched in October 2005 to enhance participation by the people in the world's largest democracy.

> Emanating from the need to empower democracy by providing a media to the people of the country to communicate with one and all, www. merinews.com is an effort to provide one such platform to interact and express. It is a news platform for collective wisdom. (Merinews.com 2009)

Within a year of its existence, the website had won an award as India's best e-content category in 2006, and in 2007 was declared an Honoree Webby Awards winner. In 2006, the Merinews.com management team announced a 'Rewards and Recognition' programme for citizen journalists whose articles featured in 'Merinews picks'. These authors are selected by the editorial board of Merinews on the basis of their topic, expression and language, and an honorarium of Rs 500 (US$ 10) is awarded to each winner. The site has established a brand name for itself and is updated regularly with news and views, and has a number of advertisements on every webpage.

In October 2006, the first bi-lingual online citizen media initiative MyNews Interactive was set up giving citizens an opportunity to provide their news, in their own words and according to their own perspective (MyNews.in 2009). MyNews.in (English) and MeriKhabar.com (Hindi) portals have a number of sections. However, the website does not provide any information about the creator of this initiative, nor does it reveal the identity of the editors who fact-check the writings submitted by citizen journalists.

Cplash.com, a citizen journalism site, started by three IT professionals, 'aims to emerge as a platform where "we the people" can express our views about events that touch our day to day life'. Cplash which is derived from citizen and splash, meaning front page news, shall feature stories that you—"the citizen shall highlight" (Cplash.com 2009). Set up in February 2008, the site daily received nearly 7000 hits in March 2009, and has a number of sections for citizens' contribution including politics, business, sports, social, technology and world news.

Then, there is WhiteDrums.com, a citizen website set up by Dhara Kothari (Editor-in-Chief) with owner Biren Shah so that 'truth can be recorded on this (Internet) global platform in the most democratic manner' (Whitedrums.com 2009). The site had about 98 members in May 2009, and encourages contributors to report news and views, and rate each other's work on the website. Then, there are a handful of Indian citizen journalism websites listed on Centre for Media and Democracy (Sourcewatch.org 2009) website such as Theviewspaper.net and citizen express.com, which does not seem to have any significant number of contributors.

Meanwhile, there are a large number of blogs, which become prominent during signpost events such as the 2005 Asian tsunami, Mumbai terror attacks in November 2008 and Indian general elections in April–May 2009. 'India Blogs' provides a list of top and most widely read bloggers in the country (labnol.org 2009). The list includes journalists, media personalities, doctors, artists, sports and film stars, as well as individuals who support their own blogging website such as Instablogs. com founded by Pramit Singh. Singh is also the founder of Bighow.com where a citizen journalist and/or blogger can find free resources on 'how to be a citizen journalist' (Pramit Singh 2008: 1).

According to Pramit Singh, there are three big portals providing blogging tools to readers: Sulekha, Rediff and Indiatimes (Ibid.). There are other groups who post their views on sites such as Desipundit.com and Blogbharati.com. Then, there are independent blogging sites such as Gauravonomics.com—a weblog on Social Media and Social Change—created by Gaurav Mishra. Mishra had also launched a campaign during the last general elections—Vote Report India—to build a grassroots movement in India with a view to encourage citizens to exercise their voting rights (Gauravonomics.com 2009). The weblog provides an aggregate service with a list of posts where 2009 elections were being discussed among citizens.

A number of not-for-profit organisations such as multi-lingual website Global Voices Online, which is funded by a number of philanthropic groups and run by a community of bloggers who aim to 'redress some of the inequities in media attention by leveraging the power of citizens' media' (Globalvoicesonline.org 2009), also created special election sections for Indian bloggers, and enlisted online space where conversations relating to elections took place in the early part of 2009. Similarly, the Indian political parties also jumped on the bandwagon to converse with their constituents on their web portals (The123network.com 2009).

As for mainstream media, *Hindustan Times* joined hands with Google to keep track of the Indian elections, while other mainstream media provided time and space to their audience to contribute their news and views on the elections. Media groups such as *The Times of India, CNN-IBN* and *BBC* have a well-established strategy to provide space for their readers' contribution, albeit these news entries, blogs and comments are edited by their editorial staff. Even in regional centres, traditional media including print and television are encouraging their readers to make contributions by filing citizens' news stories about local events. One such example is *Amrita TV*, a satellite channel based in India's southern state of Kerala, which has launched a news reality show including stories submitted by citizen journalists. The channel hosts competition among citizen journalists and rewards the winner with Rs 150,000 (US$ 2,500) cash price for their enterprising reporting of local news and events (Ccjig.blogspot.com 2009).

Meanwhile, a number of entrepreneurs have launched online sites to cover news in their local areas because they are dissatisfied with mainstream media. One such site includes Citizenmatters.com, which has an in-house editor, founder-manager, a full-time journalist and a number of freelance writers including citizen journalists and bloggers covering the city of Bangalore, providing a citizen-oriented news publication (citizenmatters.com 2009). Also, there is Himachal Pradesh's (in North India) INewsIndia.com, which attempts to promote citizen journalism in India.

There are also projects in community media where philanthropists and NGOs have launched projects such as MYOWN, Namma Dhwani etc. to assist local communities to use new technology to tell their stories. MYOWN is former journalist, Sweta Singh's initiative to train women panchayat leaders in Bihar, one of the most backward states in India, to talk about their issues and assist them in publishing a video blog so that their concerns are highlighted (Sweta Singh 2008: 1). Singh says that mainstream media 'suffers from a bias toward urban, educated, highclass male audiences', and therefore wants to 'make media use as democratic as possible and include marginalised groups especially women in the process of development' (Ibid.: 3).

Citizen journalism elsewhere in the world

For Asia at large, as in the USA and the UK, disasters have played a significant role in the growth of citizen journalism. The 2004 Asian tsunami saw a huge growth in citizen journalism and reporting of events on the ground (Johnson 2005). The effect of the online community's commitment to report the aftermath of the tsunami first hand was such that for the first time traditional media organisations all over the world relied heavily on individual citizens to bring them the news. The event reportedly contributed to a 39 per cent growth in newspaper coverage of blogs (Perlmutter and McDaniel 2005). A key generator of this growth is the heavily controlled media in much of the region. China's notoriously controlling censors have sought to stifle the internet, and the Chinese generally cannot access much international information from within the country. Despite heavy censorship of the internet, 'the blogsphere has allowed many different ideas and views to surface that previously were unavailable' (Guangqin and Clarke 2008: 10). Similarly, the incredibly high uptake and response to citizen journalism in South Korea is the result of several features of their society, with one crucial factor being their avid and loyal uptake of mobile and communication technologies (Budha 2002). Perhaps, the most instrumental factor in their drive to produce their own news is heavy censorship of media content. The lack of plurality in national media coupled with a history of intense civil rights movements have made South Koreans motivated and dedicated contributors to a new and free media. South Korea has high education and literacy rates. Fast internet access has been a key factor in the development of OhMyNews.com, which now has more than 60,000 reporters in over 100 countries.

The UK's experience in audience-generated news came in the wake of the 2005 London bombings. The inundation of user-generated content the British Broadcasting Corporation (BBC) received pushed the public broadcaster to invest in citizen journalism in a new way (Sambrook 2005). In the same year, the BBC reassessed its coverage-to-date on the Iraq war and concluded that they had failed to give an accurate depiction of the lives of Iraqis under the occupation of the Allied Forces. As a result, the citizen journalism site 'One Day in Iraq Project' was launched to give viewers a first-hand account of the situation (Anderson 2007). The BBC has since then launched many citizen journalism projects and has drastically changed the production of its news to encourage citizen participation. Similarly, *The Guardian* has also led the way in involving the public in its production through online journalism. *The Guardian*'s group blog, 'Comment is Free', now has more visitors from outside the country than from within (Ibid.).

There has been a widespread shift in North American media production and consumption that seems to recognise audience demand for interaction. In addition to a higher uptake of citizen journalism, political blogging and user-generated content, US media companies are increasingly utilising these forms within their own content. Perhaps the biggest success stories of America's movement into citizen journalism have been the many 'hyperlocal' initiatives in small communities. The MyMissourian website allows mid-Missourians to write and publish their own stories and photos, and is edited and organised by the University of Missouri's Journalism School as part of an online journalism subject. American blogs play a key role in the electorate's decision-making process during presidential elections.

Similarly in Australia, although development in citizen journalism has been patchy, online activities during the past federal election in 2007 were significant in raising the profile of citizen journalism in the country. Apart from election-focused projects such as YouDecide2007, which aimed at providing independent and representative accounts on key election issues (Rodrigues and Braham 2008), there were a number of blogging sites, such as Possums Pollytics, Larvaus Prodeo, the Pollbludger and Crikey.com, which came into the limelight during the elections. In fact, psephologist bloggers were right in predicting a victory for the Labor Party, well before the traditional media (Rodrigues 2008). Mainstream media too have adopted a strategy of co-opting this new trend in audience participation. Organisations such as Fairfax, News Ltd and the

ABC are seeking to reinvent themselves as multimedia newsrooms. The ABC is moving towards a more audience-oriented news platform, which can be tailored to suit the users' personal preferences and story 'tags'. The public service broadcaster has made significant efforts to enhance inter-action using new media communications and has recently launched its internet television service iView to cater to online interactive audience. News Ltd and Fairfax have strategies to personalise their audience's con-sumption of news and participate, if they wish to, via online feedback forums and blogs.

Comparison between India and elsewhere

Compared to other countries, India has the fortune of a thriving media environment. It is also the country, barring the impact of the current financial crisis, where traditional media (print, television and radio) is growing due to increasing literacy and economic prosperity. The Indian audiences, who can afford it, today have access to a number of media, which by default means that they have access to diverse range of views about issues of public affairs, both at local and national levels. However, in recent years, the exponential growth of media, particularly private and foreign television, has also impacted the quality of journalism prac-ticed in India. Citizen journalists and commentators believe that Indian news media as a whole, as big as it is, 'is 95 per cent drivel and five per cent news' (Pramit Singh 2008), while others believe the quality of Indian journalism has gone down due to an 'obsession of the news media with political circus and horse-trading, with crises and violence, on the one hand, and with 15-minute celebrities, on the other hand, has taken its toll' (Upadhyay in Roy 2008).

Merinews.com CEO, in an address to Convergence, Citizen Journal-ism and Social Change conference in Brisbane, Australia, in March 2008, claimed that despite the large number of regular publications in India (that being 7,000), only six groups controlled about 70 per cent of the print media in India (Upadhyay in Roy 2008). Similarly, in television, as a result of the need for sustaining ratings and keeping costs down, a num-ber of channels resorted to sensationalism in their programming includ-ing news coverage, where crime, sports and entertainment celebrities have become a staple of daily news bulletins. In the recent terrorism attacks in Mumbai, television coverage to a greater degree, and print media were criticised for unrestrained coverage of the event, which lasted for nearly three days. Traditional media practitioners generally agree that commercialism and intensification of competition has had an impact on quality of journalism in India. Commercialisation is forcing television to follow the success formula of others, leading to a 'sameness' in content.

> If a channel becomes successful in its programming, then all channels try and replicate that, and as a result, you produce a lot of one type of programming, and you lose out on variety... In television, people believe that short, sharp, sensational fare works better than something that demands concentration. (Thapar 2009)

Others believe there is a general trend in 'dumbing down' of content, particularly in 24-hour news channels. 'The whole idea is to try and reach out to as many viewers as possible and, therefore, the temptation to sensationalise, the temptation to exaggerate, to trivialise, and more and more media organisations have fallen prey to these' (Thakurta 2009). Vipul Mudgal, Editor (Research), *Hindustan Times*, says that media reflects the general decay in society, linking it to the process of 'politicisation of media' and 'mediatisation of politics' in India, where television coverage of a particular vantage point is presented as reality, which is mediated by the selective leaks, rhetoric, public relations spin doctors (Mudgal 2009). Nupur Basu, a former *NDTV* reporter agrees:

> [W]e have let the market and the competition get to us. We've completely lost track of every other objective that we could possibly have, we have lost our bearing in the sense of the best practice in journalism. It has all become a thing of breaking news—get it first even if it is right or wrong, or exaggerated or sensational or trivia. (Basu 2009)

The 2007 winner of the Ramon Magsaysay Award for journalism, literature and the creative communication arts, P. Sainath, *The Hindu*, says media's coverage of farmers' plight in India is disgraceful.

> Media is driven solely by profits rather than good journalism. You have less than six journalists covering the Vidharbha [agrarian] crisis in the middle

of 2006, but you have more than 500 journalists covering the Lakhme India fashion week in Mumbai. They (media) don't believe Vidharbha farmers make revenue for them. (Sainath in Garyali 2007)

However, there are detractors from this view. *The Times of India* Executive Editor, Arindam Sengupta (2009) says that 'journalism has improved in India. There was a time and day when all newspapers read like news agency reports, without any effort on the ground, people going out reporting extra stuff. I think competition is very healthy.' Similarly, Chandan Mitra, Editor, *The Pioneer*, points to the dichotomy:

[O]ver the past five years, print media has become much more responsible than before, whereas electronic media tends to go over the top because of this intense competition to be the first with the news. There is this need to break news with a new angle every 15 minutes. In the process, there is also this unsubstantiated news, rumours, highly exaggerated reports in electronic media, especially as you have something as dramatic and sensational like the Mumbai terrorist attacks. (Mitra 2009)

Sengupta says that while television coverage of the terror attack irritated a lot of people, and television channels made mistakes in their 60-hour on-the-spot coverage, it also brought the world's attention to the issue of terrorism in India, along with bringing the nation together.

Commentators make a distinction between print and electronic media, when describing their views about the quality of journalism at present. But, among viewers, this distinction is perhaps not well articulated, who refer to the media in collective terms. As a result of this dissatisfaction with the mainstream media, access to new media technology, and a capacity to participate on the internet platform, some have either launched their own citizen journalism and blogging websites, while others use social media sites such as YouTube, Twitter and Flickr to report their news and views.

Meanwhile, Indian traditional media, similar to their counterpart in other countries, have decided to tap into this world trend to connect with their audience via new technology by providing time and space to user-generated content. However, the growth of citizen journalism still remains patchy in India and its accessibility is limited to those who have access to new technology. As it has been mentioned elsewhere, India had a literacy rate of 65 per cent, according to 2001 Census of India, and at the same time nearly 300–350 million people in India lived below the poverty line (Asian Development Bank 2002). This means that about one-third of the population does not have the means or capacity to participate in this new media environment. Considering this, it is questionable whether these new trends in citizen journalism will have an impact on the country's public sphere for those segments of the population, which cannot reach either the mainstream media or the new media.

As for mainstream media co-opting citizen journalism into their publication or broadcast, there are some doubts about old media's intention. 'Citizen journalism fits in perfectly into this trend towards community news ... it also fits into the economic viability of a newspaper because what people want is to read about themselves' (Ninan 2009). Ninan who has authored *Headlines from the Heartland*—a publication on Hindi newspapers in India—posits that 'what the proprietors have done is changed the citizen journalist into a stringer. It is the opposite of what one would think of citizen journalism. They have made it a part of the big mainstream media.' However, Sengupta (2009) says that though mainstream media recognises the need to focus on local issues and become more accountable to its audience by providing hyper-local coverage, citizen participation in generating news content is labour-intensive for them. 'The amount of material that comes in ... it has to be culled to find any thought provoking and presentable stuff ... it is very labour intensive.' Sen (2009) agrees: 'I think what has happened is that private media has been quick to realise the importance of the local content, but they have not changed the editorial thrust, but they have increased the local content.' Similar thoughts have been expressed elsewhere too, where others have doubts about citizen journalism's capacity to contribute to the news-making process due to its chaotic articulation online in the form of too many voices and too many opinions, but little substance. Tilley and Cokley (2008: 98–99) note that the concept of citizen journalism has the potential to democratise, pluralise and enable change in traditional media, as well as to 'devalue, erode and undermine' society by enabling unchallenged and unchecked access by false 'citizen' voices with commercial or criminal interests rather than the public interest.

Conclusion

The growing dissatisfaction with the performance of traditional media coupled with the rise of the internet has fuelled people's need to react, respond, add and create news. But, does this public participation in news production via emails to media professionals, blogging and news production and commentary means we are getting closer to Harbermas's 'ideal' public sphere? Can citizens come together in an 'unrestricted fashion' and express their opinions 'about matter of general interest' rather than be mediated by a class of professionals called journalists and media owners? It could be speculated that the disparities in popularity and uptake of new participatory media forms between the US and India represent the contrasting political and social climates and cultures of the two countries, as well as a reflection of the citizens' willingness to engage in politics and national debates. In India, there is cynicism surrounding political process and, therefore, most of the middle class, who have access to new media technology, stay away from it. By the same token, Indian media, by and large, has more credibility with its audience, perhaps due to its role in the Indian independence movement, than in some advanced countries where commercialisation, corporatisation and concentration of the ownership of media industry has taken its toll on the audience's faith in mainstream media. Although, India has a diverse and plural media environment, thereby limiting the adverse impact of concentration of media ownership increasingly, the intensification of commercial pressure is being noticed in media coverages such as the Mumbai terror attacks. It remains to be seen whether Indian citizens will embrace the practice of 'online citizen journalism' as much as their counterparts in the USA, the UK and South Korea. Will their need to provide inputs to the media content be satisfied by traditional media's increasing adoption of audience participation—by providing space for comments, debates, blogging and inviting and accepting news and visual contributions from citizens within their expanding online presence?

Endnotes

1. Some of the ideas and themes mentioned in this chapter have appeared elsewhere in Rodrigues and Braham (2008).

2. According to 'State of Newspaper Scene 2007', there were 6,800 daily newspapers in India, while there were 62,483 periodical newspapers published in India (Press Council of India 2008: 7).

3. According to Minister of State Information and Broadcasting Anand Sharma, in February 2009, there were a total of 215 news and current affairs television channels available to Indian viewers, while there were 233 non-news including general entertainment and niche channels (Indiantelevision.com 2009a).

4. According to All India Radio, the public service broadcaster's website operated 229 radio stations and relay centres in the country in 2007 (All India Radio 2007), while the Telecom Regulatory Authority of India claimed that there were 245 FM radio stations and 41 community radio stations operational in the country in April 2009 (Indiantelevision.com 2009b).

5. See http://www.abc.net.au/news/indepth/featureitems/s1596452.htm for citizen contributed photos.

6. Web 2.0 applications refer to a perceived second generation of web applications that promote social networking and interactivity between users.

7. The 11 layers of citizen journalism described by Steve Outing are: *(i)* opening up to public comment; *(ii)* the citizen add-on reporter; *(iii)* open source reporting; *(iv)* the citizen bloghouse; *(v)* newsroom citizen 'transparency' blogs; *(vi)* the stand-alone citizen-journalism site: edited version; *(vii)* the stand-alone citizen-journalism site: unedited version; *(viii)* add a print edition; *(ix)* the hybrid: pro + citizen journalism; *(x)* integrating citizen and pro-journalism under one roof; and *(xi)* Wiki journalism: where the readers are editors (Outing 2005).

References

All India Radio. 2007. 'Facts at a glance', 13 November. Available online at http://www.allindiaradio.org/FACTS.html (downloaded on 28.05.2009).

Anderson, K. 2007. 'Media: Blogs to you!' *New Matilda*, 22 July. Available online at http://www.newmatilda.com/home/printarticle.asp?ArticleID=2430 (downloaded on 28.08.2008).

Asian Development Bank. 2002. 'Monthly Reports', March. Available online at http://www.abdindia.org/janeco-02.htm (downloaded on 18.02.2005).

Bowman, S. and C. Willis. 2003. *We media: How audiences are shaping the future of news and information*. Available online at http://www.hypergne.net/wemedia/weblog.php (downloaded on 05.01.2007).

Budha, K. 2002. 'Content and community: Online news in Asia', in Rao Madanmohan (ed.), *News media and new media: The Asia Pacific handbook*, pp. 79–95. New Delhi: Tata McGraw Hill Publications.

Ccjig.blogspot.com. 2009. 'Civic and citizen journalism interest group'. Available online at http://ccjib.blogspot.com/2009/02/indian-tv-station-offers-prizes-to.html (downloaded on 14.05.2009).

Citizenmatters.com. 2009. 'About us'. Available online at http://banglore.citizen matters.in/main/aboutus (downloaded on 23.05.2009).

Cook, T. 2005. 'State of play: Blogging and podcasting in Australia today', *Online Opinion*, 4 April. Available online at http://onlineopinion.com.au/view.asp?article=3307 (downloaded on 21.03.2007).

Cplash.com. 2009. 'About us'. Available online at http://www.cplash.com/about (downloaded on 16.05.2009).

Curran, J. 1991. 'Rethinking the media as a public sphere', in P. Dahlgren and C. Sparks (eds), *Communication and citizenship: Journalism and the public sphere*, pp. 27–56. London: Routledge.

Gans, H. 2003. *Democracy and the news*. USA: Oxford University Press.

Garrison, B. 2005. 'Online newspapers', in M. B. Salwen, B. Garrison and P. D. Driscoll (eds), *Online News and the public*, pp. 3–46. Mahwah, NJ: Lawrence Erlbaum.

Garyali, Natasha. 2007. 'In India, journalism equals revenue', *Asian Media*, 9 August. Available online at http://www.asianmedia.ucla.edu/article.asp?parentid+75536 (downloaded on 16.05.2009).

Gauravonomics.com. 2009. 'The report card on Vote Report India version 1.0'. Available online at http://www.gauravonomics.com/blog/the-report-card-on-vote-report-india-version-10/ (downloaded on 16.05.2009).

Globalvoicesonline.org. 2009. 'Indian elections 2009'. Available online at http://globalvoicesonline.org/specialcoverage/indian-elections-2009/ (downloaded on 14.05.2009).

Guangquin, J.Z. and J. Clarke. 2008. 'Blogging in China: A force for social change', *Australian Journalism Review*, 30 (1): 3–11.

Habermas, J. 1974 [1964]. 'Public sphere: An encyclopedia article', *New German Critique*, 1(3): 49–55.

———. 1989. *The new conservatism: Cultural criticism and the historians' debate*. Cambridge, MA: MIT Press.

Harcup, T. 2005. 'Citizens in the newsroom: Democracy, ethics and journalism', Paper presented at Association for Journalism Education (AJE) conference. Available online at http://www.ethicalspace.org/archive/2005_V2_3_feature-1.html (downloaded on 05.03.2007).

Holroyd, J. and D. Miletic. 2007. 'Bloggers go armed with mobile phones', *The Age*, 27 September.

Indian Readership Survey. 2007. 'IRS Highlights'. Available online at http://murc.net/irs/irs_highlights.html (downloaded on 16 August 2008).

Indiantelevision.com 2009a. '180 TV channels await government clearance', 26 February. Available online at http://www.indiantelevision.com/headlines/y2k9/feb/feb245.php (downloaded on 28.05.2009).

Indiantelevision.com. 2009b. '110 pay channels are on cable networks in India: Trai', 2 April. Available online at http://www.indiantelevision.com/headlines/y2k9/apr/apr18.php (downloaded on 28.05.2009).

INewsIndia.com 2009. 'Empowering Ideas'. Available online at http://www.inewsindia.com (downloaded on 31.05.2009).

Johnson, B. 2005. 'Online emergency services: As tsunami blogs fill the web', The Guardian, 6 January. Available online at http://www.guardian.co.uk/technology/2005/jan/06/onlinesupplement.insideit (downloaded on 27.10.2008).

Kellner, D. 2006. 'Habermas, the public sphere, and democracy: A critical intervention'. Available online at http://www.gseis.ucla.edu/Faculty/Kellner/essays/habermaspublicspheredemocracy.pdf (downloaded on 29.05.2009).

Kovach, B. 2005. 'A new journalism for democracy in a new age', Speech given in Madrid, 1 February. Available online at http://www.journalism.org/node/298 (downloaded on 20.02.2005).

Labnol.org. 2009. 'India Blogs'. Available online at http://www.labnol.org/india-blogs/Indian-bloggers.html (downloaded on 21.05.2009).

Lambeth, E.B., P. Meyer and E. Thorson (eds). 1998. *Assessing public journalism.* Columbia: University of Missouri Press.

McChesney, R.W. 1997. *Corporate media and the threat to democracy.* New York: Seven Stories Press.

McChesney, R.W. and J. Nichols. 2002. *Our media not theirs.* New York: Seven Stories Press.

McKee, A. 2004. *The public sphere: An introduction.* Cambridge: Cambridge University Press.

Outing, S. 2005. 'The 11 layers of citizen journalism', *PoynterOnline,* 15 June. Available online at http://www.poynter.org/content/content_print.asp?id=83126 (downloaded on 27.10.2008).

Merinews.com. 2009. 'About us'. Available online at http://www.merinews.com/aboutus.jsp (downloaded on 23.05.2009).

MyNews.in 2009. 'Frequently asked questions'. Available online at http://www.mynews.in/aboutus.asp (downloaded on 21.05.2009).

Perlmutter, D. and M. McDaniel. 2005. 'The ascent of blogging', *Nieman Reports,* Fall. Available online at http://www.nieman.harvard.edu/reportsitem.aspx?id=100641 (downloaded on 27.10.2008).

Press Council of India. 2008. 'State of newspaper scene 2007'. New Delhi: Centre for Media Studies.

Quinn, S. and D. Quinn-Allan. 2006. 'User-generated content and the changing news cycle', *Australian Journalism Review,* 1: 57–69.

Prakash, N. 2009. 'Mobile telephony', *Expresscomputeronline.com,* 25 May. Available online at http://www.expresscomputeronline.com/20090525/1000theissue30.shtml (downloaded on 29.05.2009).

Citizen Journalism and the Public Sphere in India

Rodrigues, U. M. 2008. 'Blogging comes alive', *The Hindu Sunday Magazine*, 13 January. Available online at http://www.hinduonnet.com/thehindu/mag/2008/01/13/stories/2008011350110400.htm (downloaded on 13.01.2008).

Rodrigues, U. M. and E. Braham. 2008. 'Citizen journalism and the public sphere: A study of the status of citizen journalism in Australia', *Australian Journalism Review*, 30 (2): 49–60.

Rosen, J. 1999. *What are journalists for?* London: Yale University Press.

Roy, Aniruddha. 2008. 'Citizen journalism is waiting to break the cocoon'. Available online at http://www.merinews.com/catFull.jsp?articleID=126466 (downloaded on 23.05.2009).

Sambrook, R. 2005. 'Citizen journalism and the BBC', *Nieman Reports*, Winter. Available online at http://www.nieman.harvard.edu/reportsitem.aspx?id=100542 (downloaded on 23.03.2007)

Shaffer, J. 2005. 'Citizen's media: Has it reached tipping point? New media initiatives emerge when citizen's feel shortchanged, bereft, or angered by their available choices', *Nieman Reports*, Winter. Available online at http://www.nieman.harvard.edu/reportsitem.aspx?id=100565 (downloaded on 27.10.2008).

Singh, Pramit. 2008. 'The state of citizen journalism in India part 1—Blogs, photos and videos'. Available online at http://mediavidea.blogspot.com/2008/02/state-of-citizen-journalism-in-india_9328.html (downloaded on 21.05.2009).

Singh, Sweta. 2008. 'Citizen journalism in India: From the front'. Available online at http://www.newsassignment.net/blog/sweta_singh/feb2008/09/citizen_journalism (downloaded on 21.05.2009).

Stevenson, N. 2002. *Understanding media cultures: Social theory and mass communication.* London, Thousand Oaks, California: Sage Publications.

Sourcewatch.org. 2009. 'List of citizen journalism websites'. Available online at http://www.sourcewatch.org/index.php?title=List_of_citizen_journalism_websites (downloaded on 21.05.2009).

The123network.com. 2009. 'Digitalisation of Indian elections 2009—Full list'. Available online at http://the123network.com/362/digitalisation-of-indian-elections-2009-full-list (downloaded on 14.05.2009).

Tilley, E. and J. Cokley. 2008. 'Deconstructing the discourse of citizen journalism: Who says what and why it matters', *Pacific Journalism Review*, 14 (1): 94–114.

Whitedrums.com. 2009. 'About us'. Available online at http://www.whitedrums.com/index.php?option=com_content&view=article&id=123&Itemid=433 (downloaded on 21.05.2009).

World Association of Newspapers. 2008. 'World press trends: Newspapers are a growth business', 2 June. Available online at http://www.wan-press.org/print.php3?id_article=17377 (downloaded on 25.05.2009).

Interviews

Basu, Nupur. 2009. Former NDTV senior journalist. Interviewed by author, Banglaore, 28 January 2009.

Mitra, Chandan. 2009. Editor, *The Pioneer*. Interviewed by author, New Delhi, 9 January 2009.

Mudgal, Vipul. 2009. Editor (Research), *Hindustan Times*. Interviewed by author, New Delhi, 10 March 2009.

Ninan, Sevanti. 2009. Editor, thehoot.org and media commentator. Interviewed by author, New Delhi, 12 January 2009.

Sen, Ashish. 2009. President, World Association of Community Radio Broadcasters. Interviewed by author, Bangalore, 25 January 2009.

Sengupta, Arindam. 2009. Executive Editor, *The Times of India*. Interviewed by author, New Delhi, 12 January 2009.

Thakurta, Paranjoy Guha. 2009. Media commentator and educator. Interviewed by author, New Delhi, 15 January 2009.

Thapar, Karan. 2009. Host, Devil's Advocate, CNN-IBN. Interviewed by author, New Delhi, 12 March 2009.

Chapter 7

The Naga Nation on the Net*

Maya Ranganathan

This chapter explores the ways in which Naga communities, denied space and time by the mainstream media in India, have found in the internet a way to instill nationalist ideologies among people. Building on the potential of the internet to create and nurture a nation (Ranganathan 2002), the chapter is an empirical study of how technological features of the internet are employed to position culture and history of the Naga nation to create and further Naga nationalism. Through qualitative analysis of three websites dealing with the issue, it is argued that the internet is being used much like the media that preceded it, to extend hegemony and nationalistic ideologies. What is significant in the context of the Naga nation is that first, the exercise is undertaken not by an official nation-state, but by a nation striving to transform itself into a nation-state and second, in a region which has a massive 'infrastructure deficit' (*Business Week* 2007) typifying the use of a 'post modern medium' for the achievement of 'traditional political goals' (Karatzogianni 2006: 3). Drawing from Anderson's seminal work, 'Imagined Communities', this chapter explores the hegemonic articulation and the antagonistic dynamic between the Indian nation-state and the minority Naga nationalism online (Anderson 1991), through a rhetorical analysis of three Naga websites.[1]

The Naga movement

The demand for a union of all the Naga inhabited areas surrounding the present so-called 'neo-colonial' structure of Nagaland as recognised by

---

*This chapter arose out of a post-graduate dissertation submitted by Shiva Roy-Chowdhury, supervised by Maya Ranganathan and passed by Manipal Institute of Communication, Manipal University, Karnataka, India in 2008. An earlier version of this paper was published as a special article in *Economic and Political Weekly*, 19–25 July. XLIII (29): pp. 61–68.

the Government of India, has largely been ignored by the powers that be as well as the mainstream media (Bezboruah 2006: 91; Hazarika 2006: 357), forcing them to adopt the internet that provides 'easier and cheaper means of political communication' (Karatzogianni 2006: 7) to create and perpetuate Naga nationalism. A study of online Naga nationalism becomes a study of how public opinion is generated—a part of Habermas' 'public sphere' which delineates public opinion with its consequent transformation and creation of identity and identity politics.

Comprising 16,527 square kilometres, Nagaland was carved out of Assam on 1 December 1963 and accounts for 0.17 per cent of India's total population.[2] The demand for unification of all the Naga-inhabited areas under a single administered state, either 'autonomous or independent' depending on who is making the demand, is the bone of contention in the north-east of India (Choube 1985: 163). The Nationalist Socialist Council of Nagalim—Isaak, Muivah or NSCN-IM—is at the forefront of demanding Greater Nagaland based on the claim that the Nagas were, prior to the 'unwelcome annexation' by India, a territory under British governance. Prior to India's Independence on 15 August 1947, the Nagas also declared their independence, which to date has not been recognised (Worldstatesmen). Statehood within the framework of India's Constitution has been unacceptable to the leaders and the founding fathers of the NSCN-IM—namely, Thuengaling Muivah and Isak Chisi Swu.

Naga nationalism dates back to mid-20th century when, following World War I, some Nagas were sent abroad by the British as part of the Labour Corps, thus exposing them to 'currents and political changes' (Hazarika 2006: 356). Upon their return to India, twenty Nagas came together and formed the Naga Club which presented a memorandum to the Simon Commission in 1929 stating, 'when the British leave, they should leave the Nagas as they were before the colonial powers came to the hills' (Hazarika cited in Hazarika 2006: 356).The Naga Hills District Tribal Council was established on the initiative of the British Deputy Commissioner in April 1945. In February 1946 the council renamed itself the Naga National Council (NNC) and organised itself as a federation of several tribal councils and brought out a small newspaper called the *Naga Nation*, the first step towards dissemination of Naga nationalism. (SACW 2003). In the 1940s, A.Z. Phizo assumed leadership of the NNC and met British officials to persuade them of his convictions and dreams that 'they should be as independent of India as India was to be of Britain' (Hazarika 2006: 356).

The plebiscite of 1951, when volunteers of the Naga National Council went to far-flung villages to collect thumbprints of every Naga to announce that 99.9 per cent of the Nagas sought independence, 'emotionally integrated the various Naga tribes' (SACW 2003). When Phizo and the NNC persisted with their campaign by 'boycotting the general elections in 1952 and launched (sic) a violent secessionist movement,' the first clashes erupted in the Naga Hills District of the state of Assam.[3] New Delhi rushed troops to tackle what was a 'political challenge' thereby unfolding a history of violence and terror in the North-East of India (Hazarika 2006: 357).[4] According to websites Nagalim.nl and Nagarealm.com, the NNC set up the Federal Government of Nagaland (FGN) and unfurled its flag and proclaimed a president, parliament and ministers under the leadership of Phizo on 22 March 1956 with a military wing called the Naga Federal Army (NFA) to drive out Indian forces. The NFA eventually succumbed to the Indian military might. To deal with the situation, the Armed Forces (Special Powers) Act, 1958, was subsequently enacted by the Government of India (INSAFIndia: online).[5] Phizo, however, escaped to the then East Pakistan in December 1956 and, subsequently, to London in June 1960. In the meantime, some Nagas took stock of the situation, and resolved that 'even if independence was not possible, the land, identity and individuality of the Naga people should never be compromised'. In mid-1957, moderate leaders headed by Dr Imkongliba Ao came to the fore (Chandra et al. 1999: 114). The result was the agreement that led to the creation of the state of Nagaland by India in 1963, which 'gave the Nagas worth and significance in the eyes of the world' (SACW 2003).

After numerous attempts at pacifying Naga resistance in 1972, the Centre banned the NNC, the NFG and the NFA as 'unlawful associations' under the Unlawful Activities (Prevention) Act of 1967. The security forces launched a massive counter-insurgency operation and forced the insurgents to the negotiating table. An agreement known as the 'Shillong Accord' was signed between the Centre and a section of the NNC and the NFG on 11 November 1975, according to which the NNC-NFG accepted the Indian Constitution and agreed to come out of hiding and surrender their weapons (SATP: online). However, a group of about 140 activists of the NNC, who had gone to China for training, 'repudiated the Shillong Accord and refused to surrender.' They formed a new underground organisation called the National Socialist Council of Nagaland (NSCN) under the leadership of Thuengaling Muivah, Isak Chisi Swu and S.S. Khaplang on Burmese soil in 1980. Today, the NNC and the NSCN have both split further, with each competing for 'supremacy and legitimacy as the official representative of the Naga independence movement' (SATP: online).

The Naga nation

The construction of a distinct Naga identity online needs to be examined in the light of challenges posed by intrinsic factors like 'tribal particularism and inter-tribal rivalry' (Chaube 1985:165). The Naga nation comprises thirty nine tribes (Daga: online). During the colonial rule, Nagas lived atop mountains with signs of fortification still intact and head-hunting, an institutionalised form of inter-village warfare, occasionally taking place even though it was criminalised by the colonial state. According to Hutton, neighbouring villages spoke 'dialects or languages totally incomprehensible to one another,' and in their communications involving war-making or alliance-building, they relied on sign language, which 'reached a high state of development' (SACW: 2003).

The 'exclusion', that initially began with the Inner Line Regulations of the British administration, 'kept Indian culture and religion on the other side of the fence' and created a controlled environment for the Christian Missionaries to proselytise and the 'administrators to provide enormous thrust to conversion' (Jafa 2006: 78). The missionaries 'collaborated with the colonial authorities and helped keep the nationalist influence out of tribal areas,' besides 'encouraging their isolation from the rest of the population of Assam and India (Chandra et al. 1999: 111).' Therefore, even long after the British left India, the hill tribes of Assam had no cultural affinity with the Assamese and Bengali residents of the plains. The tribals also 'feared losing their identities and being assimilated by what was seen as a policy of Assamisation' (Chandra et al. 1999: 113).Today, Christianity is an essential part of Naga identity.

Groups such as the Naga National Council (NNC) lace their separatist rhetoric with free use of Biblical imageries. Isak Chisi Swu NSCN-IM's chairman was the one to coin the phrase, 'Nagaland for Christ,' which found its way into the NSCN's lexicon. The slogan 'Nagaland for Christ' hangs over churches in the NSCN camps (APCSS: online). The Christian identity, which distinguishes the Nagas from the mostly Hindu and Muslim population of the Indian heartland has been partly an act of cultural resistance that also parallels the political and armed resistance. Thus, the British with their socio-political, cultural policies and most decisively, religion, have played a significant role in the construction of a distinct Naga identity. The Naga groups advocating independence began using the term 'Nagalim' to describe the Naga homeland and to distinguish it from the Indian state of Nagaland, and adopted English. 'Lim' is a word in the Ao dialect that refers to land. While the term Nagalim had been used by Naga student leaders for a while, in 1999 the NSCN-IM began formally calling itself the National Socialist Council of 'Nagalim', instead of 'Nagaland'.

The nation on the Net

In the following sections, the exploration of Naga nationalism online is placed in the context of the constraints faced by the dominant media in India in covering the Naga issue; the need for an alternative national construct; the challenges faced in forging a Naga identity; and the manufacturing of consent. Three websites are chosen for discourse analysis, the first being the NSCN online (http://www.nscnonline.org), the official website of NSCN-IM that continues to demand an independent Greater Nagaland and aims at 'promoting independence for a region including Nagaland and some of the surrounding areas'.[6] The second is 'Nagalim.nl' (http://www.nagalim.nl) which deals with Nagaland's past, present and future, or Greater Nagalim. The third, 'Nagarealm' (http://www.nagarealm.com) declares no political affiliation but nevertheless seems to defend the Nagalim movement, albeit in a subtle manner. The exploration of Naga nationalism on the websites is presented in the following pages in three sections: first, the laying down of the political agenda, second, the use of technological features of the internet and third, the content presented. This chapter delineates the process of construction and dissemination of Naga nationalism online and does not deal with negotiation of the websites by the members of the Naga nation.

Political agenda

The 'first historical steps of informational societies,' according to Castells, is the tendency to 'characterise them by the pre-eminence of identity as their organising principle' (Castells 2000: 22). Clearly, the most significant 'aspect of identity making is the naming process' and the websites flag Nagalim (Everard 2000: 58). Nagalim.nl registered in the Netherlands is owned by the Naga International Support Centre (NISC), which it claims has been set up 'to focus attention' on 'Nagalim, homeland of the Nagas'. The home page further asserts, 'NISC stands by the oppressed Naga people'. Nagalim.nl is clearly critical of India as at the outset it states that Nagalim is 'landlocked and inaccessible to outsiders, because of India's travel restrictions' and that Nagalim 'has been practically isolated from the outside world'. It also claims that 'in 1954 India invaded Nagalim'. It states, 'NISC wants to make it known that the human suffering in Nagalim and the rest of North-East India should stop'.

The site's home page links to a news archive and lends further support to the political agenda. Of the 15 news items uploaded on 16 October 2007 in the archives page, at least 13 were in support of the movement. One of the two stories, which gave the Indian government's point of view, was 'China abetting insurgents in North-East' from the local newspaper, 'The Nagaland Post'—dealt with the issue of a secret dossier. This allegedly prepared by the 'Indian Intelligence Bureau'—on how the 'insurgency in the north-eastern States had been compounded by suspected covert support from Chinese authorities and the prevailing geo-political situation in the immediate neighbourhood, particularly in Bangladesh and Burma.' Among the four stories that were clearly in defence of the movement or organisation, the article, 'Centre has no policy on North-East subversives' from the magazine 'Organiser' alleged that the Naga groups were 'clueless about the intent and purpose of the Union Home Ministry' (Organiser: online). The author argued that the groups who had laid down arms were 'confined in camps with no signal from the Centre' for their rehabilitation and that 'frustrated leaders and cadres of two outfits' were contemplating a change of heart after the treatment meted out to the groups by the local and Central governments, thus underlying the futility of towing the Indian line. Another story, though unrelated to Nagaland, titled, 'PREPAK to end fund drive 9 October next year; offers to give up struggle if unsuccessful by 2015', related to the banned People's Revolutionary Party of Kangleipak (PREPAK)'s demands for the establishment of an independent state of Manipur.[7] The fact that Nagalim.nl carried the press release of a 'banned organisation' signified its defiance of the Indian Constitution.[8]

Nscnonline declares in a banner on top of the home page that it is the official website of the NSCN. The URL also indicates that it belongs to the NSCN-IM. Its stated aim is 'promoting independence for a region including Nagaland and some of the surrounding areas'. It is hosted from Bangkok in Thailand.[9] On the home page, the NSCN-IM declares: the Indo-Naga issue is neither a question of 'separation' nor 'secession' from India... Nagalim was and is never a part of India and as such, Naga independence is neither a question of separation nor secession from India.

The next section contains the preamble adopted by the NSCN-IM, which declared Nagalim to be 'an Independent Sovereign Christian Socialist Democratic Republic' on 6 April 1996. Nscnonline asserts that it has been struggling for 'self-determination against colonisation in the region' and that the plebiscite of May 1951, yielding a 99.9 per cent vote in favour of independence from India, justifies its struggle. The five stories uploaded on 18 October 2007 on the home page shared either the views of NSCN-IM or were clearly in support of the Nagalim movement.

Nagarealm which, unlike the other two websites does not have a political declaration on its home page, reveals its political affiliation subtly in its content. It is hosted from Kohima, which is the capital of the Indian state of Nagaland (Nagarealm.com: online). Out of the three websites chosen for this study, Nagarealm is the lone website operating from within the nation. Nagalim.nl and Nscnonline, although dealing with issues specific to Nagas in India prefer operating from beyond the legal domain of India, perhaps to avoid legal action. The focus of the site is on news, information and entertainment. Yet, five out of 10 of the stories on the home page of Nagarealm accessed on 18 October 2007 were found to be in support of the Nagalim movement.

Technological features

While the internet has presented the Naga nationalists with new opportunities, it must be noted that 'the nature of the medium does not appear to affect the essentially modernist nature of the game' (Karatzogianni 2006: 7). In the sections that follow, I delineate the employment of some of the technological features of the internet in support of a traditional political goal, 'power'.

Hyperlinks

Contrary to enabling greater pluralism through 'off-site linking', hyperlinks are used in the Naga websites to provide navigational interactivity leading to a carefully structured navigation of the site, leaving no room for the reader to manipulate meanings (Brunsden and Morley 1978: 23). The hyperlink on the bottom of the Nagalim.nl home page links to a page in a book titled 'Enter the Forbidden land: The Quest for Nagalim'. Of the nine active links that link to off-site webpages, there are four that link to sites with similar opinion, leading to 'solipsism'. The potential to provide more information irrespective of approval is clearly ignored and the 'history' page on Nscnonline links to nine more on-site pages. The forum and gallery pages are only accessible to members who register with the site. Despite the possibility of debating information—through a facility for discussion on Naga history, culture, news and even general chat—there were no comments as on 20 October 2007 (Aelst and Walgrave 2002: 465–93). The 'Top ten page' innovatively positions content by ranking the most viewed article or section on Nscnonline, simulating the 'we write, you read' dogma of the press (Deuze 2003: 22). Nscnonline too, offers no off-site hyperlinks to the reader. Nagarealm's link to the commercial news agency Reuters website can perhaps be seen as an attempt at creating a notion of objectivity. Apart from links to four ethnic websites, Nagarealm links to sites like Nagalim.nl and Nscnonline, which are clearly inclined towards the idea of greater Nagalim. In effect, hyperlinks, though innocuous in their presence, attempt to reinforce opinion rather than accommodate different views.

Feedback

If the core concept of interactivity, that sets the internet apart from the traditional media, is 'feedback', there is little evidence of an understanding and appreciation of the concept among the Naga websites. In its contact page Nagalim.nl merely provides four email links to the organisation, its secretary and webmaster, treasurer and chairman, leading primarily to nominal interactivity. However, Nscnonline displays a greater awareness of the interconnectedness of relationships, and provides a feedback page that allows a registered user to send messages to the organisation, either as 'private messages' or posting as 'news' (Rafaeli and Sudweeks 1997: online). It also has a 'forum' for registered users which features discussions on Naga history, culture, news and press releases and 'general' topics such as 'Friends of Nagas in Europe', thus facilitating 'reciprocity' and 'contribution to debate', two features that define public sphere (Jankowski 2002: 43).

The news section on the home page allows registered readers to post comments on the stories and articles which are later displayed below the story. Spontaneity is curbed to the extent that to access this site one has to be a registered member but comments which are posted are displayed instantaneously.[10] Nagarealm, on the home page, has a 'News submission' link to user submitted articles thus providing facility to exchange roles in mutual discourse (Williams et al. 1998: 10). The website also had a discussion forum where 'How to survive as a student in the Big Indian Cities? The funny side!!!' was found to be the most popular topic on 21 October 2007. The most interesting feature however, is the 'surveys and polls' page which seems to 'accommodate increasingly complex and divergent social interests without conceding independent political space for opposition or dissent' (Rodan 1996: 105). On 18 October 2007 the website featured 44 polls on a range of issues such as 'Naga factions leaders/cadres are abusing their power and status for personal ends' which had eighty-one, votes of which 83.95 per cent believed that Naga factions were indeed abusing power.[11] The polls present a contrasting picture of current Naga sentiments underscoring the potential of the medium to allow pluralism.

Images

The most effective use of images among the pictures of men and women in traditional attire on Nagalim.nl is on the 'Maps page'.[12] The page effectively depicts the asserted 'Naga nation' (Nagalim) in the first map which includes major chunks of the neighbouring states of Manipur, Assam and Myanmar, presenting 'a scientific abstraction of reality' (Thongchai cited in Anderson 1991: 173). The second map highlights the boundaries of the 'so-called Nagaland' and 'Indo-Burma' borders. The third map shows, what the NISC describes as the arbitrarily formed Indian state of Nagaland. The Nscnonline website uses its leader Th Muivah's 'mug shot' as its site icon which is displayed in the address bar of the browser as well as on the page tabs, thus creating a national leader. The banner displays the NSCN-IM's self-styled government's 'National Flag' which is incorporated as an iconic representation with every news item in the news section, indicating the nation's 'quasi-developmental capabilities for forming, supporting and enforcing a common will' (Oommen 1997: 14). The NSCN's gallery page has 5 sections allowing for the 'veneration and exaltation' of the land and people that make the nation (Smith 1991: 9). The section featuring pictures of the Naga landscape is called 'Natural Beauty' which is a celebration of the land, depicting vast expanses of green and blue-top hills spawning with flora and fauna (NSCNonline: online). The section featuring Naga culture contains pictures of Naga traditional dancers in rich ethnic wear. The 'People's movement' section features pictures of Nagas protesting with placards and cloth banners with slogans demanding peace. The page also carries photographs of Naga leaders, Th Muivah and Isaac Chisu Swu. The 'consultations and meetings' page seeks to highlight the credibility of the movement's leaders as representatives of the Naga people. Among the pictures is a photograph of NSCN leaders with India's Union Home Minister Shivraj Patil and the Indian Prime Minister Manmohan Singh, thereby indicating the Naga leaders' 'official status' as the prime movers of the Naga Movement. Nagarealm has very few graphical enhancements on its pages, unlike Nscnoline. However, it has an extensive gallery with similar sections to those of Nscnonline with additions like sections on tourist attractions, North-East Tribals, North-East-Seven Sister's Abode, and news snapshots.

Personalisation

While the use of interactive elements is minimal in Nagalim.nl, Nscnonline imbibes the medium's ability to permit personalisation and customisation. Nscnonline allows the users to 'login' to their 'personalised' accounts. Sections like 'Feedback', 'Forum', 'Journal', 'Submit news' and 'Surveys' are only accessible to registered users. Once users log into Nscnonline, they have access to their private space on the website and can send private messages to other registered users and deactivate the public message broadcast. The user can configure the length of other people's comments and also send personal messages. The site also allows the user to customise the look and feel of his/her personal space on site by giving the option of 'themes'. The user can also maintain a 'journal' on the site, which can be made public or private, representing 'a shift in the author-reader relationship' (Everard 2000: 155). Nscnonline features a 'Music' section with song titles like 'My land and people', 'Oking the shifting capital', 'The Nagalim song', 'The weeping Nagalim' and 'Trumpet of victory.' Most of these songs are written in English, perhaps considering the lingual-diversity of the Naga tribes and in order to reach a wider audience. The titles indicate the attempt by the NSCN-IM to evoke the spirit of Naga nationalism through the medium of entertainment using rock and pop music to attract the youth. The extensive use of interactive elements in Nscnonline is an attempt to ensure that all the online needs of the user are taken care of, which may dissuade him/her from leaving the site. Nagarealm also offers personalisation and customisation, the significant feature being its feedback forms. The use of technological features by the Naga websites can be seen as nationalism as 'a discursive formation' shaping the form of representation (Calhoun 1998: 124).

Presentation of content

Alternate expressions: The portrayal of the internet as an 'alternate media' stems from the possibility that 'unmediated, unadorned and unreported' documents which find it difficult to penetrate mainstream media, can thrive on the Net—unquestioned and unmonitored (Lister et al. 2003: 177). NISC's website, Nagalim.nl and NSCN-IM's official website

Nscnonline, registered in Netherlands and Bangkok respectively, beyond the control and purview of the Indian government, makes it possible for them to disseminate the political ideologies of these organisations without fearing reprisal from those critiqued. While Nscnonline, the official website of NSCN-IM, which is in the forefront of the Naga movement states on its home page that 'Nagalim was and is never a part of India and as such, Naga independence is neither a question of *separation* nor *secession* from India' (Emphasis added), the official website of the government of the Indian state of Nagaland describes Nagaland merely as 'a vibrant hill state located in the extreme North Eastern end of India' in an attempt perhaps to convey the indifference of the Indian government to the demands for Nagalim.[13] Nscnonline, ironically draws support for its demands by quoting the Father of the Indian nation, Mahatma Gandhi: 'I will come to the Naga Hills; will ask them to shoot me first before one Naga is shot' reacting to the alleged 'forceful union' of the Naga Hills with India.[14] Abstracts of documents like the 'cable to the excellency' after the self-styled declaration of Naga independence is featured in 'Naga history' on Nscnonline: Benign Excellency (.) Kindly put on record that Nagas will be independent (.) Discussions with India are being carried on to that effect (.) Nagas do not accept Indian Constitution (.) The right of the people must prevail regardless of size (.)[15]

These documents are not attributed to sources, raising doubts as to their credibility. Nevertheless, they indicate the website's efforts to provide an alternate voice. Similarly, the website accommodates press releases denied space and time by the dominant media. Nagarealm, the site hosted from within the Indian state of Nagaland, comprises information about its districts, festivals, educational institutions, economy, jobs, church news and Nagaland/Naga history. However, it puts across its views on Naga history in an extremely subtle manner, unlike the other two websites. It is not clear whether the subtlety is due to constraints it faces owing to the fact that it functions from within the geographical boundaries of the nation or because of its convictions. But a conscious effort on the part of all three websites to justify the Naga claim for self-determination, thus revealing antagonistic world views, is evident (Laclau and Mouffe 1985).

The 'other': In all the websites, the Nagas are the 'we' with the Indians becoming the 'other'. The websites speak for the Nagas who are unlawfully being subjugated by the Indians. Interestingly, Nagalim.nl takes the position of a bystander to educate the readers about the Nagas, who are referred to in the third person. Although the presence of one group, the Nagas, automatically indicates the presence of the 'other', the 'other' is not mentioned in the discourse but is left to be understood by the reader. For instance, the account of history is presented thus:

> The Nagas have lived under the pressure of invasion for more than fifty years. To come out of the isolation forced upon them - and the international community to recognize their struggle for self determination, they need your attention and help. The Naga International Support Centre is determined to make the Nagas and their struggle known to the world. To enable us to project their rights there are several intriguing opportunities to consider.[16]

The 'deixis' of the homeland is embedded in words such as 'they' and 'their', rather than 'we' and 'our', although clearly indicating that the Nagas are the 'oppressed' and leaving little doubts as to who the oppressor is (Billig 1995: 94). The home page of Nscnonline on 24 October 2007 carried a piece written by NSCN-IM leader Th Muivah in which he said,

> [G]od has stood by us ... he has hitherto won all the battles for us from then up to now. He has also softened, to a measure, the hearts of the 'opponents' and made them admit the hard fact that the solution to the Indo-Naga issue is not in the military might of India but in the positive political approach.[17]

Read in the context of the other material on the websites, a complete picture of the discursively manufactured distinction between the Nagas and the 'other' emerges. The distinction laces every argument and is clear in some articles. In the article titled, 'The need to introduce Naga history in school text books: A political perspective' on Nscnonline, a poser reads: 'We the Naga study Indian history, but do we study Naga history in school or college level?'[18] The pronoun 'we' is used with calculated effect to draw clear the distinction.

History: The process of unification of the nation through a constant process of conveying a common historic fate, common triumphs of the past, national history speaking of grandeur, a national mission, and assurance of the nation's worth for mankind, is evident in all the websites (Gerth and Mills 1954). The narration of history projects 'equilibrium' in the past, prior to the advent of the British, the 'degradation of the situation' and the 'state of disequilibrium' in the present and an attempt to re-establish the 'initial equilibrium' (Todorov 1990: 29). Naga history effectively begins from the British invasion of the Naga Hills. It stops short of terming it a 'conquest' perhaps to indicate that the Nagas were never under the dominion or rule of any Indian or British Empire. However, it must be noted that the British indirectly ruled the Naga tribal areas through the village elders who were heads of the tribal village councils. Nagalim.nl, in its 'history pages', discusses the basis of the claim of Greater Nagalim from the perspective of cultural differences and the ways in which the British treated the Nagas. For instance, laws passed by British India or the Assemblies under the 1919 Indian Home Rule and the Government of India Act 1935, were not made applicable to the Naga areas. Apparently, this was in recognition of the fundamental differences underlying the social and cultural practices between Hindu and Naga societies. Nscnonline also maintains that the 'North and Eastern part—(of the Naga Hills) which formed the larger part of the Naga territory, was left uncontrolled and unoccupied by the British'. This area 'remained almost unvisited, entirely self-governing and completely independent even when India attained her independence from Great Britain in 1947'.[19] The 'Naga history' which the site refers to as 'Nagalim history' has instances of uprisings against the British by the 'Zeliangrong Nagas'—spearheaded by 'Jadunang' who was later hanged by the British. The site terms it a 'heroic revolution' on account of the 'staggering number of Nagas who were shot dead, hanged or otherwise imprisoned' and allegedly 'never made public by the British authorities.' Nscnonline accuses India of betraying the 'ten years agreement' which according to the site, guaranteed,

> [T]he Government of Indian Union will have a special responsibility for a period of ten years to ensure the due observance of this Agreement; at the end of this period, the Naga National Council will be asked whether they require the above agreement to be extended for a further period, or a new agreement regarding the future of the Naga people be arrived at.[20]

But as things turned out, according to the site, 'the agreement was no longer considered to exist by the Indian Government' and the Naga Hills were forcefully annexed by India, causing widespread resentment. The 'degradation of the situation' is recounted through a narration of the incidents of 'massive indiscriminate ransacking and ravaging of Naga villages' by the Indian armed forces (Todorov 1990: 29). It further claimed that on 18 October 1952 'Mr Zasebito of Zotsoma village was shot dead on the main road at Kohima by a sub-inspector of Indian police.' He was a judge of the Kohima Central Court and was the first Naga to be shot. The website goes on to name the victims of rape committed by the first Maratha Regiment and presents a statistical and descriptive account of the atrocities that allegedly went on unabated in 'Free Nagalim'.[21] Nscnonline further accuses the then Prime Minister of India, Pandit Jawaharlal Nehru of being in cohorts with the Prime Minister of Burma, Thakin U. Nu, and completing the division of the Naga Hills. It further goes on to condemn the 'Shillong Accord' as 'the most ignominious sell-out ever made in the history of the proud Nagas.' Nagarealm, however, is less blatant than the other two websites. In its 'history page' it states:

> In spite of all setbacks, behind the suspicion and the anxiety over the political issues, social crisis, changes to the Naga society in recent years, the Nagas throughout the decades have grown in knowledge and freedom, which many would agree is the real point of the Naga History.[22]

All three websites can be seen to be involved in the 'construction of a new common sense' changing the identity of the Naga groups (Laclau and Mouffe 1985: 183).

Culture: Given the diversities among the tribal groups that constitute Nagalim, the 'process of construction of meaning on the basis of a cultural attribute or related set of cultural attributes' is indeed difficult (Beniger 1986: 6). However, this is attempted in the websites by drawing out similarities among the different tribal groups and underscoring the differences with the Indians. The page on culture in Nagalim.nl describes the word 'Naga' as a 'collective name of many tribes' descending from a common ancestor. The introductory page displays pictures of a Naga man and a woman in tribal attire. It goes on to declare 'Nagalim' as their ancestral homeland and describes the ancestral symbols of common origin found in 'Makhrai-Rabu-Khyafii,' a Mao-Naga village in the state of Manipur, partly hinting that the village is an integral part of the Naga Nation. The Nagas are described as 'tough and defiantly self-reliant people.'[23] Describing their resemblance to South Asians, the difference in their physical appearance with the Indians is reinforced. Attention is drawn to the life-style of the Nagas—their warring and head-hunting ways—and the strategic locations of their towns perched atop peaks living in isolation resulting in the evolution of a diversity of languages. It is asserted that today 'Nagamese' is the common language and that although they comprise 16 major tribes speaking different languages, they 'forged a common identity during the British colonial period'.[24] As 'nationalism is primarily a cultural doctrine or, more accurately, a political ideology with a cultural doctrine at its centre', Nscnonline, even when it does not carry a separate section on Naga culture, features pictures of Naga traditional dances and rituals in the 'Gallery page' (Smith 1991: 74). On the home page, the 'Naga National Flag' enshrines the colours— yellow, blue, green, red and white—predominantly used by the Nagas in their handloom works. Nagarealm also does not have a section dedicated to Naga Culture, but has a section featuring 'Naga festivals' that states 'Nagaland is replete with festivities all through the year as the tribes have their own festivals'.

The unifying issue however is religion. The only state with over 80 per cent Christian population in a Hindu-dominated country, Nagaland remains a devout Christian state free from religious extremism (CensusIndia: online). Nagalim.nl in its 'history pages' refers to the Nagas, 'egalitarian communal social structure' which 'differed greatly from the stratified caste system of Hindu society.'[25] The page further alleges that it was 'impossible for them to live together in harmony' based on claims that the Hindus and Muslims hated the Nagas because of their consumption of 'beef' and 'pork'. Nagalim.nl alleges that soon after the British left India and 'Free Nagalim' was annexed as the Naga Hills district of Assam, India began attempts to 'inculcate' Indian nationalism by converting the people to Hinduism. It also accuses the Indian government of 'bringing Hindus into the region in administrative positions and introducing Hinduism as a compulsory subject in schools. Christianity, it claims, was banned as a 'foreign religion', including the reading of the Bible and Christian burials, thus appealing to the religious sentiments of the masses by identifying the nation with the religious community (Smith 1991: 49).

Nscnonline, in its preamble on its 'home page' declares in the 'Manifesto of the NSCN' that it attempts to constitute an Independent Sovereign Christian Socialist Democratic Republic. The NSCN-IM charges: 'the forces of Hinduism viz., the numberless Indian troops, the retail and wholesale dealers, the teachers and the instructors, the intelligent, the prophets of non-violence, the gamblers and the snake-charmers, Hindi songs and Hindi films, the rosogula makers and the Gita are all arrayed for the mission of supplanting the Christian God, the Eternal God of the universe.'[26] The website cites the 'freedom of Religion Bill, 1978' which was introduced in the Indian Parliament and forbids further conversion to Christianity as an indication that the Indian Constitution can be changed by the majority to suit their purpose. However, Nagarealm details the role of the American Baptist Missionaries in educating the Nagas and evangelising them at the same time. 'Education' was a tool the missionaries used effectively. 'Literacy was the stamp of authority that gave Christianity supremacy over traditional customs and belief.'[27] Nagarealm has a separate section on its website dedicated to news from the Church.

News: The Naga nationalism project is most apparent in the extensive coverage of news. Nagalim.nl does not have news on its home page but incorporates it in archives. An article titled 'Jamir should say sorry: NSCM-IM' featured in all three websites repeats the NSCN-IM allegation that the Naga politicians are betraying Nagas for their own political interest. Another story, headlined 'NSCN-K claims "victory"' featured by both Nagalim.nl and Nagarealm, details how NSCN-K managed to score some political points over its rival, the IM faction, by 'claiming to have extracted an assurance from Delhi to dismantle all "unauthorised camps" of its rival'.[28] Understandably, Nscnonline did not publish this story. Instead, it published a story on 22 October 2007 dated to '22 October 2004', titled 'NSCN-IM accepts PM's invitations to visit India', which is a significant development in the Indo-Naga peace process when the leaders of NSCN-IM, Th Muivah and Isaac Chisu Swu accepted the Indian Prime Minister's invitation to visit India for furthering the talks. The news offered on the websites presents a political debate for the readers who can leave comments, if they wish to do so, thereby providing a space for interaction to take place between the users. But more importantly the websites construct and convey particular ideologies.

Conclusion

The nation of Nagas, with a specific geographical demarcation in which people are integrated by a combination of several objective relationships and are striving to achieve their political aspiration for independence, has found in the internet a potential tool for nation-building. A post modern tool is employed for a traditional demand. This is especially significant as the movement for Nagalim runs counter to the official Indian nationalism propagated by the dominant media in India. Thus, the Naga websites, often registered outside the geographical boundaries of the Indian nation-state where the writ of the Indian government does not run, employ the different features of the internet to propagate Naga nationalism. While the very names of the websites reveal their political agendas, the content presented defends the movement for Nagalim either overtly or covertly, thus countering the dominant media's portrayal of the movement as unlawful. In this context, the alternate media of Naga websites seem to be engaged in a dialogue with the dominant media, thus contributing to some extent, to the creation of a public sphere. The technological features of the internet which have spawned visions of the creation of a Habermasian public sphere, are used, ironically, to reinforce particular viewpoints. Thus, hyperlinks which could be employed to present an array of information to readers, thus enabling them to make their own judgments, are employed by these websites solely to link to on-site material, leading to solipsism. Similarly, the form of the provision of feedback in the websites indicates notional interactivity as there is no evidence of its democratic potential being realised.

Typically, the websites are dominated by content that is clearly not the staple of the dominant media. Given the fact that some of the websites are registered outside India, they prove to be a storehouse of information that would never be featured by the mainstream media operating within Indian laws. Indeed, a constant distinction is sought to be created between 'us', the Nagas, and 'them', the Indians. This is attempted through a rendering of a detailed history which sets the Nagas' past apart from the Indians', justifying the turmoil in the present and leading to hopes for a different future. Interestingly, the commonness among the Nagas is sought to be created, not by presenting a unifying a culture, but by laying stress on the common religion practised by them. The differences in languages and customs between the different tribes is sought to be downplayed by stressing that Christianity binds them as one. The nationalism project is however, most apparent in the presentation of news in which the support for Nagalim is conveyed both overtly and subtly. News items are so chosen as to convey first, the aspiration for a separate nation-state and second, the ways in which the aspiration can be realised. Thus, an exploration of the Naga websites in the context of nation-building reveals that while the Nagas seem to have found a potential tool in the internet to 'rearticulate social reality using an alternative national construct', they are however yet to employ the medium to the fullest (Sutherland 2005).

Endnotes

1. See Sutherland, 2005 for the appropriateness of discourse theory to study nationalism as an ideology.

2. Calculated against India's estimated population as on July 2007 which was 1,129,866,154 according to Worldstatesmen.

3. The state of Nagaland that we know today was carved out of the state of Assam's Naga Hills District which was formed after the British left India.

4. See also SATP: online.

5. The Act gives sweeping powers to the Indian Army and paramilitary forces to control insurgency in the North-East. See http://www.insafindia.org/publication/afspa%20license%20to%20kill.htm downloaded on 13.10.2007.

6. http://whois.domaintools.com/nscnonline.org accessed on 10 October 2007. WHOIS is a TCP-based query/response protocol which is widely used for querying a database in order to determine the owner of a domain name, an IP address, or an autonomous system number on the internet.

7. *Kangleipak* is the ancient name of Manipur. See http://www.ipcs.org/agdb1 1-prepak.pdf downloaded on 17.10. 2007. The story however, is an announcement by the group that 'it would stop all coercive collection of funds from 9 October 2008.' It goes on to declare a 'deadline of 2015 to fight with all its

might to achieve its cherished goal of restoring independence to Manipur,' failing which it would leave the path of revolution forever. This story was originally published in yet another local newspaper based in Manipur called the 'Imphal Free Press.'

8. Article 19 Clause 2 of the Indian Constitution states, 'laws may be passed by the state imposing reasonable restrictions on the freedom of the press in the interests of the security of the state, the sovereignty and integrity of India', which is why press releases issued by 'banned or proscribed organisations' do not find their way into the mainstream media or in this case the print media. See Basu 2003, 19th edition, 103–04 and also Newswatch: online.

9. http://whois.domaintools.com/nscnonline.org downloaded on 18.10.2007.

10. Roy-Chowdhury registered under a fictitious name and managed to easily post comments which were generated instantaneously.

11. http://www.nagarealm.com/index.php?name=Polls&req=results&pollID=50

12. See http://www.nagalim.nl/naga/maps/maps.html

13. See http://www.nagaland.nic.in/

14. See http://nscnonline.org/modules.php?name=News&file=article&sid=188 downloaded on 22.10.2007.

15. Ibid.

16. http://www.nagalim.nl/naga/objectives/objectives.html

17. http://www.nscnonline.org/modules.php?name=News&file=article&sid=320 &mode=thread&order=0&thold=0 downloaded on 24.10. 2007.

18. http://www.nscnonline.org/modules.php?name=News&file=article&sid=248 &mode=thread&order=0&thold=0 downloaded on 24.10. 2007.

19. http://nscnonline.org/modules.php?name=News&file=article&sid=186 downloaded on 24.10.2007.

20. Ibid.

21. http://nscnonline.org/modules.php?name=News&file=article&sid=199 downloaded on 24.10. 2007.

22. http://www.nagarealm.com/index.php?module=htmlpages&func=display& pid=2 downloaded on 24.10. 2007.

23. http://www.nagalim.nl/naga/culture/culture.html downloaded on 24.10.07.

24. http://www.nagalim.nl/naga/culture/naga2.html downloaded on 24.10.07.

25. See http://www.nagalim.nl/naga/history/historical_context.html downloaded on 24.10.2007.

26. http://nscnonline.org/modules.php?name=News&file=article&sid=165 downloaded on 24.10.2007.

27. http://www.nagarealm.com/index.php?module=htmlpages&func=display& pid=2 downloaded on 24.10. 2007.

28. http://www.nagalim.nl/news/news.html downloaded on 24.10.2007.

References

Aelst and Walgrave. 2002. 'The role of Internet in shaping anti-globalisation "movement"', *Information, Communication and Technology*, 5(4): 465–93.

Anderson, B. 1991. second edition, *Imagined Communities: Reflections on the origin and spread of nationalism*. London, New York: Verso.

APCSS. Available online at http://www.apcss.org/Publications/Edited%20Volumes/ReligiousRadicalism/PagesfromReligiousRadicalismandSecurityinSouth Asiach10.pdf (downloaded on 15.10.2007).

Basu, D.D. 2003. *Introduction to the Constitution of India*. 19th edition. Nagpur: Wadhwa.

Beniger, J.R. 1986. *The control revolution: technological and economic origins of the information society*. Cambridge, MA: Harvard University Press.

Bezboruah, D.N. 2006. 'India's forgotten corner', in Asharani Mathur (ed.), *The Indian media illusion, delusion and reality essays in honour of Prem Bhatia*, pp. 86–97. New Delhi: Rupa & Co.

Billig, M. 1995. *Banal nationalism*. London: Sage Publications.

Brunsden, C. and D. Morley. 1978. *Everyday television: Nationwide*. London: British Film Institute.

Business Week. 2007. ' The trouble with India', 19 March. Available online at http://www.businessweek.com/magazine/content/07_12/b4026001.htm (downloaded on 12.4.2010).

Calhoun, C.J. 1998. *Nationalism*. Minneapolis: University of Minnesota Press.

Castells, M. 2000. *The information age: economy, society and culture, Vol. 1*. Oxford: Blackwell Publishers.

CensusIndia. Available online at http://www.censusindia.gov.in/Census_Data_2001/Census_data_finder/C_Series/Population_by_religious_communities.htm (downloaded on 24.10.2007).

Chandra, B., Aditya Mukherjee and Mridula Mukherjee. 1999. *India after independence*. New Delhi: Viking.

Choube. S.K. 1985. *Electoral politics in North-East India*. India: Universities Press (India) Pvt. Ltd.

Daga. Available online at http://daga.dhs.org/daga/readingroom/justpeace/nagaland/nagalim.htm (downloaded on 14.10.2007).

Deuze, M. 2003. 'The web and its journalisms: considering the consequences of different types of newsmedia online', *New Media and Society*, 5(3): 203–30.

Everard, J. 2000. *Virtual states: the Internet and boundaries of the nation-state*. London: Routledge.

Gerth, H. and C.W. Mills 1954. *Character and social structure*. London: Routledge and Kegan Paul.

Hazarika, S. 2006. 'Terrorism and Sub-alternity - III: India and the sub-nationalist movements in Mizoram and Nagaland', in Imtiaz Ahmad (ed.), *Understanding terrorism in South Asia: beyond statist discourses,* pp. 345–70. New Delhi: Manohar Publishers & Distributors.

INSAFIndia. Available online at http://www.insafindia.org/publication/afspa%20 license%20to%20kill.htm (downloaded on 13.10.2007).

Jafa, V.S. 2006. 'Insurgencies in North-East India: Dimensions of discord and containment', in S.D. Muni (ed.), *Responding to terrorism in South Asia,* pp. 77–115. New Delhi: Manohar Publishers & Distributors.

Jankowski, N.W. 2002. 'Creating community with media: history, theories and scientific investigations', in Jankowski (ed.), *Handbook of new media: social shaping and consequences of ICTs,* pp. 34–49. London, New Delhi: Sage Publications.

Karatzogianni, A. 2006. *The politics of cyberconflict.* UK: Routledge research in Information Technology and Society.

Laclau, E. and C. Mouffe. 1985. *Hegemony and socialist strategy.* London: Verso.

Lister, M., Jon Dovey, Seth Giddings, Iain Grant and Kieran Kelly. 2003. *New media: A critical introduction.* London: Routledge.

Nagarealm.com. Available online at http://www.nagarealm.com/index.php (downloaded on 19.10.2007).

Newswatch. Available online at http://www.newswatch.in/news-analyses/ethics-and-freedom/8753.html (downloaded on 18.10.2007).

NSCNonline. Available online at http://www.nscnonline.org/modules.php?name= coppermine&file=thumbnails&album=1 (downloaded on 19.10.2007).

Oommen, T.K. 1997. *Citizenship and national identity: from colonialism to globalism.* New Delhi, Thousand Oaks: Sage Publications.

Organiser. Available online at http://www.organiser.org/dynamic/modules.php?name =Content&pa=showpage&pid=206&page=12 (downloaded on 17.10.2007).

Ranganathan, M. 2002. 'Nurturing a nation on the net: The case of Tamil Eelam', *Nationalism and Ethnic Politics,* Summer 8 (2): 51–66.

Ranganathan, M. and Shiva Roy-Chowdhury. 2008. 'The Naga nation on the Net', *Economic and Political Weekly,* XLIII (29): 61–68.

Rafaeli, S. and F. Sudweeks. 1997 *Networked interactivity.* Available online at http://www.ascusc.org/jcmc/vol2/issue4/rafaeli.sudweeks.html. (downloaded on 21.06.2008).

Rodan, G. 1996. 'State-society relations and political opposition in Singapore', in G. Rodan (ed.), *Political oppositions in industrialising Asia,* pp. 95–127. London, New York: Routledge.

SACW. 2003. 'Confronting constructionism: Ending Indiaís Naga war'. Available online at http://www.sacw.net/peace/baruahMay2003.html (downloaded on 13.10.2007).

SATP. 'Nagaland Backgrounder'. Available online at http://satp.org/satporgtp/ countries/india/states/nagaland/backgrounder/index.html (downloaded on 13.10.2007).

Smith, A.D. 1991. *National identity*. London: Penguin Books.

Sutherland, C. 2005. 'Nation-building through discourse theory', *Nations and Nationalism*, 11(2): 185–202.

Todorov, T. 1990. *Genres in discourse*. Cambridge, New York, Melbourne, Sydney: Cambridge University Press.

Worldstatesmen. Available online at http://www.worldstatesmen.org/India_states. html (downloaded on 12.10.2007).

Williams, F., R. E. Rice and E. Rogers. 1988. *Research methods and the new media*. New York: Free Press.

3

The Cultural Aspect

Chapter 8

Towards a More Inclusive Indian Identity?

A Case Study of the Bollywood Film *Swades*[*]

Maya Ranganathan

Introduction

The changing political and economic scenario worldwide since the 1990s has necessitated changes in the articulation of Indian national identity. This has been reflected politically by the Government of India's passing of the Dual Citizenship Act in 2003. Such political measures have also been accompanied by an articulation of the changed national identity by the media, particularly Hindi cinema that has come to have worldwide appeal and viewership. However, the inclusive identity attempted now is not entirely 'new' but draws heavily from the 'inherited culture' of the nation to provide the 'adaptive leverage' to meet the western standards of progress (Chatterjee 1986: 2). This is brought to light in this chapter through a case study of the popular Bollywood film *Swades* which was released a year after the passing of the Dual Citizenship Act.

Although the idea of the nation[1] is based mostly on the 'other' in the case of nation-states-to-be, the 'other' plays a significant role in the crystallisation of national identity even in the case of established nation-states.[2] Established nation-states often invoke images of the demonic

[*]An earlier version of this chapter is published in *National Identities*, Vol. 12, Issue 1, March 2010, pp.1–20. The author thanks Judhajit Bagchi of Manipal Institute of Communication whose dissertation titled *Inclusive national identity in Bollywood films: A case study of Swades* submitted to the Manipal Institute of Communication in 2005 partially fulfilling the requirements for the post-graduate degree, forms the background for this chapter.

'other' to perpetuate nationalism and secure the unswerving loyalty of its citizens. If nation is indeed an imagined and abstract community, the 'emotional attachment' to it is furthered by constantly emphasising the real or imagined commonness among its people vis-à-vis the 'others'. While the collective identity that the people of a nation may acquire based on real or perceived similarities may change from one nation-state to another, the role of the 'other' in the creation and sustenance of national identity remains constant. The people of the nation are often made to remember and nurture their national identity based on what they are not as much as what they are.

The concept of the 'other' is generally articulated and reiterated through mass media, besides state education.[3] Although mass media is largely outside the purview of governments, especially in liberal democracies, the fact that those working in the media have internalised the concept of the 'other' ensures the sustenance of the 'other'.[4] Hegemonisation results in further reflection of the government ideology in newspaper writings, contemporary literature, films, and television soaps, encouraging the people 'to see the world in national terms in general and to think in patriotic terms about their own nation in particular' (Billig 1995: 115). Indeed, every media discourse can be read as a text for, every discourse makes the distinction between 'we' and 'they' clearly underscoring the 'other' (Fairclough 1995).

However, with 'transnational cultural flows and mass movements of population', definitions of nation and national identity are challenged by 'a dazzling array of postcolonial simulacra' that necessitate the constant redefinition of the 'other' (Gupta and Ferguson 1992: 6–23). While much attention has been focused on how the 'pace of border-crossings' or what Said called 'a generalized sense of homelessness' has led to a transfiguring and recreation of new representations of migrants' 'selves, their pasts and their new milieu', this chapter looks at how a change in the definition of a 'national' necessitated by political and economic compulsions is conveyed through popular media (Rayaprol 1997: 1–2; Said 1979: 7–58;). It traces how national identity that is based on differences or diversities undergoes subtle but significant changes with some exclusions becoming inclusive over a period of time (Geertz 1986: 105–23).[5] It also asserts that the core of the changed identity draws heavily from the traditional past placing it at the same time within the western framework of 'progress'.

Indian national identity

As pointed out in Chapter 2, Chatterjee argues that 'eastern' type nationalism has been accompanied by an effort to 're-equip' the nation culturally, unlike western nationalism which had 'little need to equip themselves culturally by appropriating what was alien to them' (1986: 1–2). However, this meant not a blind aping of the alien culture but adapting of the inherited culture of the nation to create a distinct identity.[6] Although Indian national identity is a larger question that cannot be legislated, I use the Constitution of India as a starting point for the discussion. The Constitution divides the population into two classes: citizens and aliens. While citizens are those who enjoy full civil and political rights and compose the state, aliens do not enjoy all of them (Basu 2004: 74). According to Basu, the Constitution sought to 'confer certain rights and privileges' upon the Indian citizens and place aliens under certain disabilities. The definition of an Indian citizen, according to the Constitution contained in Articles 5–8, emphasises domicile in India as a major pre-requisite.[7] It rules out double citizenship. The Government of India has its own term for its people who are scattered across the world. It defines them as Non Resident Indians (NRIs) or People of Indian Origin (PIO) under the Foreign Exchange Regulation Act of 1973 (Rajagopal 2001).

The Indian Constitution's definition of citizenship fits the 'rational ideological framework for the realisation of rational, and highly laudable, political ends'. The 'over-riding political needs of the time' led to the creation of a pan-Indian identity that played down diversities among the people within the state at the same time endowing them with an identity distinct from those without (Ganesh 2005: 21). If national identity is taken, as Scott said, as the 'referential sign of a fixed set of customs, practices and meanings, an enduring heritage and a set of shared traits and/or experiences', it explains the need for domicile in the state to be an important criterion for citizenship in an age when physical location could alone ensure that nationals were shaped by the culture of the nation they lived in (Plamenatz 1976: 23–36; Scott 1995: 5). The wave of modernisation that has resulted in mass migrations for political and economic reasons and the breakdown of the traditional structures of society, thanks to technological advancements have however, now rendered 'culture' non-synonymous with 'nationality'. 'Pride in one's heritage', which is an important ingredient in citizenship, has now been divested of passport nationality or physical location (Scott 1995: 5). Thus, while on the one hand, technological advancements have made physical location almost insignificant, on the other, mass migrations have called for a reconstruction of difference. The impossibility of a fully inclusive political community has led to the creation of a 'constitutive outside, an exterior to the community that is the very condition of its existence' through a construction of 'we' as distinguished from 'them' (Mouffe 1995: 36). Different identities have been produced by 'discrimination' which is what has led to the constant redefining of the 'other', based not only on a new understanding of pluralism, but an acknowledgement of 'the constitutive role of power and antagonism' (Ibid.: 33).

The changes in political thought in India since Independence have led to a redefinition of Indianness and even Indian citizenship. Although the fundamental fabric of the Constitution which advocates unity in diversity within the state has remained intact, the advent of globalisation has resulted in visible, invisible, intentional and accidental changes in political thought. This has necessitated adaptation or 'creation for the growth of a certain degree of individual initiative and choice, and for the introduction of science and modern education' (Chatterjee 1986: 3). A major step has been the economic liberalisation in India in 1991 dictated by globalisation that has resulted in far-reaching changes not only in the area of India's economic policies, but also in political and cultural fields.[8] With liberalisation making foreign investments imperative for economic growth, 'national' could no longer be 'some kind of a quintessence, resisting contamination by the global,' but had to represent 'a special sense of being that transcends nationalities and cultures' (Gooptu 2006: 10). In the economic climate when the country had to look to contributions from Indians abroad, political thought had to change towards a more inclusive national identity, culminating in the passing of the Dual Citizenship Bill in 2003.[9] However, this national identity cannot vary distinctly from the identity already created, but can only adapt it to meet new challenges. Thus, the new Indian national identity has come to stress on the need for participation in the making of the nation, preferably through domicile in the state. The fact that the Act facilitates economic participation but denies voting rights and public employment makes it seem as an instrument of 'economic citizenship'. It is in this context that I place the study of the Indian identity as articulated in the Bollywood film *Swades*. *Swades* has been chosen as a representation of the 'political culture', a source of imagery for the public consciousness, playing a highly 'personal role in the psychological development of the individual'.[10] Although the advancements in technology giving rise to a variety of communication systems that defy the control of the state seem to challenge the concept of hegemonisation, in India where access to communication systems is concentrated in the cities and among the educated elites, media, particularly the larger-than-life films 'occupy a special place in the social ritual' of the populace and continue to function effectively as tools of hegemonisation.[11]

Bollywood and nationalism

In the largest film-producing country in the world, films have played a role in the democratisation of culture and taken over and even eclipsed other forms of cultural productions, particularly in the realm of nationalism.[12] While the media in general construct and celebrate the nation, 'for millions of Indians, wherever they live, a major part of India derives from its movies' forming a vital part of what Appadurai calls the 'ethnoscape' (Appadurai 1991: 191–210; Rajadhyaksha and Willeman 1999: 10). They lead to the 'imagination' of the nation complementing perhaps the personal experiences of the first generation of migrants and leading to new images for the second and subsequent generations of Indians whose knowledge of the nation is dependant more on secondary sources. For the second and subsequent generation of migrants, the films also help develop their own identity.[13] The new heights that Hindi films have reached in recent times signify the transgression of geographical and language barriers by the Hindi films and most importantly indicate Bollywood's growth into the most famous international brand making possible a crossover to globalised mainstream cultures of the West.

Khan and Debroy, in a detailed study titled, 'Indian economic transition through Bollywood eyes: Hindi films and how they have reflected changes in India's political economy' establish that Hindi films have always reflected the dominant political themes of their time.[14] In almost all such films, nationalism was a 'projection of cross-border conflict between

India and Pakistan and Indianness, a consciousness that was defined in opposition to the "other"' (Gooptu 2006: 10). Indeed, the 'other' in such films that recorded a nascent nation's assertion to sovereignty was the Pakistani or the white man or more surprisingly, the Indian who had 'deserted' his/her land for better economic prospects. For instance, *Purab Paschim*'s (1970) story line emphasised the need to remain in India even if it meant a life of untold sufferings. In Mahesh Bhatt's *Naam* (1986), the protagonist who migrated was shown as turning into a criminal after leaving India. During the 1980s the term 'brain drain' gained currency when media discourse discouraged Indians from moving overseas. Thus, anti-nationals were not merely the stereotypical enemies of the country, but also portrayed as those who were unable to resist the global. The image of the anti-national drew heavily from Articles 5–8 of the Indian Constitution that dealt with citizenship and the Citizenship Act, 1955 which laid down the ways by which Indian citizenship may be lost.

The economic liberalisation of 1991 that necessitated among other things, drawing investments to the country from abroad also led to a redefinition of the 'other'. The stereotypical media image of the callous and selfish Indian abroad of the eighties when the Indian economy appeared to be doing well had to give way to a more tolerant image of the NRI following the waking up of the Indian government to the need of involving the huge NRI population in the process of nation-making.[15] A study done in 1993 with regard to investments in Indian securities revealed that the NRIs preferred holding securities in other countries than those they stayed in and especially in India (Hiremath 1997: 385). The second generation of migrants are also known to be pumping in huge money into the Indian economy and contributing to a greater international awareness of India (Khadria 1999). A more recent trend has been that of 'reverse migration' where NRIs have been returning to India, though not in sizeable numbers, especially owing to the slowing down of the western economies and picking up of the Indian economy (NRIinformation.com). It is in this scenario that the erosion of the stereotype of the Indian who moves abroad must be evaluated.

Liberalisation was also accompanied by yet another phenomenon, that of the Hindi films becoming popular abroad. With an increase in the number of Indians moving overseas for study and employment, Hindi films transformed into a source of cultural sustenance for overseas

Indians, preparing them perhaps for the 'return visit' which is an essential part of the migration experience (Baldassar 1997: 69–93). Bollywood films not only enable them to maintain ties with their geographically distant country of origin, but these 'ties to the old homeland' often even define the development of ethnic identity in the new homeland (Ibid.: 70). Indeed, 'connections to place, even if only imagined, are of central importance to migrants lives' (Gupta and Ferguson 1992: 6–23). Thus, the market for Hindi films has extended and grown beyond the boundaries of the country to not just South Asia and South East Asia, but also to East Africa, Mauritius, the Caribbean, the Middle-East, Britain, Canada, United States and even those countries associated with the former Soviet Union (Moti and Dissanayake 1998: 8). In an article published in the Indian monthly *Filmfare* titled 'How the West was won', Naheem (1998: 121–24) writes:[17]

> [F]ilms open here (USA) the same day they do in India, and the first nights often dictate their fate. With about 40,000 Indians and Pakistanis and perhaps 10,000 Afghanis scattered across the large Washington metropolitan area, going to a Hindi film is first and foremost a major commitment of time.

With the Indians abroad becoming an important market of popular cinema as well as site for its production, a spate of films began to be made on the lives of Indians abroad like *Dilwale Dulhanya Le Jayenge* (1994), *Hyderabad Blues* (1996), *Pardes* (1997), *Aa Ab Laut Chale* (1999), *Kabhi Khushi Kabhi Gham* (2001), *Kehta Hai Dil Bar Bar* (2001), *Kal Ho Naa Ho* (2003), *Swades* (2004), *Hyderabad Blues II* (2005) and *Kabhi Alvida Na Kahana* (2006).

But for the Indians abroad, they provided a link to their home country. Hindi films that celebrate and reiterate traditional Indian values and culture appeal to the often sentimental Indians abroad and enable what Schutz termed 'consociation' (Naheem 1998:121 and Schutz 1967: 109). Hindi films have thus been 'coloured by questions of Indianness and identity' as also technological advancements and connections with the global culture (Ganesh 2005: 23). Bollywood film-makers, in their effort 'to provide a level of content which will guarantee the widest possible acceptance by the largest possible audience' had, to perforce shed the stereotypical image of the NRI as the 'other' and 'reflect a more inclusive Indian identity (Jowett and Linton 1989: 83). It can thus be argued that first, the shift in economic and political ideologies and second, the increasing market for Hindi films abroad dictated a gradual shift in the treatment of the Indian national identity consequently changing the definitions of 'Indianness' and the 'other'.

The first step towards a more inclusive national identity was taken with films like blockbuster *Dilwale Dulhanya Le Jayenge* (1995) where the west-settled Indian protagonist who comes to India to find a bride also contemplates setting up a beer company of 80 million pounds, a contribution to the country of his origin. The runaway success *Hum Aapke Hain Kaun* (1994) touched upon joint ventures and foreign collaborations while *Duplicate* (1998) dealt with the concept of Foreign Direct Investment (FDI). The Indian settled abroad who came back to make such contributions was treated with a mixture of admiration and jealousy.

> Overseas Indians were expected to pay back their debt of gratitude to their country of origin for the investments made by it in their formative years by way of such things as subsidized higher education. It is envisaged that this repayment could take various forms such as making available to India the technological know-how acquired aboard; remittance home of a part of their savings for the support of their families in India; foreign currency deposits in various kinds of NRI accounts to ease the country's shortage of foreign exchange; and investments in Indian securities or directly in industrial ventures. (Hiremath 1997: 385)

The hitherto demonised or ridiculed Indian who had moved abroad, i.e., the 'other', could become 'national' by repaying his/her debts to the country. The definition of 'Indianness' thus moved towards the transcendental (Gooptu 2006: 10). A superficial reading of the film *Swades* brings to light the ways in which the 'other' could shed his 'otherness' to become a national. But what is significant is that in this age of migrations and technological advancements that are shrinking physical distances and in a political climate when the Indian nation-state is offering dual citizenship for Indian migrants to the west, the film advocates return of the migrant to the homeland to make a significant contribution to the country's development and sets it up as an hallmark of Indian identity. Even if the film, steering away from the stereotypical image of the Indian migrant as one to be shunned, portrays the Indian migrant as a person to be wooed back to the country, it continues to valorise

'Indian traditions' and reinforces a highly problematic and essentialised notion of Indianness.

Swades

Swades is significant in this context because the protagonist of the film is an Indian settled in the US returning to India not to just find a bride or celebrate his marriage in the Indian way, but with the express intention of contributing to the development of the nation (See Appendix 1 for storyline of the film). In this aspect the film differs from the earlier Hindi films of the genre.[17] The film was released on 17 December 2004 within a span of one year of the passing of the Dual Citizenship Act in Parliament, although it is not clear if it was indeed inspired by it. According to the then Deputy Prime Minister L.K. Advani, the main aim of the Dual Citizenship Bill was to attract Indians abroad to contribute 'to the cause of India's development' which precisely is the storyline of *Swades* (Indiaday: online). But it must be remembered that the film is not about citizenship, for nowhere in the film is there a discussion on citizenship. The film is about Indian national identity which, as pointed out earlier, cannot be legislated for. The film raised expectations also because its director Ashutosh Gowarikar's previous film *Lagaan* (2004), which incidentally 'threw up grey areas which could not easily be fitted into the self-other paradigm' thanks to the presence of some positive white characters, had been nominated for the Academy Awards in the best foreign film category (Gooptu 2006: 10). In India, *Swades* won the jury award for the 'best film of the year 2004' in the 50th Filmfare awards. The film also fetched the 'Filmfare best actor award' for Shah Rukh Khan who played the protagonist, Mohan Bhargav. In the following sections, I first highlight how familiar and often accepted images are used to articulate a seemingly more inclusive national identity before pointing out how stress is particularly laid on domicile to participate in the process of nation-building.

Invoking *parampara*

The most significant aspect of the film is that the film while seemingly attempting a redefinition of Indianness in no way argues against the

Indian world view dictated by *parampara*, translated in English as tradition, which connotes 'a flow, a vertical transmission in time and a spatial spread horizontally' (Vatsyayan 2005: 41). Indeed the film's storyline reflects the 'ambiguous and painful relation' with the epitomes of western world—institutional order, reason, science, and cultural self-assertion—that has marked Indian nationalist discourse at the outset (Hansen 2004: 29). Mohan Bhargav, the protagonist is torn between his desire for the orderliness and the prosperity of the western world and the cultural superiority of the land that he 'belongs' to. Also it falls in line with what Chatterjee identified as a unique feature of anticolonial resistance: the creation of an 'inner' culturally sovereign realm while competing with the west in the 'outer' realm of politics and economy. Thus, the parameters of development identified in the film as desirable are western, however, the way in which it is to be reached is through Indianness.

The definition of Indianness prompted by the transnational dimension of cultural transformation leading to the 'construction of culture, the invention of tradition, the retroactive nature of social affiliation and psychic identification' draw on familiar symbols in literature, art, music, life and death (Bhabha 1995: 49). For one, the title consists of two parts: the main title, *Swades*, and the tag line, 'We, the people.' In most Indian languages, there is a clear distinction between *desh* (homeland) and *videsh* (foreign land) (Oommen 1997: 151). *Swades* is an extension of the word *desh* which means 'our own land'. *Desh* is a common enough term used often to refer to communities with identities (Hansen 2004: 43). However, these identities have been fluid. They represent anything from a native village to a state to a region that one belongs to.[18] Thus, although the action in the film is located in the fictitious village of Charanpur in Uttar Pradesh, the village can be taken to represent any village in India. A particular regional identity is sought to be subverted by naming one of the main characters Kaveri, after the river Cauvery that flows in southern India. To Mohan, an Indian-born American who left India 12 years ago, and to others like him, *Swades* can only mean India. It can be presumed that Mohan is an American as he is shown as employed in National Aeronautical and Space Agency (NASA). Ironically, Mohan could not have laid claim to India as his own before 2003, for, on acquiring US citizenship his Indian citizenship should have been terminated as per the 1955 law of citizenship. It is after the passing of the Dual

Citizenship Bill in 2003 that India could have rightfully become Mohan's *Swades*. Second, the tag line of the film—'We, the people' in English 'a local as well as global medium'—has direct reference to the Preamble of the Indian Constitution that spells out the essence of the provisions as well as the main objectives of the Indian Republic.[19] The inclusiveness of the national identity becomes clear here, for, Mohan's *Swades*, which excluded him till now thanks to his opting for the citizenship of another country, now reciprocates his feeling of belonging. This is reiterated when the title reappears in the screen in 11 Indian languages.

The India that Mohan comes back to is a village where the 'interpretations of relation between the greater nation and its constituent communities' emerging as a continuum can be seen (Hansen 2004: 45). It is at a modest house in a typical Indian village that Kaveri *amma* (Mother Kaveri) clad in a saffron-coloured sari and a green blouse, colours in the tricolour welcomes him with *diya* (earthen lamp), sweets and flowers to Charanpur, which literally means 'land that offers refuge'. In contrast, the US where Mohan comes from is the land of glass and chrome, devoid of Gandhi's cultural nationalist tradition that distinguishes India.[20] Thus, when Mohan thinks of India it is of photographs of Gita, Nandan and Kaveri *amma* and the frames of agricultural, rural India, landless labourers and the aged.

'The recurrent metaphor of landscape as the inscape of national identity' is apparent when Mohan's recollection of India includes Charanpur and the house of Kaveri *amma*, the Ram temple, the box that Gita had gifted him, the train, hills, rivers, Mohan's trips in the train, bus, boat and Melaram's M-80 (a typical hardy Indian rural two-wheeler) and the song '*Yun hi chala chal…*' that describes the topography of the nation (Bhabha 1994: 143).

If Kaveri *amma* is taken as a metaphor for India, India nurtures her children from their childhood and makes them independent in life, much the same that Kaveri *amma* had done for Mohan. The arrangement of elements in the scene in which Kaveri *amma* is introduced in the film forms a syntagmatic chain. The paradigms are Kaveri *amma* cooking or sleeping or chatting. The scene of Kaveri *amma* tending a baby conveys the unconditional love of a mother for her child, drawing forth on the concept of *Bharat mata*, the country as a mother nurturing all her children. What is more significant is that Kaveri *amma* is shown tending another woman's baby. Mohan is also not her own son. Kaveri *amma* stays with Gita and Nandan, again not her children, to take care of them. In the film, there is not one who enjoys blood relations with her but she is still portrayed as a woman who showers love and affection on any and everyone. Like a dutiful son, Mohan attempts to take Kaveri *amma* to US with him and give her all the comforts that she deserves. However, the director, through Kaveri *amma*'s refusal offers another solution, that of Mohan returning to his *Swades* and taking care of her and her people. The 'corrosive feelings of guilt' that mark nationalism is on display when in the US, Mohan agonises over the life of Kaveri *amma* (read India) who is no blood relation of his, but a woman who took care of him when young (Kedourie 1970: 2). In an interlude, Gita points out to the customs and tradition that endow soul to the body of the nation (See Appendix 2). And interestingly it is *Gita*, (also referring to the celestial song that contains Lord Krishna's teachings to the world) who enlightens Mohan of his duty to his homeland. The inclusiveness is based on a cast of characters, symbols and spatial strategies that are identifiable as Indian.

Mohan himself espouses the significance of the underlying concept of 'unity in diversity' in India's national identity when the Panchayat chief and members resist the admission of Dalit children to the school and again in the song *'Yeh tara woh tara har tara...'* A selective general transformation of the 'pre-existent cultures' is used to indicate the inclusiveness (Gellner 1983: 48). An ancient Indian sport *kusthi*, i.e., wrestling, considered to be a test of manliness is also employed as a test of Indianness. The first time that Mohan is invited to match his skills with Nivaran Dayal Sharma, he is the 'other' and naturally he loses. As Mohan sheds his 'otherness', he manages to win a match with Nivaran Dayal.[21]

However, the erosion of the structure of the traditional society in response to the changing political and economic compulsions becomes clear when Gita spurns a marriage proposal almost borrowing the west's argument for women's emancipation or in the turn around of Melaram who belongs to the lower caste (Gellner 1964). Gita tells the prospective groom, 'Besides looking after the home, I want to work outside the house also...our parents educate us with the same kind of love and affection (that they bestow on men) and they want us to be independent and self-dependent. If your son wants to make his name in the society why can't I? Our hands are not merely meant to be decorated…why should one sacrifice more than the other?' Melaram who faces discrimination in the village and dreams of escaping to the US gives up his dream when Mohan offers to sponsor him. He says, 'No Sir, now there is no need for it, I am fine here. Thanks to you, some things have changed in the village.' The message here is clear. A few 'traditional' structures have to be done away with in the process of modernisation of the nation where 'public concern' rather than the idea of common good cements the political community (Mouffe 1995: 37). Thus, although the film focusses on a few traditional practices that are undesirable, it makes a stronger argument for the retention of others that bestow soul on the nation.

The role of symbolism

An interesting aspect of the study, perhaps borrowing heavily from film analysis techniques, is the use of symbolism to indicate the 'otherness' and the inclusiveness. If the film can be read as the progress of the protagonist from the 'other' to 'us', it becomes evident that western images and things are used to portray the 'otherness'.[22] Mohan, when he comes driving a caravan through the by lanes of Charanpur unable to let go of the mineral water bottle and his Marlboro cigarettes, is clearly the 'other'. It is when he gives them up along with the American notion of Spartan cleanliness during the course of the film that he sheds his 'otherness' that allows complete integration with India. Mohan is expected to melt 'like ice in water', as the elderly woman Fatima tells Kaveri *amma*, by returning to the homeland spurning the comforts of the US of A before he can prove his Indianness. Surprisingly, although Mohan derives his 'otherness' from being a citizen of the US, the US, the 'other', is depicted positively, as a developed nation that offers comforts and opportunities to all who chose to migrate to it. It is the transposition of the American lifestyle into the Indian milieu, as signified by the caravan that Mohan lives in, during his initial days in India that presents a conflict. This is resolved by Mohan's declaration when he moves into Kaveri *amma's* house to sleep, 'why do you wake me up Kaveri *amma*? I have not slept so well in days.' Mohan's contentment stems from the fact that for the first time he has slept in the lap of his nation.

The distinction and greatness of the two countries is again brought to light in the discussion Mohan has with the villagers on *Vijayadasami*, the auspicious day when children begin their formal education by being admitted to schools. When the Panchayat chief comments that India is the best in terms of culture and traditions, Mohan replies,

> I don't think that our country is the best in the world, but I admit that we have the potential to be the best. America and India are completely different from each other. Americans have developed based on their strengths…and they have their own culture. So it will be incorrect to say that their culture is inferior (to ours). Whenever we Indians are about to lose a challenge we take shelter in our culture and tradition. We distinguish between human beings on the basis of caste and creed. Everywhere in India people say, 'nothing is going to happen to this country'. But our duties do not end with saying this. We all, including me, are responsible for the current state of the nation. We all have to do something for this country. We are escapists and always lay blame on others.

Unlike in films of the past, the country that Mohan derives his 'otherness' from, is not demonised, owing perhaps to the understanding that in the era of globalisation, India is irreversibly committed to progress in western terms. Neither is Mohan ridiculed for his western ways.

However, with clever use of the tri-colour, India is flagged throughout the film. In the plane shot when Mohan is on his way back to India, the mise-en-scène shows the combination of three colours – green, white and saffron. As Mohan looks down from the plane, patches of white clouds and green fields can be seen far below and the next shot shows the plane, saffron bordering the white windows. Also Gita's parting gift to Mohan quintessentially sums up all that is Indian with the colours of the flag being prominent.

Domicile

What is interesting in the film is that such subtle changes are accompanied by jingoistic and parochial notions of identity. Even in this age of migrations and technological advancements, the film in no way undermines the stress on domicile laid down in the Constitution. On the contrary, it reiterates the need for Indian citizens to return to the country and physically situate themselves within its boundaries to contribute to the development of the country. A turning point in Mohan's progress towards integration is when he is sent to Chudi village by Kaveri *amma* to collect the lease amount on Gita's land from farmer Haridas. Moved by Haridas' plight, Mohan gives him some money and returns to Charanpur empty-handed. While Kaveri *amma,* symbolising India, appreciates his gesture she also points out that this is the condition of most of the people in the region. And she speaks of how Mohan could contribute to the development of the people and place, in effect his *Swades.* When Mohan is ready to leave for the US, she declines to accompany him and says, 'Your absence will be felt here. Had you stayed on, everything would have been settled.' Again the contribution that Indians within and without India can make to the nation is brought out by Gita and Kaveri *amma* in a conversation with Mohan, where Mohan almost denies that he is an Indian (See Appendix 2).

The importance of staying within the boundaries of the country is brought out again when Mohan crosses swords with the Panchayat members on the issue of admitting Dalit children to school, and he is told, 'Hey, who are you to tell me what I have to do and what I should not do for this village? I know that this is your birthplace, but that does not mean that you are capable of taking everyone's welfare into consideration. What decisions I have to take in respect of the village I know very well…see Mohan, you are here only for a few days… roam around and see the village…why do you involve yourself in these problems?' Mohan's initial effort to change attitudes is met with resistance and he is instantly excluded on account of his not living in the village. It is much later that he is accepted. In the sequence when Mohan is leaving, the head (*sarpanch*) of the Panchayat says, 'Mohan, we had come to forget that you are a foreigner. A guest comes to go'. Studies have established that Indians who migrate to the west do not want to return and if they do, 'hasten back after a short trial period because of the difficulties encountered here of a personal or professional nature' (Hiremath 1997: 385). The above interlude also touches upon this aspect.

However, what is problematic and is left unsaid in the film is that the solution does not lie in Mohan's return to the country for good from the land he has migrated to. It lies in his relinquishing his American citizenship and taking up Indian citizenship, which is glossed over in the film. As an OCI, Mohan will be able to contribute economically to the development of his motherland which does not essentially necessitate his returning to live in it. In fact, considering the foreign exchange rate, his contribution is likely to be more significant if he remains in the west. His return in order to live and work for the development of India as an OCI will not only rob him of his earnings in US dollars but also restrict his participation in the nation-building. For, even if he is accepted by the villagers of Charanpur as one of 'them', as an OCI he will not be able to participate in the political process or even gain employment to public office. His contribution is thus limited. The film in fact seems to advocate a giving up of citizenship of western countries and opting for Indian citizenship alone. This is ironical considering the increased migrations to the countries of the west and the passing of the Dual Citizenship Act extending privileges to the Indians abroad.

Conclusion

It is clear that economic and political compulsions are pushing the Indian nation-state to make its national identity more inclusive. Challenged by mass migrations and technological advancements that allow for 'psychological make-up manifested in a common culture' even when removed from the geographical boundaries of the nation, a study of 'popular culture' as represented by the Bollywood film *Swades*, indicates that the Indian national identity is moving towards greater inclusiveness. This has called for a redefinition of the 'other', through an articulation of a greater acceptance of the Indian leaving the geographical boundaries of the nation. However, such inclusiveness is still governed by some traditional beliefs and fundamental beliefs enshrined in the Indian Constitution. This was explored in this chapter through an analysis of the Bollywood film *Swades*.

The film was released within a year of the enactment of the Dual Citizenship Act, when the issue was current. The film deserves attention firstly, for steering away from stereotypical image of Indians who migrate to the west as selfish and uncaring and secondly, for laying down the ways in which they can contribute to the nation's development. However, what is significant is that while the film may indicate a greater tolerance towards and acceptance of the Indian who has made her/his home in the west, it still roots Indianness in tradition (*parampara*), and the established tenets in the Indian Constitution. Even as more people are sought to be brought within the purview of the 'Indian national', an expectation of contributing to the nation's progress by physically living within its boundaries is sought to be built. The film propagates that 'otherness' can be shed only by a return to the nation and complete integration. Thus, the protagonist Mohan, although he works on a prestigious project in NASA, remains the 'other' in his country of birth where he longs to be accepted, till he is willing to give it all up for the sake of his homeland. It must however be noted that the tolerance and acceptance does not extend to all Indians who have left the country, but is conditional. While Mohan, an NRI is able to return and eventually integrates, his friend Vinod, who does not display Indian sensitivities as in a love for the motherland, remains the 'other' throughout. The film advocates changes in a few of the traditional structures, but it reiterates other traditional concepts like the efficacy of the panchayati raj system and the importance of culture and tradition in the making of the nation.

In the process, the film almost seems to be arguing against the provisions of Dual Citizenship Act, for the Act allows overseas Indians to retain the citizenship of the countries they have migrated to and yet claim citizenship of India. But the protagonist in this film has to relinquish the comforts of the foreign land and return to the rustic and not-so-comfortable life in India to make a contribution to his motherland. His acceptance by his homeland is dictated by his willingness to give predominance to his Indian identity over his American citizenship. This is indeed ironical as the protagonist's contribution to his homeland arises out of what he has learnt and earned in the west. The west where Indians settle down is indeed shown as a much desirable place. But then the film advocates that test for the true Indian lies in giving it all up for his country. Mohan's plans in the film while returning to India to either work in the Vikram Sarabhai Centre or continue with NASA even while in India are indeed beyond the realm of possibility. To work in the former, he must give up his American citizenship and to work in the latter must remain an OCI which will restrict his role in contributing to India, which is the very purpose of his return. Thus, although the film seems to attempt an articulation of an inclusive national identity, on closer analysis it seems to argue against staying in the west and advocates returning to India forsaking the conveniences of the west and contribute to the Indian nation.

Appendix 1

Narrative of *Swades*

This is a film about an overseas Indian, Mohan Bhargav, who leaves his comfortable life in Washington, USA and returns to India, to contribute to India's development. Director Ashutosh Gowarikar contrives situations to make Mohan realise that he must return to India for the greater common good. Throughout the film, the director takes care to ensure that the viewer knows what the two countries can offer their citizens.

To sum up the narrative, Mohan is a manager working for the National Aeronautic Space Agency (NASA)'s Global Precipitation Measurement project. Everyone in the Goddard Space Research Centre is happy with his work. The film introduces Mohan as a hard-working scientist. But at the same time he is worried about Kaveri *amma*, who looked after him in his childhood and is now in an old-age home in Delhi. His friend Vinod compels him to take leave of absence from work for a week to go to India and bring back Kaveri *amma*. Thus Mohan leaves for India.

In India Mohan finds that Kaveri *amma* no longer lives in the old-age home and has shifted to a small village, Charanpur, in Uttar Pradesh. In his friend Rahul's bookstore he meets Gita, the female protagonist of the movie. Mohan decides to go to Charanpur. On his bidding, Rahul arranges for a caravan as Mohan is apprehensive about the conditions in the village. Mohan reaches Charanpur and meets Kaveri *amma*. There he comes to know that Gita is his childhood friend and she is the person who had brought Kaveri *amma* from the old-age home.

Gita lives with her brother Nandan, fondly referred to as Chiku. Gita's parents have built a small school in Charanpur and in their absence Gita runs it. Mohan, feeling guilty for neglecting Kaveri *amma*, seeks her apology and asks her to accompany him to the US. She says that she will think about the matter. A few days pass by and Mohan spends his time interacting with the villagers, specially the five Panchayat members, the postmaster Nivaran Dayal Sharma and the cook belonging to the backward classes, Melaram, who dreams of making it big in America by setting up a restaurant. Nivaran Dayal Sharma is concerned about the development of the village both in terms of infrastructure and literacy. But the Panchayat members are orthodox in their thinking and resist change.

Mohan spends his nights in the caravan. With the passage of time he begins to sleep inside the house but continues to drink mineral water. Gradually he falls in love with Gita. When Gita rejects a marriage proposal with a prospective groom because of his narrow-mindedness, Mohan is elated. He finds out that Kaveri *amma* cannot go with him because of two problems: one is Gita's marriage and the second is the school. The Panchayat orders the school to be removed from the place where it currently functions if Gita fails to enrol a certain number of students within a given time. Mohan and Kaveri *amma* divide the problems between them and Mohan goes about the task of bringing students to the school.

In the course of time he gets into confrontation with the Panchayat but still manages to gather a considerable number of students for the beginning of a high school in the village. In this whole process, several basic questions like the inclusion of the backward classes in mainstream society, the necessity for mass education and the involvement of the people at the grassroots level come up. As Mohan involves himself with the matters of the village his return to the US keeps getting postponed. But he continues his work on the GPM project through the internet. At this point of time Kaveri *amma* sends him to Haridas, a villager who lives in Chodi village, a few miles away from Charanpur. Haridas had taken Gita's land on lease but has defaulted on the lease amount. Mohan goes with Melaram to collect the money but is moved by the wretched living conditions of Haridas and returns empty-handed after giving money from his pocket to Haridas. While returning by train he meets a child vendor selling drinking water. For the first time, he leaves his mineral water bottle aside and buys water from the boy.

As the narrative unfolds Mohan involves himself with a greater task of bringing electricity to the village. He succeeds in his mission. By now, Gita has also fallen in love with Mohan. But when he plans to return to the US, neither Kaveri *amma* nor Gita agree to accompany him. Instead they ask him to stay back in India. Mohan leaves alone for the US.

After returning to the US, he accomplishes his project of GPM successfully but cannot resist the urge to return to his homeland India and decides to come back. He returns without a proper plan and wants to work either for Vikram Sarabhai Space Centre or to continue his work with NASA from India. The film ends with Mohan winning the game of wrestling (*kusti*) against the postmaster Nivaran Dayal Sharma in Charanpur.

Appendix 2

Mohan: Such attitudes, customs and tradition are fetters that do not allow the country to move forward.

Gita: Excuse me, without its customs and traditions, our country would be a human body without a soul.

Mohan: What soul are you talking about Gita? Illiteracy is rampant, there are administrative problems here and we are still underdeveloped.

Kaveri *amma*: Yes, poverty and illiteracy are interrelated here.

Mohan: Kaveri *amma*, your village still has no electricity … this caste and creed, increasing population, unemployment, corruption. Our condition is very bad, it's pathetic.

Gita: The government is trying to solve these problems.

Mohan: Infrastructure that the government has is not enough to cope with even one-fourth of the existing population.

Gita: The government is trying and is drafting schemes.

Mohan: Just drafting plans and collecting funds for them is not the duty of the government. Should not the government also ensure that the schemes are implemented properly at the grassroot level and that the common people benefit from them?

Gita: But just what do you think of the government? Government is a system of which the people are also a part. I, you and all the people here are also part of this system. If there is something lacking in this system then the responsibility is as much ours as the government's.

Kaveri *amma*: God does not help those who don't know how to help themselves.

Mohan: But here nothing is going to change, people don't want to change.

Gita: It's very easy to spot the errors, are you doing anything to rectify them?

Mohan: Excuse me, at least I am not protecting the government like you, I am building satellites.

Gita: But you are doing all these things over there. At least, I am working at the grassroots level, I am trying to make this a better place.

Mohan: Gita, you are a typical Indian, you Indians never accept your mistakes.

Kaveri *amma*: You Indians?

Mohan: Sorry, I mean, 'we' Indians.

Endnotes

1. The terms 'nation' and 'state' are used interchangeably in this chapter.
2. This is an inversion of the orientalist epistemology of 'other' by Hansen (2004). Hansen points out to Inden's observation of the European 'we' being in opposition to the dominant utilitarian and rationalist imaginations of India. Europe saw India as spiritual as opposed to the materialist Western world. This distinction was taken forward in the Indian nationalism project by Jawaharlal Nehru, Bankim Chandra Chatterjee and Swami Vivekananda. Indian national identity during the Independence movement and post-Independence was constructed in terms of the 'other' and it is in this sense that the term is employed in this paper.
3. A case in point is the way Mohammed Ali Jinnah, founder of Pakistan and Mahatma Gandhi, father of India, figure in the official accounts of the history of the respective nations. Jinnah, for instance, who is eulogised in Pakistan is treated as a symbol of Partition that lead to huge loss of lives by both Indian historians and Indian media. So much so that the Bharatiya Janata Party (BJP)

leader, L.K. Advani created a furore, when on a visit to Pakistan in June 2005, he termed Jinnah 'secular'. The newspaper *The Hindu* reported: 'A PTI report said Mr Advani described Jinnah as "a great man" who had espoused the cause of secular Pakistan in an address to his country's Constituent Assembly. Jinnah's 11 August 1947 address was really 'a classic, a forceful espousal of a secular state in which while every citizen would be free to pursue his own religion, the state should make no distinction between one citizen and another on grounds of faith'. See *The Hindu* 2005.

4. For example, an oft-repeated criticism against the Indian media is that it toes the official line in its reportage of Kashmir. See Singh 1996: 7. This is a fall-out of the fact that all Indian journalists have, over the course of their life and career, subconsciously internalised the successive Indian governments' line on Kashmir thereby subscribing to and actively perpetuating the image of Pakistan as the villain.

5. Geertz says, 'like nostalgia, diversity is not what it used to be'. People use the past in highly selective ways to construct a present identity which is mostly drawn from several cultures and experiences. Consequently, diversity does not remain the same over a period of time and is constantly defined and redefined in different ways.

6. Theorists have pointed out the contradiction in the attempt. Plamenatz (1976: 23–36) argues that while the attempt accepts the standards set by the alien culture, here the western model, it rejects the alien intruder who nevertheless is to be imitated and surpassed by his own standards and rejection of ancestral ways which are at the same time seen as hindering progress and as a distinct mark of identity. Hansen traces this in his chapter on 'Modernity, nation and democracy' (2004) and Vatsyayan (2005: 39–50) also points to this dichotomy in his arguments on fluidity and dynamics of tradition in the role of culture in identity-making in contemporary India.

7. Under Articles 5–8 of the Constitution, the following persons became citizens of India at the commencement of the Constitution—*(i)* A person born as well as domiciled in the territory of India – irrespective of the nationality of his parents (Art 5a); *(ii)* A person domiciled in the territory of India, either of whose parents was born in the territory of India, – irrespective of the nationality of his parents or the place of birth of such person (Art 5b) and *(iii)* A person who or whose father was not born in India but who *(a)* had his domicile in the 'territory of India' and *(b)* had been ordinarily residing within the territory of India for not less than 5 years preceding the commencement of the Constitution.

8. In the years 1985–90, the Gross Domestic Product (GDP) grew at the rate of 5.5 per cent a year permitting India to remain in its cocoon of protectionism. However, over-borrowing and over-spending led to the economic crisis of 1991 when the Reserve Bank of India had to sell some of its gold reserves so that the country would not default on its international debts (Mohan 2003: 130 and

Chandra et al. 1999: 363). In order to gain assistance from the World Bank and other international financial institutions, India had to sign an agreement with the World Trade Organisation (WTO) which essentially opened the doors to multi-national corporations. Liberalisation also meant seeking investments from abroad necessitating the wooing of the foreign investor, significant among who is the non-resident Indian.

9. The Bill amends the Citizenship Act, 1955 and simplifies the procedure to re-acquire Indian citizenship by adults who are children of Indian citizens and former Indian citizens. The concept of dual citizenship grants overseas citizenship to persons of Indian origin belonging to certain countries as well as Indian citizens who may take up the citizenship of these countries in future. This facility is being extended to People of Indian Origin (PIO) of 16 specified countries, including United States of America. The benefits and privileges that will be available to the overseas Indians wanting to reside in India are that of the issuance of a registration certificate on being granted overseas citizenship and issuance of an overseas citizen passport, which incidentally is to be a different colour than the regular passport. There is no requirement of visa for travel to India, there are no registration formalities for staying in India and no separate documentation required for admission to colleges/institutions or for taking employment. Parity will also be maintained in respect with non-resident Indians in the case of facilities available to the latter in the economic, financial and educational field. Thus the loss of Indian citizenship on the basis of termination will not happen and in turn people will be favoured with citizenship of both the countries. See Basu 2004: 76. However, the Overseas Citizen of India (OCI) cannot vote and gain public employment.

10. According to Hansen, 'political cultures are a sort of political common sense or political doxa: a widely dispread, fuzzy, and yet pervasive and naturalized sense of what politics is about, how it should be properly performed, what a good leader is, what true justice is and so on'. (2004: 27–28 and Jowett and Linton 1989: 85).

11. I would however like to clarify that I do not argue that this film is disciplined and directed reason made specifically to either propagate the dual citizenship act or has been funded by any organisation to expressly persuade Indians settled abroad to return to India. D.G. Lilleker defines hegemonisation (2006: 91) and G. Jowett and J.M. Linton speak of the power of movies (1989: 19).

12. India produces around 800 movies every year. According to unofficial estimates available in January 2001, the Indian film industry has an annual turnover of Rs. 60 billion (approximately US$1.33 billion). It employs more than 6 million people, most of whom are contract workers as opposed to regular employees. See Indiaonestop online. Nationalism has been the staple of Hindi cinema for long which has mostly reflected the dominant ideologies of its time. Whether it was Bhalji Pendharkar's *Vande Mataram Ashram* (1926) in

the pre-Independence days or Chetan Anand's *Haqeeqat* (1964) that cashed in on the resurgence of nationalism in the wake of the Chinese aggression in 1962 or J.P. Dutta's *Border* (1997) based on the India-Pakistan war of 1971 or the more recent Yash Chopra's *Veer Zarra* (2004) based on the thawing of relations between India and Pakistan, Hindi films have proven to be a 'microcosm of the social, political, economic, and cultural life of the nation'. See Rajadhyaksha and Willemen 1999: 280 and 350 and Chakravarty 1996: 5.

13. In another context, Hannerz (1992: 133,199) used the term 'double vision' to refer to the consequences of the second generation migrants' first 'return visit' to their homeland.

14. For instance, the Requisition and Acquisition of Immovable Property Act, 1952 was followed by *Do Bigha Zameen* (1953) which is about a small land owner who goes to work in Kolkata to repay his debts and buy back his land; the Food Adulteration Act (1954) led to the making of the film *Jagte Raho* (1956); the Essential Commodities Act (1954) found reflection in films such as *Mother India* (1956) and *Boot Polish* (1954) while *Naya Daur* (1957) was in response to Industrial Policy Resolution (1956) and *Pyaasa* (1957) poignantly drew attention to the Public Employment Act (1957). The trend followed into the sixties and seventies. The developing nation's initial steps towards political and economic growth were recorded in various films—*Upkaar* (1967) on the Green Revolution; *Sabse Bada Rupaiya* (1976) on rupee devaluation (1966) and bank nationalisation (1969); *Zanjeer* (1973) on Anti-Corruption Law (1967) and Indian Patents Act (1970); *Deewar* (1975) on the Gold Control Act (1968) and *Namak Haram* (1973) on the Manufacturers and Retailers Trade Practices Act (1969) and the Contract Labour (Regulation and Abolition) Act, 1970 was represented. Almost every act enacted by the government found reflection in the films of the time. Thus, *Johny Mera Naam* (1970) reflected the Antiquities and Art Treasures Act, 1972; *Aandhi* (1975) referred to the Election Laws, 1975; *Kala Pathar* (1979) reflected the Coking Coal Mines Act, 1972 and Coal Mines Act, 1974; *Amar Akbar Anthony* (1977) was based on the Smugglers and Foreign Exchange Manipulators Act, 1976; and *Mr. India* (1987) was prompted by the Terrorist And Disruptive Activities Act in 1985 and Terrorist Affected Areas Act in 1987. See Khan and Debroy: online.

15. Indeed successive Indian governments, immaterial of the party at the helm, have attempted to woo Indian investors abroad. Concerted efforts to include the Indians abroad in the making of the nation included setting up a website exclusively for them. See *The New Indian Express* 2000: online.

16. Increasingly Bollywood films are also watched by non-Indians. In an interview featured in Nasreen Munni Kabir's documentary film '*The Inner/Outer World of Shah Rukh Khan*' (Nasreen Munni Kabir Redchillies Entertainment 2005), an American woman revealed that she had driven nine hours from her home to watch a Hindi film, which she would not ever do for a Hollywood film.

17. Yet another film that urges NRIs to return to India has hit the screens worldwide at the time of revising this paper. 'Singh is Kinng' (sic) does not quite reverse the earlier trend of the NRIs being the 'baddies', but does make a case for the return of the Indians abroad to return to India and contribute to nation-making by living in the country. See 'NRIs return home to after watching Singh is Kinng' on TheBollywoodActress.com: online.

18. The awareness of the existence of different perceptions on nationalism and the need to bring them under the umbrella of Indian nationalism has dictated discourses on Indian nationalism. However, over the years, prime ministers like Jawaharlal Nehru, Indira Gandhi and Rajiv Gandhi have underscored the 'divisive' and 'disruptive' potential of diversities within the state (Phadnis 1990: 86–87). This remains the basis of Indian nationalism to this day.

19. For a discussion of the role of English in the Indian cultural milieu see Mukherjee 2005: 109. The Preamble is the introductory part of the Constitution of India, though not an operative part. The Preamble is not enforceable in court of law and talks about the moral duty of an Indian citizen towards the country. It reads:

> We, the people of India, having solemnly resolved to constitute India into a sovereign socialist secular democratic republic and to secure to all its citizens: Justice, social economic and political; Liberty of thought expression, belief, faith and worship; Equality of status and of opportunity; and to promote among them all; Fraternity assuring the dignity of the individual and the unity and integrity of the nation. In our Constituent Assembly this 26th day of November, 1949, do hereby adopt, enact and give to ourselves this Constitution.

Incidentally, the American Constitution also contains these words. In this context however, the reference to India and her Constitution is clear. Basu 2004: 20, 21.

20. Hansen (2004: 50) argues Gandhi saw 'the essence of the nation as residing in India's cultural communities, whereas the political realm of the colonial state remained a morally empty space, a set of lifeless procedures and culturally alien institutions that could only be given life and indigenous meaning by a vibrant national community outside the political realm'.

21. Interestingly, the camera looks down on Mohan making him look 'small, insignificant and vulnerable' when he loses the match with Nivaran Dayal and looks up at him when he is completely integrated. See Hansen A. et al. (1998: 134) for significance of camera positions.

22. For an analysis of the film in terms of title, lyrics, dialogues and film techniques see Bhagchi 2006.

References

Appadurai. A. 1991. 'Global ethnoscapes: notes and queries for a transnational anthropology', in R.G. Fox (ed.), *Recapturing Anthropology*. Santa Fe, New Mexico: School of American Research Press.

Baldassar. L. 1997. 'Home and away: Migration, the return visit and transnational identity', in Ang Ien and Michael Symonds (eds), *Home, Displacement and Belonging*, pp. 69–93. Australia: University of Western Sydney.

Bagchi, J. 2006. 'Towards a more inclusive identity? A case study of *Swades*'. Dissertation passed by the Manipal Institute of Communication.

Basu, D.D. 2004. *Introduction to the Constitution of India*, New Delhi: Wadhwa and Company Law Publishers.

Bhabha, H. 1994. *The location of culture*, New York, London: Routledge.

Billig, M. 1995. *Banal nationalism*, London, New York, New Delhi: Sage Publications.

Chandra, B., M. Mukherjee and A. Mukherjee 1999. *India after independence*, New Delhi: Viking, Penguin India.

Chakravarty, S.S. 1996. *National Identity in Indian Popular Cinema 1947–1987*, Bombay, Calcutta, Madras: Oxford University Press.

Chatterjee, P. 1986. *Nationalist thought and the colonial world*, Oxford: Oxford University Press.

Fairclough. N. 1995. *Media discourse,* Edward Arnold: London, New York.

Ganesh, K. 2005. 'Fields of culture: conversations and contestations', in Kamala Ganesh and Usha Thakkar (eds), *Culture and the making of identity in contemporary India,* pp.14–38, New Delhi, Thousand Oaks, London: Sage Publications.

Geertz, C. 1986. 'The Uses of diversity', *Michigan Quarterly Review*, xxv (1) (Winter): 105–123.

Gellner, E. 1964. *Thought and change*, London: Weidenfeld and Nicholson.

———. 1983. *Nations and nationalism*, Oxford: Basil Blackwell.

Gooptu, S. 2006. 'Transcending nationalism', *The Times of India*, Mangalore edition, Feb 10, p. 10.

Gupta and Ferguson. 1992. 'Beyond "Culture": space, identity and the politics of difference', *Cultural Anthropology*, 7 (1): 6–23.

Kedourie, E. 1970. 'Introduction', in Ellie Kedourie (ed.), *Nationalism in Asia and Africa*, London: Weidenfeld and Nicolson.

Hannerz, U. 1992. *Cultural complexity: Studies in the social organization of meaning.* New York: Columbia University Press.

Hansen, A., S. Cottle, R. Negrine and C. Newbold. 1998. *Mass communication research methods.* London: Macmillan Press Ltd.

Hansen, T.B. 2004. 'The saffron wave: democracy and Hindu nationalism in modern India', in *The Hindu Nationalist Movement and Indian Politics 1925 to the 1990s*, an omnibus, pp. 3–290. New Delhi: Penguin Books Ltd.

Towards a More Inclusive Indian Identity?

The Hindu. 2005. 'My respectful homage to this great man'. Available online at http://www.hindu.com/2005/06/05/stories/2005060507210100.htm (downloaded on 28.02.2006).

Hiremath, J.R. 1997. 'India and Overseas Indians', in Mansingh Lalit et al. (eds), *Indian Foreign Policy: Agenda for 21st Century,* pp. 365–394. New Delhi: Konark Publishers Private Ltd.

Indiaday. 2007. 'Brand success' Available online at http://www.indiaday.org/government_policy/dual_citizenship.asp (downloaded on 20.09.2005).

Jowett, G. and J.M. Linton 1989. *Movies as mass communication.* London, New Delhi: Sage Publications.

Khadria, B. 1999. *The migration of knowledge workers: Second-generation effects of India's brain drain.* New Delhi: Sage Publications.

Khan, A.U. and B. Debroy *Indian economic transition through bollywood eyes: Hindi films and how they have reflected changes in India's political economy.* Available online http://www.bazaarchintan.net/pdfs/paper1_bollywood.pdf/paper1_bollywood.pdf+conflict+resolution+through+Hindi+films&hl= en (downloaded on 08.09.2005).

Lilleker, D.G. 2006. *Key concepts in political communication.* London, Thousand Oaks, New Delhi: Sage Publications.

Mohan, T.K. 2003. *Multi-nationals and their roles.* Sikkim, Sikkim-Manipal University.

Mouffe, C. 1995. 'Democratic politics and the question of identity', in John Rajchman (ed.), *The identity in question,* pp. 33–46. NY and London: Routledge.

Moti, K.G. and W. Dissanayake 1998. *Indian popular cinema.* New Delhi, India: Orient Longman Ltd.

Mukherjee, M. 2005. 'Divided by a common language: the novel in India, in English and in English translation', in Kamala Ganesh and Usha Thakkar (eds), *Culture and the making of identity in contemporary India,* pp.108–124. New Delhi, Thousand Oaks, London: Sage Publications.

Naheem, S. 1998. How the west was won, in *Filmfare, Vol. 47,* pp. 121–124. Bombay: Bennet, Colman Com. Ltd.

The New Indian Express. 2000. *And now, an exclusive website for the Indian Diaspora,* Dec 22, Chennai, India. Available online at http://www.newindpress.com (downloaded on 22.12.2000).

NRI information.com. 'Return to India: Reverse immigration, Guide for NRIs'. Available online at http://www.nriinformation.com/nrireturntoindia.php (downloaded on 09.10.2008).

Oommen, T.K. 1997. 'Citizenship and National Identity: Towards a Feasible Linkage', in T. K. Oommen (ed.), *Citizenship and National Identity: From Colonialism to Globalism,* pp. 143–172. New Delhi, California, London: Sage Publications.

Phadnis, U. 1990. *Ethnicity and nation-building in South Asia.* New Delhi, Newbury Park, London: Sage Publications.

Plamenatz, J. 1976. 'Two types of nationalism', in Eugene Kamenka (ed.), *Nationalism: the nature and evolution of an idea*, pp. 23–36. London: Edward Arnold.

Rajadhyaksha, A. and P. Willemen. 1999. *Encyclopaedia of Indian Cinema.* New Delhi: Oxford University Press.

Rajagopal, A. 2001. *Politics after Television: Hindu Nationalism and the Reshaping of the Public in India.* Cambridge: Cambridge University Press.

Rayaprol, A. 1997. *'Negotiating identities: women in the Indian diaspora'*, pp.1–2. New Delhi, Calcutta, Chennai and Mumbai: Oxford University Press.

Said, E.W. 1979. 'Zionism from the standpoint of the victims', *Social Text*, 1: 7–58.

Scott, J.W. 1995. 'Multiculturalism and politics of identity', in John Rachman (ed.), *The identity in question*, pp. 3–14. NY and London: Routledge.

Schutz, A. 1967. *The phenomenology of the social world.* New York: University of Chicago Press.

Singh, T. 1996. *Kashmir: the tragedy of errors.* New Delhi: Penguin.

Vatsyayan, K. 2005. 'From interior landscapes into cyberspace: fluidity and dynamics of tradition', in Kamala Ganesh and Usha Thakkar (eds), *Culture and the making of identity in contemporary India,* pp. 39–50. New Delhi, Thousand Oaks, London: Sage Publications.

Chapter 9

Public Service Broadcasting in India

Doordarshan's Legacy

Usha M. Rodrigues

Introduction

In the face of tremendous technological advances and severe competition from the airwaves since 1991, Doordarshan has survived and revived itself many times in the past five decades since its inception in 1959. As the former monopolistic public service broadcaster in the largest democracy in the world, it continues to struggle to fulfil its role as a mass medium for education and entertainment. This chapter explores the role of public service broadcasting using Doordarshan as a case study, particularly following the advent of private and foreign television in India. It examines the changing role of Doordarshan from serving as a tool for 'development communication', to being a mouth-piece of the government of the day; from being a monopoly to being a government owned network in a predominantly commercially driven multi-channel market;[1] and from being a government propaganda tool to a network striving to attain autonomy from its funding source (the government, on behalf of the public of India). The chapter explores Doordarshan's position as a monopoly before 1991 and later, as one of the players in a multi-channel market to understand whether this monolithic giant fulfills its mandate to serve all sections of the Indian population.

Public service broadcasting—the concept

It has long been argued that public service broadcasters should be free from revenue raising concerns if they are to achieve their goal of providing 'comprehensive, varied and balanced television and radio programs of high quality for reception by the entire public' (Mendel 2000).

A public service broadcaster's specific functions include provision of 'regular news services, a central educational role, promotion of national culture and identity, entertainment, and serving the needs of minorities and other specialised interest groups' (Ibid.). It is seen as a powerful means of reflecting and shaping the cultural identity of a nation, where public service broadcasting has 'the central role of providing space for a diverse range of experiences, perceptions and arguments' (Norris et al. 2003: 1).

The main principles of public service broadcasting were identified in the United Kingdom's Broadcasting Research Unit (BRU) in the mid-1980s. The BRU document supported the approach that broadcasting should be seen as a comprehensive environment and it should be:

1. Universally accessible (referring to its geographic availability).
2. Universally appealing (cater to many tastes and interests in society).
3. Attentive to the interest of minorities in society, especially those disadvantaged by physical and social circumstances.
4. Contributing to a sense of national identity and community.
5. Distanced from vested interests.
6. Funded directly and by all public.
7. Encouraging competition in quality programming rather than quantity.
8. Liberating rather than restricting programme makers (Raboy 1999; Tracey 1998).

Similarly, the World Radio and Television Council (2000)[2] identified three basic principles or essential goals of public broadcasting: universality, diversity, and independence (Price and Raboy 2003). Price and Raboy feel that, in this era of the co-existence of public and private broadcasters, a fourth essential feature of public broadcasting is distinctiveness.

One of the essential principles of public broadcasting is that it should be accessible to every citizen in the country. This refers to geographic availability and to programmes that appeal to the largest possible number of people in the country. In Doordarshan's case, the network boasts of reaching 100 per cent of the population with 30 channels,[3] a number of them in regional languages. However, that was not always the case, because Doordarshan expanded its reach in urban areas first, and broadcasted New Delhi-centric Hindi programmes to other regional centres (Mitra 1986; Singhal and Rogers 1989). Doordarshan claims to telecast a variety of programmes from entertainment, education, information and culture across India (Prasar Bharati 2007), whereas critics say that Doordarshan programmes often lack creativity (Ninan 1995). Doordarshan can be most criticised for not being independent of political influence vis-à-vis the Information and Broadcasting Ministry. As a government funded broadcaster, it has never been free to circulate a variety of opinions, information and, particularly, criticisms of the ruling party (Doordarshan Handbook 1997; NAMEDIA 1986; Indiantelevision. com 2009b). In terms of maintaining distinctiveness, Doordarshan, in the nearly two decades between 1990 and 2009 has distinguished itself from other commercial players by offering more national interest and culture-based programmes (Doordarshan 2001; Prasar Bharati 2007). However, it has increased the proportion of entertainment programmes to education or information oriented programmes (see Table 1).

Public service broadcasting—funding debate

As for financing, in these times of economic rationalism, privatisation and globalisation, governments across the world are becoming hesitant to fund public service broadcasters from general revenue. On the other hand, those who do not regularly listen to or watch public radio/television are reluctant to pay a compulsory fee for the service. There is also

Table 1: Doordarshan's programming structure

Programme Genre	1988	1996	2001	2007
Informative	21%	23%	38%	38%
Development Orientation	24.4%	14%	15%	11%
Art and Culture	23%	12%	—	—
Entertainment	24.5%	40%	47%	51%
Advertising	7%	11%	—	—

Sources: Doordarshan Online 2001; Johnson 2000; Prasar Bharati 2007.

the administrative cost of collecting the broadcasting fee that govern-ments can no longer justify. Of course, there is the conservative political ideology, which believes that market forces can achieve everything that public service broadcasting is trying to achieve, at a lesser cost to the tax payers. As a result, funding for public service broadcasting is drying up. As Mendel notes in a UNESCO study:

> The main threat today to the ability of public service broadcasting organi-sations to fulfil their mandates stems from the financial restraints that are increasingly being placed on them. In these times of austerity, and with pre-vailing views relating to government downsizing, many public service broad-casting organisations are being called upon to maintain previous levels of service while at the same time the level of public financial support for them is decreasing. (Mendel 2000)

The pendulum of public policy on funding public service broad-casting seems to have moved towards commercialisation. Competition from private broadcasters and the need to incorporate rapidly chang-ing technological advances are forcing public broadcasters to boost their funding by selling their products and services in the commercial mar-ket. This in turn is making the private sector envious because it sees public broadcasters using their public and commercial funding to gain or retain market share in the entertainment business—the bastion of private television. In a relatively new trend, private television owners in a number of countries have begun lobbying governments to give them the public funding to provide public service broadcasting at a lower cost (Cox 2003; Hassan 2005). The current discourse is to take fund-ing away from public service broadcasters and allocate it for public service programming irrespective of who produces it. Under the cir-cumstances, many have raised the public policy question: is there a need for the maintenance of a public service broadcasting institution in the commercially driven multi-channel television environment? If so, then what should be the role and shape of such a public service broadcaster? (Graham 2000; Hargreaves Heap 2005; Norris et al. 2003).

Funding pressures for public service broadcasters in developing coun-tries are further compounded by the fact that governments are cash-strapped and have a priority to meet many basic needs of their people.

India is no different. It is the most populous democracy and still has more than a quarter of a billion people living below the poverty line (Asian Development Bank 2002). Although the Indian government after independence in 1947 accepted the principle of 'public service' broadcasting, it did not jump on the bandwagon of introducing a television service in the country until 1959. When the government did introduce television technology in the country, it did not want the private sector to own the broadcast media because of its potential power to persuade the masses. However, developments in the 1990s have had an enormous impact on the Indian television industry and the public service broadcasters had to let go of their monopoly and learn to survive in a commercially driven multi-channel market. In 2001–02, about 30 per cent of Prasar Bharati's expenses were paid by the central exchequer on behalf of the taxpayers, whereas as much as 70 per cent of its revenue came from commercial activity (Indiantelevision.com 2002a). Similar is the story in 2005–06, for which the available data reveals that about 30 per cent of the Corporation's expenses are still being funded by the government.[4]

Commercialisation of Indian public service broadcasting

All India Radio (AIR) was established under the British rule in India in 1936 to disseminate information with a view to strengthening its rule. In subsequent years, apart from 'reiterating the paternalistic role of the state', AIR as a public service broadcaster became a means to forge and disseminate 'indigenous Indian culture' (Gupta 1998:18). However, by 1957, AIR introduced Vividh Bharati, which broadcasted programmes on popular culture of Indian films and film songs. A decade later, in 1967 advertising was introduced on AIR, 'which was partly a reflection of the emerging consumer market and a growing middle class in India' (Gupta 1998: 19). Later, in 1959, India launched television by utilising the equipment left behind by a multi-national company. The inception of Indian television was largely supported by foreign agencies and foreign governments (Gupta 1998; Ninan 1995; Singhal and Rogers 1989).

One way to understand the development of broadcasting in India is through its socio-political history. Being a poor country with a rapidly increasing population, its leaders saw television as a luxury that a developing country could ill afford, irrespective of whether it was a private or a public enterprise (Gupta 1998). Therefore, until the early 1970s, television remained an education-facilitating medium for a small population around Delhi. The Indian government's broadcasting policy was also influenced by the general world view at the time, i.e., broadcasting technology, especially through the television, could be effectively used to impart education to the masses. Launching of productions such as *Krishidarshan* in 1967 and later on Satellite Instructional Television Experiment (SITE) in 1975 on Doordarshan were examples of this policy of using television as an educational tool. However, the progress in space technology during the 1970s nudged the Indian government to expand the reach of television in the country. With the success of the SITE project (NAMEDIA 1986), the idea that television could be used for developmental (and political) purposes was accepted. In mid-1975, the country was placed under a 'State of Emergency' by the Congress party leader and Prime Minister Indira Gandhi, and her party used both AIR and Doordarshan (the two public service broadcasters in the country) to the maximum to spread its message (Ninan 1995). In 1976, Doordarshan started broadcasting imported programmes. Later, to fund this new initiative, Doordarshan started accepting advertisements, which were initially aired during imported programmes. In the 1980s, two technological changes expanded Doordarshan's reach—first, was the introduction of colour television and second, the launch of India's first domestic communication satellite Insat-1A. By 1985, Doordarshan could reach up to 50 per cent of the population, resulting in a viewer number of 60 million. This programme of expansion and modernisation in the mid-1980s forced Doordarshan to raise more revenue via commercialisation. In effect, there were two opposite trends in Doordarshan's attempt at modernising—on one hand, it began raising revenue from sponsorship and advertising and on the other, it continued to telecast tightly monitored and censored news and current affairs programmes.

The commercialisation process proved to be a success as Doordarshan, which first began by offering free commercial time to the sponsors, was able to increase its advertising rates three times during the broadcast of the Hindu epic *Mahabharata* in 1988–89. A study of the impact of television on the rural Indian population by Johnson (2000) found that although all members of rural families were influenced by advertisements they saw on television, children and teenagers were more swayed than others and wanted to emulate the metropolitan lifestyle depicted therein. However, it needs to be remembered that it was not television advertisements alone that gave rise to a desire to imitate the urban lifestyle, but the entire programming genre. The tension between balancing its role as an educational and developmental tool and as an entertainment medium has continued for Doordarshan since the beginning. During the 1980s, as its viewer numbers increased, so did its commercial revenue, as big business houses did not have any other audio-visual medium by which to advertise their products. The pub-caster enjoyed a monopoly and to some extent became complacent in its programming. However, in the early 1990s, the Indian monolithic giant had to wake up to competition.

The introduction of VCRs in 1984 and later the expansion of local cable networks seriously threatened Doordarshan's monopolistic status in the market. The Persian Gulf crisis of 1991 further escalated the spread of cable networks to other parts of metropolitan India even as Li Kasing launched his STAR TV (later bought by Rupert Murdoch) operation from Hong Kong, a beaming multi-channel television over the South Asian region, including India. Reddi argues that it was the 'coupling of satellite and cable television' that brought about this huge change in the Indian broadcasting scenario (Reddi 1996: 237). Without the cable television networks, satellite television would not have gone far in India. Within a couple of years, satellite and cable television had created a situation of 'de facto deregulation of control of the airwaves' by breaking Doordarshan's monopoly (Ibid.: 238). In response to this competition from the skies, the Indian government allowed Doordarshan to expand its reach, by multiplying the number of channels available to national and regional viewers and increasing the number of entertainment programmes broadcast on Doordarshan. A government committee specifically looked into the proposal to allow further private sponsorship of its programming to counter the competition from overseas (Varadan 1991). Following lengthy discussions, 'governmental instruction to Doordarshan was to increase substantially its entertainment content during prime-time evening slots, by making changes in schedules and by reducing the time devoted to news' (Reddi 1996: 241), taking it further away from its goals of providing developmental programming.

Doordarshan expanded its service with the help of satellite technology. On the programming and advertising fronts, Doordarshan began relaxing its rules and criteria to allow advertisements of foreign films, banks and airlines among others. Critics examining the development of Indian television say that as television grew, development alternatives steadily skewed (Rajgopal 1993). Doordarshan, however, had little choice, as government funding was reduced and market conditions worsened. The 1990s saw an end to Doordarshan's monopoly with the advent of many private and foreign television channels like CNN, BBC, STAR, *Zee* and *Sony*. Doordarshan officials boasted of successfully safeguarding its revenue by adopting various market-friendly policies. The broadcaster's website states:

> Doordarshan is a public service broadcaster and hence revenue earning can only be a by-product of its mission and objectives, but it does not undermine the importance of revenue earning. Revenue earning may not be an end in itself, but it is a powerful means to its ultimate end. (Ddindia.net 2003)

The implication is that Doordarshan needs to make 'a significant contribution to accelerate socio-economic change, promote national integration and stimulate scientific temper' (Ddindia.net 2003). Whether Doordarshan presently meets this objective is a debatable issue, despite its rising commercial revenue (see Table 2).

Table 2: Doordarshan's Commercial Revenue

Year	Rupees in Million
1976–77	7.70
1980–81	80.80
1984–85	314.30
1988–89	1612.60
1992–93	3602.30
1996–97	5727.30
2000–01	6375.10
2005–06	9600.00

Sources: Ddindia.net 2003 and Exchange4media.com 2006.

Autonomy for Indian public service broadcasters

The call for an autonomous public service broadcasting system in India was finally heeded in 1997, with the formation of the Prasar Bharati Board (Broadcasting Corporation of India). After the state of emergency in mid-1970s, Doordarshan was massively used as a propaganda machine for the ruling party. The Congress government led by the late Indira Gandhi was defeated in the 1977 elections. The new Janata party-led government commissioned a 'white paper' on the misuse of the broadcast media during the Emergency period. It also established a committee to look into the issue of autonomy for the broadcast media. This committee, headed by a former newspaper editor B.G. Verghese, recommended that Doordarshan should be run as an autonomous organisation (Verghese 1978).

However, the recommendation to give more autonomy to Doordarshan and AIR was not implemented till the end of 1997, when the left-wing government in New Delhi decided to keep its election promise and ratified the long-pending Prasar Bharati Act 1990, which facilitated the formation of the Prasar Bharati Board. Doordarshan and AIR both came under the management of this autonomous board. This, in turn, raised viewers' and media critics' expectations about the autonomy of Doordarshan in general and enhanced editorial freedom in covering news and current affairs. Sinha and other media analysts described 'the Government's decision to implement Prasar Bharati—with the prospect of greater autonomy for Doordarshan and AIR'—as 'a momentous step in the history of public service broadcasting in India' (Sinha 1998: 22).

Even after the formation of the Prasar Bharati Board, the ruling party's influence on Doordarshan programming remained via its power to select members of the Prasar Bharati Board. Viewers in the audience survey in 1998 believed that Doordarshan's coverage of news had improved, but they wanted further improvements ((Rodrigues) Manchanda 1998). However, it is important to note that Doordarshan gained credibility by contracting out news and current affairs coverage to private producers and allowing them more and more editorial freedom over the years. Previously, independent news programme producers were forced to submit their tapes for a preview to Doordarshan before they could go on air. Since 1998, however, Doordarshan began establishing itself 'as a free credible channel, and the greatest example of this is that Aaj Tak, which is an independently made news programme on Doordarshan, now boasts of its freedom' (Thapar 1998). On the other hand, NDTV proprietor Prannoy Roy, who produced a news and current affairs programme for Doordarshan in 1997, believed otherwise (Roy 1998). In contrast, the changes in Doordarshan's own in-house produced daily news programmes were much slower because of a lack of equipment and trained manpower and, perhaps because it produced a large number of news programmes in various languages, having to meet its 'social objectives' at the same time (Churchill 1998). One of the reasons why Doordarshan functions the way it does, according to critics, is that, 'given the security of tenure government employees enjoy regardless of performance, and the virtual absence of incentives for merit, there is a powerful tendency towards institutional inertia' (Rajgopal 1993: 93). A decade on, in 2009, a number of media commentators believed that Doordarshan had lost out in the current competitive environment and is usually ignored by at least the urban population. Critics have also raised serious questions about the continual interference by the government of the day in the working of Prasar Bharati (Indiantelevision.com 2009b; Mitra 2009; Mudgal 2009; Ninan 2009; Thapar 2009).

Public service broadcasting in India—the rhetoric

The best way to understand the concept of public service broadcasting as applied in the Indian context is to look at the 'functions and powers' of the Prasar Bharati Board (Broadcasting Corporation of India), which manages the two public service broadcasters (pub-casters) in India— Doordarshan (television) and AIR (radio).[5] The Prasar Bharati Act 1990 states that 'it shall be the primary duty of the corporation to organise and conduct public broadcasting services to inform, educate and entertain the public and to ensure a balanced development of broadcasting on radio and television' (Prasar Bharati Act 1990, 2000: 12). The Prasar Bharati board, when discharging its functions, is expected to be guided by a number of objectives including, 'safeguarding the citizen's right to be informed freely, truthfully and objectively on all matters of public interest, national or international, and presenting a fair and balanced flow of information including contrasting views without advocating any opinion or ideology of its own' (Ibid.).

The objectives entrusted to the corporation are similar to some of the expectations and scope of public service broadcasting envisaged in Australia and the U.K. The Indian public service broadcasters need to provide a comprehensive service to all communities and sections of society, a principle identified by Tracey (1998: 26) when defining public service broadcasting.

> Public broadcasting has historically sought to ensure that its signals are available to all. It is axiomatic to the public broadcasting community that no one should be disenfranchised by distance or by accident of geography. The imperative which guides this principle is not that of maximizing customers in a market but of serving citizens in a democracy.

The 'universality' principle as discussed by Tracey (1998) and others includes the expansion of broadcasting infrastructure in India, under which the AIR and Doordarshan both claim to reach 100 per cent of the geographical area and population (at least one national channel). So, public service broadcasting in India is 'universal' and not dependent on the private entrepreneurs' cost-benefit analysis of its profitability. Similarly, public service broadcasting in India is 'comprehensive', as it is expected to cater to all communities and their interests—rural, remote, minorities, women, children, various tribes and the aged. Indian public service broadcasting is based on the principle of 'serving the national diversity of a society' as described by Tracey (1998: 27). The public broadcaster's role in India is also to 'uphold the unity and integrity of the country' by producing and broadcasting programmes which speak to all citizens, thereby giving 'a burning sense of the collective, of belonging to the national-as-community' (Ibid.: 28). Doordarshan's attempt at creating programmes such as *Hum Log* (We the People) and *Buniyaad* (The Foundation Stone) in the 1980s were successful examples of this principle.

The other concept which is relevant in the Indian context is that of 'governmentality' as described by Jacka (1997: 9) in a working paper on Australian public service broadcasting. She points to the role of a public service broadcaster as an educator, of being part of 'governmentality'—

'that is part of the scrutiny of populations with a view to intervention in their civic and moral training'. Jacka refers to a speech by ABC chairman, Dr James Darling (in Jacka et al. 1997: 11), to explain the educational role of a public service broadcaster in society.

> The influence of the medium is great, particularly since Television. The voice and picture from our transmitters penetrates into the homes of the public, they attach both eye and ear, they carry on hour after hour, day after day, week after week: they impose, if not views, at least impressions, consciously and sub-consciously: they have become in many cases the substitute for theatre and cinema, for public meetings, for books and even for newspapers. They can affect all who can hear or see, and their influence is not confined to the literate. In the hands of those who might be ready to use the medium for purposes of propaganda they can be a very powerful instrument.

Indian public service broadcasting was initially developed as a tool for educating and informing the masses—as a development communication tool.

Public service broadcasting in India—the practice

From the beginning, Indian public service broadcasting has been controlled by the government to ensure that it met the social objectives set out in its charter. The social, economic and political atmosphere in the 1950s and 1960s was such that nation building was the paramount principle. One tool of nation building was to unite and integrate the citizens of the country by disseminating a unified message as far and wide as possible via the broadcast media. Since the press or the print media were already in private hands, a need was felt to keep the broadcast media in public ownership. Although AIR and Doordarshan were and are still answerable to the Indian parliament, in reality these public institutions have become hostage to the governing political leaders (Gupta 1998; Indiantelevision.com 2009b; Mitra 2009; Mudgal 2009; NAMEDIA 1986; Ninan 1995; Reddi 1996; Sinha 1997; Thapar 2009). Perhaps, it is an indictment of the nature of democracy in India, that it has been difficult to separate the power of the parliament and the ruling party/parties. 'The tight control over Doordarshan's finances has been one of the instruments through which the government has controlled the growth and development of television in India' (Sinha 1997: 135).

In 1976, the government decided to allow Doordarshan to accept advertising to boost its revenue and partly abandoned the principle of public funding for public service broadcasting. By 1994, following the principles of self-sufficiency in a market economy, Doordarshan was ordered by the Planning Commission to raise revenue for its future expansion. Unfortunately for Doordarshan, this push for self-sufficiency coincided with the entrance of commercial satellite channels into the market. Ninan comments: 'Just when you needed money the most, it began to be withdrawn' (Ninan 2003). This trend towards commercialisation of Doordarshan continued even after the formation of Prasar Bharati Board to oversee the management and functioning of the two public service broadcasters in India (Doordarshan and All India Radio). There are two views about the commercial success of Prasar Bharati Board. One view is that the Board has been successful because, in 2005–2006, Prasar Bharati's revenue was pegged at Rs 12,300 million, whereas its running cost was between Rs 17,000 million to Rs 18,000 million (exchange4media.com 2006). Considering the competition from nearly 400 other channels in the commercial market, it had done well to earn and maintain about 70 per cent of its income.

On the other hand, critics say that though it is understandable that Prasar Bharati would want to raise its revenue to reduce its dependence on the government subvention, it is another matter when it proposes to auction its entire prime time slots to private bidders and 'relinquish all responsibility and control over the content for the sake of raising its commercial revenue' (Gill 2001). S.S. Gill, former Prasar Bharati CEO, points out that India, as a developing country, still needs a powerful public service broadcaster to foster a climate of tolerance and social harmony, to strengthen the roots of a democratic ethos, highlight its cultural heritage and promote the values of multi-culturism in a highly diverse society (Ibid.). Similarly, B.G. Verghese, the architect of the 'White Paper on the Misuse of the Mass Media during the Emergency [in 1975]', has been critical of the functioning of the Prasar Bharati Board as an autonomous body. Verghese says that the Prasar Bharati Board needed to get its priorities right in accordance with its charter.

Its programming, including news and current affairs, must uphold plurality and diversity, and air contrasting voices, giving the government its due. It must devolve more autonomy on its regional and local kendras [centres], emphasise local, community and instructional broadcasting as a means of grassroots articulation and empowerment of the voiceless and under-privileged. It has to cater to the citizen and not merely the consumer or those in power. (Verghese 2003)

The misuse of public broadcast media by local, state and federal ministers and bureaucracy continues today, pressuring Doordarshan and AIR employees to publicise their programmes and successes in the name of educating and informing the masses (Indiantelevision.com 2009b; Raman 2005). As a result, the network is seen as a government-owned, rather than as a tax-payer funded institution.

Besides the political interference issue, Doordarshan continues to struggle with inadequate and inefficient manpower and equipment issues. Recently, a parliamentary committee criticised the government for not filling the vacant posts in Prasar Bharati, noting that 'the Committee is extremely unhappy that a large number of creative young women and men are denied the chance to be part of the public broadcasting service in the country' (Indiantelevision.com 2009b). Deputy Director General of Doordarshan, Usha Bhasin, who oversees Doordarshan's new profitable Development Communication Division set up in 2001, too is not satisfied with the state-of-play, where she has to work with ageing and de-motivated manpower. 'In DD (Doordarshan), one major issue is that there has been no recruitment for the past 19 years. So, here we are talking about an organisation which is 45-plus, and in the private sector production personnel are young, vibrant' (Bhasin 2009). According to Bhasin, who has managed a high-profile, multi-award winning, health-focused series *Kalyani*, produced by Doordarshan for India's nine most backward states, her development communication presently earns 26 per cent of Doordarshan's revenue, where it markets the network's air-time to government departments for their public-interest messages and programmes.

The future of public service broadcasting in India

After losing its monopoly in the 1990s, Doordarshan has survived and has revived as a significant player in a competitive multi-channel market. It has expanded its reach by utilising its capacity to reach 100 per cent of the population with a combination of terrestrial and satellite technology. It has 30 channels broadcasting a large number of entertainment and information oriented programmes in a number of languages, many produced and sponsored by private production houses. Media critics and academics may mourn the fact that television in India has moved away from the public service principles of educating and informing the masses. It is, however, a fact that since the advent of commercial television in India, television's viewership numbers have expanded to about 500 million (Indiantelevision.com 2008). Although, Doordarshan continues to remain a significant player in non-cable-satellite households because of its terrestrial reach across the country, other private channels with a commercial agenda and leaner organisations are more profitable operations. Opinions are divided as to whether Doordarshan is meeting its public service objectives. A media critic, Bajpai (2003), says there is no competition between Doordarshan and other channels.

> The kind of programs they (Doordarshan channels) still offer or alternatives they offer are still not available on satellite (channels). They are the ones that will bring you the Winter Olympics, Indian soccer, make space for programs on national dance or music, classical etc. So, to that extent their own mandate being different, they really are not in competition except in terms of commercial revenue. (Bajpai 2003)

Bajpai even welcomes Doordarshan's 'boring' news bulletin since it provides straight-forward facts compared to the sensational news presented by private channels. Similarly, Bhasin defends Doordarshan's main channel DD1's lack of personality, as it has to meet the needs of a large and diverse population, owing to its accessibility by the 100 per cent of the population.

> Private channels, when they have general entertainment channel, they do general entertainment, but when it comes to DD1, there are thousands of pressures for time on DD1, that a general entertainment private channel cannot think of, so how do you withstand all these pressures and also meet the commercial demands... we have several activities that are not commercially viable because we are the public service broadcaster. (Bhasin 2009)

Critics point out that Doordarshan is suffering from a lot of ailments.

> It is an extremely corrupt organisation. When there is corruption, obviously creativity takes a back foot. So it's losing the battle there—in terms of creativity, in terms of keeping good content consistent. All those things are slipping... their studios are not shiny, their guys don't speak English in an American accent. They are not elite, no elite consensus in their coverage. Surprisingly, they have the masses with them. (Mudgal 2009)

Nupur Basu (2009), former NDTV (a private news television network in India) journalist agrees saying: 'But they never seem to get their technology right, they never seem to change their style... it is like a barometer of how things have not changed...their readers have no personalities, they are like robots, just reading from the autocue.' Ninan believes that Doordarshan has become a purely government channel. 'They plug government programs... they have just totally abandoned the whole thing about autonomy... the CEO is always a retired government person... many of the board vacancies are never filled.... The only channel people watch on Doordarshan network is the Lok Sabha channel' (Ninan 2009). Thapar (2009) says 'Doordarshan lacks credibility, even now in news because it seems to be a government owned channel and whoever, the government of the day, determines what line it takes.... And, most people in urban India do not watch Doordarshan.' Similarly, Mitra (2009) opines that at least a few years ago, Doordarshan's programming used to be 'very good, in fact they used to set the trend in modern television in India,' but now, 'I'm afraid, Doordarshan has lost out comprehensively, which is a pity because, although it is state funded, it has a bias towards the ruling party of the time, it has a reach that is unparallel in India.'

Doordarshan's efforts to meet some of its social objectives of promoting rural development and social change at the local level are, however, not so visible. Following the SITE Project, Doordarshan was part of another pioneering experiment, in using television for educational purposes in the early 1980s. The Kheda Communication Project was based on the idea of participatory communication, where villagers in Kheda district, an area near Ahmedabad city (in the west of the country), were encouraged to participate in the project as actors, writers and producers

(Singhal and Rogers 2001). Some of the issues dealt with in this project were caste discrimination, minimum wages, alcoholism, family planning, gender equality and elections, using various formats such as puppet shows, dramas and entertainment-education serials. However, the award winning community-level programme model was not replicated in other parts of India due to commercial imperatives, when the Kheda transmitter was transferred to a city to facilitate a second entertainment channel for its urban residents (Ibid.: 98). Similarly, at present, Doordarshan does broadcast the Lok Sabha channel and an education-based channel called DD-Gyandarshan ('To Experience Knowledge') launched in January 2000. And, it is cashing in on the need for development focused budget of government departments by producing and telecasting programmes such as *Kalyani* (Bhasin 2009).

It is, however, the issues of lack of credibility and political interference, which still plague public service broadcasters in India.

> State ownership and control was long justified on the grounds that radio and television are a public service. But it was the State itself, by virtue of its dominance of the country's political economy has been the biggest threat to public broadcasting during the past 45 years. (Sinha 1998: 23)

In fact, some Indian media commentators believe that 'autonomy is just a concept, it does not exist. And, I don't think it exists anywhere in the world frankly' (Abraham 2003). Some critics say that the Prasar Bharati Corporation and the experiment in providing autonomy to public service broadcasters in India have failed, because of the corporation's inability to divest itself of government power and control. On the other hand, Gupta contends that,

> ...the battle is not about ratings and advertising revenue. It is really about 'determining the framework for debate' and, for the present at least, Doordarshan has lost this battle. It has accepted the new rules of the game as defined in terms of revenue maximisation and shifted its agenda to providing entertainment rather than enlightenment. (Gupta 1998: 77)

Although this decline of the public service orientation of national broadcasting systems is a worldwide phenomenon, Doordarshan's fate was sealed a long time ago when, in the days of no-competition from the

commercial and foreign channels, it under-utilised its capacity to produce quality entertainment programmes. What did not help the Indian
public service broadcaster, besides the constant interference and reliance
on the government of the day to dictate day-to-day decisions, was a
short-sightedness in understanding the role of a public service broadcaster and a failure to create brand loyalty with the public similar to that
created by the British Broadcasting Corporation in the U.K. and the
Australian Broadcasting Corporation in Australia. In 2002, the Prasar
Bharati chief executive, K.S. Sarma, expressed a view that, although
public service broadcasting no longer enjoys a monopoly status,

> ...it will always remain an important reminder of the social and cultural
> responsibilities of the media in an age when the thrust is overwhelmingly
> oriented towards consumerism. The more commercial the television market
> becomes, the role of a public broadcaster correspondingly becomes that
> much more necessary. (Indiantelevision.com 2002b)

However, the question he did not answer was: Who would save public
service broadcasting from commercialisation? Media analysts argue that
even in this digital multi-channelling era, public service broadcasters
should be supported by public funding as a force for the development
of citizenship and as an insurance against market failures to meet the
needs of various populations (Graham 2000; Hargreaves Heap 2005;
Holland 2003). Others argue that the setting up of an Arts Council to
fund public service programming is a more efficient and accountable
process (Cox 2003).

Considering the imperatives of commercial revenue for the Prasar
Bharati Corporation and its need for self-sufficiency to gain real autonomy from politicians, it seems Doordarshan needs parallel emphasis,
where it maintains its competitiveness in the advertising market and yet
meets its charter obligations. This is difficult, but not impossible, if one
is to consider the coexistence of the advertising and editorial departments in a newspaper organisation. The independence of the editorial
department in selecting news and views for the paper's editorial pages is
paramount, but the paper cannot survive without the revenue it earns
from advertisements placed in the media. The ideological struggle between the independence of news and information, against the need to

raise revenue, continues at a number of quality newspapers in the world. In the end, it is the management's commitment to bring out a quality newspaper, where the editorial department is largely free from being concerned about raising revenue, which can maintain the balance. Similarly, in the case of Indian public service broadcasters (AIR and Doordarshan), it is the 'independent' Prasar Bharati Board, which can bring a balance between meeting the 'social change' needs of the deprived one-third of the population living below or near the poverty line, and the rest who can afford a television set and cable subscription (the middle class, which may prefer entertainment to educational programmes on television).

Similarly, the Indian government, which has an obligation to meet the developmental needs of the large population of poor in the country, must facilitate and encourage public service broadcasting through Doordarshan and AIR and other private and community broadcasters. First and foremost, it needs to put in place a legal framework, which provides for a plurality of voices and decentralisation of broadcast industry, rather than let the *de facto* deregulation continue (which it has since 1991).[6] In fact, various government committees have recommended such a move, where private, non-commercial community players such as universities, local governments and non-government agencies are given licences to broadcast their television signals in India (Paswan 1996; Varadan 1991). Five decades of experience of the blurring of lines between public-owned or government-funded broadcasting cannot be erased, but self-sufficiency of Doordarshan and AIR may put some distance between the political party in power and the broadcasters' trustees (Prasar Bharati Board).

On the public service programming front, it is worth visiting some of the ideas and experiments tried in other countries. The Indian government could look at the option of prescribing certain levels of public service broadcasting (in consultation with the public) by all broadcasters, not just Doordarshan and All India Radio, including specifying levels of local content and children's programming. It could consider the idea of setting up a contestable fund for public service programming open to all players, with the aim to lift the standard of innovative education and development oriented programming. The long-pending Broadcasting Bill 1997 had foreshadowed such a move, when it stated that licences could be granted for broadcast over limited areas using terrestrial broadcasting systems, including institutions which provided education, community service, environment protection or health awareness (The Broadcasting Bill 1997). Whether it is the institution of public service broadcasting in the form of Doordarshan or AIR, or the emphasis on the need for public service broadcasting programming irrespective of who produces it, the Indian government is obliged to make a commitment to the existence of public service broadcasting in the country. Ultimately, what is required is the political will, accentuated by enlightened public pressure, to allow public service broadcasting in India to fulfil its objective of 'informing, educating and entertaining' the entire population.

Endnotes

1. According to Minister of State Information and Broadcasting, Anand Sharma, in February 2009, there were a total of 215 news and current affairs television channels received by Indian viewers, while there were 233 non-news channels, including general entertainment and niche channels (Indiantelevision.com 2009a).

2. See World Radio and Television Council 2000.

3. Doordarshan network consists of 30 channels—five all India channels, one parliament channel —Lok Sabha channel—11 regional language channels, 11 state networks, one educational channel—Gyandarshan—and one international channel (Prasar Bharati 2007: 9).

4. Prasar Bharati's commercial revenue for the year ended 31 March 2006, was at Rs 1,230 crore as against Rs 831.47 crore. Doordarshan's commercial revenue was at Rs 960 crore, where All India Radio earned Rs 271 crore. Prasar Bharati's expenditure for the year 2005–06 stood between Rs 1,700 and Rs 1,800 crore, with a deficit of around Rs 500 crore paid by the central government, according to CEO, K.S. Sarma (exchange4media.com 2006).

5. *Objectives Guiding the Functioning of Prasar Bharati Corporation*

> 1. Upholding the unity and integrity of the country and the values enshrined in the Constitution;
>
> 2. Safeguarding the citizen's right to be informed freely, truthfully and objectively on all matters of public interest, national or international and presenting a fair and balanced flow of information including contrasting views without advocating any opinion or ideology of its own;

3. Paying special attention to the fields of education and spread of literacy, agriculture, rural development, environment, health and family welfare and science and technology;

4. Providing adequate coverage to the diverse cultures and languages of the various regions of the country by broadcasting appropriate programmes;

5. Providing appropriate coverage to sports and games so as to encourage healthy competition and the spirit of sportsmanship;

6. Providing appropriate programmes keeping in view the special needs of the youth;

7. Informing and stimulating the national consciousness in regard to the status and problems of women and paying special attention to the uplifting of women;

8. Promoting social justice and combating exploitation, inequality and such evils as untouchability and advancing the welfare of the weaker sections of the society;

9. Safeguarding the rights of the working classes and advancing their welfare;

10. Serving the rural and weaker sections of the people and those residing in border regions, backward or remote areas;

11. Providing suitable programmes keeping in view the special needs of the minorities and tribal communities;

12. Taking special steps to protect the interests of the children, the blind, the aged, the handicapped and other vulnerable sections of the people;

13. Promoting national integration by broadcasting in a manner that facilitates communication in the languages in India; and facilitating the distribution of regional broadcasting services in every State in the languages of that State;

14. Providing comprehensive broadcast coverage through the choice of appropriate technology and the best utilisation of the broadcast frequencies available and ensuring high quality reception;

15. Promoting research and development activities in order to ensure that radio and television broadcast technology are constantly updated; and

16. Expanding broadcasting facilities by establishing additional channels of transmission at various levels.

Source: Prasar Bharati Act 1990, 2000: 12–13.

6. See Chapter 12 for detailed discussion about Television policy in India.

References

Asian Development Bank. 2002. 'Monthly Reports, March 2002.' Available online at http://www.abdindia.org/janeco-02.htm (downloaded on 18.01.2005).

Cox, B. 2003. 'Four lectures on TV in the digital age', *Guardian Media* supplement, 28 January; 4, 11 and 28 February.

Doordarshan Handbook .1997. *Doordarshan 1997 annual report.* Audience Research Unit, New Delhi: Doordarshan.

Doordarshan Online. 2001. 'Doordarshan – at a glance'. Available online at http://www. ddindia.net/RealContent/about/content.html (downloaded on 20.01.2003).

Ddindia.net. 2003. 'Doordarshan commercial service – an overview'. Available online at http://www.ddindia.net (downloaded on 12.11.2003).

Exchange4media.com. 2006. 'Prasar Bharati gets marketing savvy, brings about a revenue turnaround'. 6 April. Available online at http://www.exchange4media. com/e4m/news/fullstory_band.asp?section_id=6&news_id=2-577&tag= 15304# (downloaded on 29.05.2009).

Gill, S.A. 2001. 'Directionless Prasar Bharati'. *The Hindu,* Opinion, 17 July. Available online at http://www.hindunet.com/2001/07/17/stories/05172523. htm (downloaded on 19.02.2005).

Graham, A. 2000. 'The future of communications: Public service broadcasting', a discussion document presented at Balliol College. Oxford.

Gupta, N. 1998. *Switching channels: ideologies of television in India.* Mumbai: Oxford University Press.

Hassan, T. 2005. 'ABC have to fight for Asia Pacific TV', *PM, Australian Broadcasting Corporation,* 23 June. Available online at http://www.abc.net.au/pm/ content/2005/s1398332.htm (downloaded on 23.06.2005).

Holland, P. 2003. 'Conceptual glue: public service broadcasting as practice, system and ideology', paper presented at MIT3 Television in Transition 2003, pp. 1–15. Massachusetts: Massachusetts Institute of Technology.

Harvgreaves Heap, S. P. 2005. 'Television in a digital age: what role for public service broadcasting?', *Economic Policy,* 41: 111–57.

Indiantelevision.com. 2002a. 'Prasar Bharati chalks plans to push revenue', Breaking News, 28 November. Available online at http://www.indiantelevison.com/ headlines/y2k3/nov/nov125.htm (downloaded on 28.02.2004).

———. 2002b. 'Thursday world television day', Breaking News, 20 November. Available online at http://www.indiantelevison.com/headlines/y2k3/nov/ nov86.htm (downloaded on 15.11.2003).

———. 2008. 'IRS 2008 R2: the lowdown on TV viewership', 5 November. Available online at http://www.indiantelevision.com/headlines/y2k8/nov/ nov63.php (downloaded on 15.12.2008).

Indiantelevision.com. 2009a. '180 TV channels await government clearance', 26 February. Available online at http://www.indiantelevision.com/headlines/ y2k9/feb/feb245.php (downloaded on 28.05.2009).

Indiantelevision.com. 2009b. 'Prasar Bharati should have more autonomy: Parliamentary committee', 25 February. Available online at http://www.indiantelevision. com/headlines/y2k9/feb/feb224.php (downloaded on 28.05.2009).

Jacka, E. and Public Service Broadcasting Research Group. 1997. *Australian public service broadcasting in transition: 1986–1996 Working Papers*. Presented at '40 years of television conference in April 1996', Australia.

Johnson, K. 2000. *Television and social change in rural India*. New Delhi: Sage Publications.

(Rodrigues) Manchanda, U. 1998. 'Invasion from the skies', *Australian Studies in Journalism*, 7: 136–163.

Mendel, T. 2000. 'Public Service Broadcasting: a comparative legal survey', *UNESCO, Asia Pacific Institute for Broadcasting Development*. Available online at http:// www.unesco.org/webworld/publications/mendel/compana.html (downloaded on 07.03.2003).

Mitra, A. 1986. 'For a new kind of software', *A vision for Indian television*, NAMEDIA, Media Foundation of the Non-aligned: New Delhi.

NAMEDIA. 1986. *A vision for Indian television*. New Delhi: NAMEDIA, Media Foundation of the Non-aligned.

Narayanamurthy, N.R. 2000. *Prasar Bharati review committee*, Ministry of Information and Broadcasting, National Informatics Centre: India, pp.1–52. Available online at http://mib.nic.in/informationb/AUTONOMOUS/nicpart/pbintro. html (downloaded on 06.01.2005).

Ninan, S. 1995. *Through the magic window: Television and change in India*. New Delhi: Penguin Books India (P) Ltd.

Norris, P., B. Pauling, R. Zanker and G. Lealand. 2003. *Future of public service broadcasting:Experience in 6 countries*. Wellington: NZ on Air.

Paswan, Ramvilas. 1996. 'Working paper on national media policy (Paswan committee)', at *Indiantelevision.com*, legal resources. Available online at http:// www.indiantelevision.com/indianbrodcast/legalreso/Ramvilaspaswan.htm (downloaded on 14.11.2004).

Prasar Bharati 2007. 'Annual report 2006–2007'. New Delhi: Prasar Bharati Secretariat.

Price, M.E. and M. Raboy. 2003. *Public service broadcasting*. New York: Kluwer Law International.

Raboy, M. 1999. 'What is public service broadcasting?', *Public service broadcasting in Asia: surviving the new information age*. Singapore: An Asian Media Information and Communication Centre (AMIC) compilation.

Rajgopal, A. 1993. 'The rise of national programming: the case of Indian television', *Media, culture and society*, 15: 91–111.

Raman, A. 2005. 'Rahul Gandhi associate will guide DD's Bihar poll coverage', *Indianexpress.com*, Front page, 25 January, p. 1. Available online at http:// www.indianexpress.com/full_story.php?content_id=63392 (downloaded on 24.06.2005).

Reddi, U. V. 1996. 'Rip van winkle: a story of Indian television', in D. French and M. Richards (eds), *Contemporary television: eastern perspectives*, pp. 231–245. New Delhi: Sage Publications.

Singhal, A. and E. M. Rogers. 1989. *India's information revolution*. New Delhi: Sage Publications.

———. 2001. *India's communication revolution: from bullock carts to cyber marts*. London: Sage Publications.

Sinha, N. 1997. 'India: Broadcasting and National Politics', in D. Atkinson and M. Raboy (eds), *Public Service Broadcasting: The challenges of the twenty-first century*. Paris: UNESCO Publishing.

———. 1998. 'Doordarshan, public service broadcasting and the impact of globalisation: a short history', in M. E. Price and S. G. Verhulst (eds), *Broadcasting reform in India*, pp. 22–40. Mumbai: Oxford University Press.

The Prasar Bharati Act (1990). 2000. Ministry of Information and Broadcasting, India: New Delhi.

The Broadcasting Bill. 1997. 'The Broadcasting Bill 1997', at *Indiantelevision. com*, Legal Resources. Available online at http://www.indiantelevision.com/ indianbrodcast/legalreso/broadcast.htm (downloaded on 10.01.2005).

Tracey, M. 1998. *The decline and fall of public service broadcasting*. New York: Oxford University Press.

Varadan, K.A. 1991. 'Introducing competition in the electronic media', at *Indian television.Com,* Legal Resources. Available online at http://www.indian television.com/indianbrodcast/legalreso/kavaradan.htm (downloaded on 14.11.2004).

Verghese, B.G. 1978. 'Excerpts from "major recommendations" of the working group on autonomy for Akashwani and Doordarshan', at *Indiantelevision.com.* Available online at http://www.indiantelevision.com/indianbrodcast/legalreso/ verghesereport.htm (downloaded on 14.11.2004).

———. 2003. 'Which master's voice?', *The Indian Express,* 20 August. Available online at http://mail.sarai.net (downloaded on 27.01.2004).

World Radio and Television Council. 2000. 'Public Broadcasting, Why? How? 2000', Centre d'études sur les médias, Canada: Quebec. Available at http://portal. unesco.org/ci/en/files/18796/11144252115pb_why_how.pdf/pb_why_ how.pdf (downloaded on 25.04.2003).

Interviews

Abraham, T. 2003. Managing Editor, *Indiantelevision.com.* Interviewed by author, Mumbai, February 2003.

Bajpai, S. 2003. Media critic and commentator. Interviewed by author, New Delhi, March 2003.

Basu, Nupur. 2009. Former *NDTV* senior journalist. Interviewed by author, Bangalore, 28 January 2009.

Bhasin, Usha. 2009. Head of Development Communication Division, Doordarshan. Interviewed by author, New Delhi, 12 January 2009.

Churchill, J. 1998. Head of news, Doordarshan. Interviewed by author, New Delhi, January 1998.

Mitra, Chandan. 2009. Editor, *The Pioneer*. Interviewed by author, New Delhi, 9 January 2009.

Mudgal, Vipul. 2009. Editor (Research), *Hindustan Times*. Interviewed by author, New Delhi, 10 March 2009.

Ninan, S. 2003. Editor, *thehoot.org* and media commentator. Interviewed by author, New Delhi, 5 March.

———. 2009. Editor, *thehoot.org* and media commentator. Interviewed by author, New Delhi, 12 January 2009.

Roy, P. 1998. Proprietor, *NDTV*. Interviewed by author, New Delhi, January 1998.

Thapar, K. 1998. *BBC* current affairs talk show host. Interviewed by author, New Delhi, January 1998.

———. 2009. Host, Devil's Advocate, *CNN-IBN*. Interviewed by author, New Delhi, 15 March 2009.

Chapter 10

The Archetypes of Sita, Kaikeyi and Surpanaka Stride the Small Screen

Maya Ranganathan

Introduction

If votaries of liberalisation and news reports are to be believed, globalisation has thrown open opportunities for women. Hitherto confined to the home and hearth, Indian women in the era of globalisation have 'progressed' to take up jobs in areas that were the preserve of males. Surprisingly, this reality is not reflected in television. In Indian television (TV), by far dominated by cinema and serials, the 'progression' remains superficial and does not permeate. Neo-liberalism is confined to demeanour and occupations that the women are shown to be engaged in. On closer analysis, it becomes apparent that not only are the women in television archetypes of the mythological characters of Sita, Kaikeyi and Surpanaka of the Ramayana, but also that the traditional values associated with 'good' Indian women are being touted as the solution to ills plaguing the society today. This chapter details how hegemony operates in Indian television, focussing particularly on the mega serials telecast on Tamil satellite television.

On 12 January 2006, *The Hindu* carried the results of a 'scientific study' conducted by the Indian Science Monitor (ISM) on the perception of women viewers of Tamil TV serials, in which it was revealed that 70 per cent of those who watched the TV serials were unhappy with the characterisation of women in them (Varma 2006). This survey was quoted by the Women's Alliance for Rationality (WAR) in the US, in its online petition, against the portrayal of women in Tamil TV serials to the producers of Tamil serials and the 'respective regulatory agencies' in the Tamil Nadu government (Chelliah: Petition online).

The main complaint was that Tamil serials portrayed a sizeable number of women as dependants, and oppressed by men and society, thus, reinforcing the stereotypical image of Tamil women as 'weak'. The petition drew attention to the fact that the portrayal of women reiterated the traditional virtues of the meek and the patient emerging successful in the end, while portraying the ambitious and the achiever as avaricious and without scruples. WAR was particularly incensed because such portrayal was too far from reality for the Tamil diaspora in the West, concomitantly presenting a 'dilemma and a false sense of Tamil culture'. It said in the petition,

> ...it is not only illogical but also commercially unviable when these Tamil channels from India try to churn out the same stereotypes that are being aired in India. The petition ended with a plea to the powers-that-be to change the portrayal, besides a call to reflect the tradition and values of our rich Tamil culture and history. (Chelliah: Petition online)

More than a year later, on 27 October 2007, Chennai Television, an online portal, attributed two factors to the phenomenal popularity of the Tamil serials.

> First, serials are realistic–and therein lies (sic) their strength. Unlike the movies, where the hero goes from rags to riches in one song, serials exert a realistic nature–that shows the characters as ordinary people just like us–struggling to make a living, while achieving our dreams. (Chennai Television 2007)

Pointing out that Tamil serials were popular worldwide, the article added, 'Second, the serial offers surrealism – something which is totally different. Serials show us a world where people are just like us, but these people are able to demonstrate extraordinary things'.

Both assertions pose challenges for academic scrutiny. With the definition of 'Tamil culture' steeped in confusion and contradiction, it is almost pointless to argue whether the TV serials represent Tamil culture or not, or indeed, if they should and how.[1]

While most women agree that the portrayal of women in the serials leaves much to be desired, this in no way deters them from watching the serials. This phenomenon is not restricted to Tamil Nadu or even to India, but extends to the diaspora women who have become avid consumers of Tamil serials. The spread of satellite television worldwide explains their popularity as the staple of Tamil TV channels—Tamil films and film-based programmes and TV serials. Indian grocery stores abroad, which lend recordings of such serials, do brisk business with many members of the diaspora becoming subscribers who pick up the latest episode of the serials along with their weekly provisions.[2] The 'identity-conscious' Tamil woman in the West does not desist from watching the serials made predominantly for the Indian audience.

If Tamil films are the forte of the male hero, TV dramas which have metamorphosed into 'mega serials', belong solely to women. Even if they are not always made by women, they are definitely 'for' and 'of' women. This, perhaps, explains the forays of former Tamil film actresses into television. The preoccupation of television dramas with women is not unique to Tamil TV or even Indian TV. Studies elsewhere have established soap operas as the medium of and for women.[3] Blumenthal traces the popularity of the genre to the attraction of 'feminine-oriented emotionality' and gender identification that they induce (1997).[4] The fact that Tamil serials, like the western counterparts, focus on the home and family, and define a successful woman as one who manages the home front and relationships satisfactorily, indicates that they are perhaps following a time-tested formula for a successful television drama (Cantor et al. 1983: 48–53; Rogers 1992: 54–56).

If the formula for a successful soap opera in the West has been adapted to suit the Indian cultural milieu to make the popular Tamil TV serials of today, then Tamil TV serials lend themselves to analysis within the framework of cultural feminism, literary theory, audience responses, ideology of mass culture, historicity and national identity.[5] This chapter, while acknowledging the wealth of meanings and understanding that can be gained from such analyses, singles out the ways in which hegemony operates in the Tamil TV serials. It argues that while TV serials in the era of globalisation seemingly make allowances for the changes taking place in Indian society and consequently the roles of women, they still hold that the solution to the ills plaguing the society lies in a return to traditional values, if not traditional roles, for women.

Evolution of 'mega serials'

Indian television serials are of comparatively more recent origin. They began in the days when the public service broadcaster, Doordarshan, held sway over Indian audiences. With Doordarshan clearly being non-commercial and professing lofty aims of mass education and fostering national unity, the first serial *Hum Log* traced the life of a middle class family through three generations. It was followed by equally popular and well-made serials such as *Buniyaad* and *Nukkad*, which portrayed the emerging middle class in urban India. Also notable were the *Ramayan* and *Mahabharat*, serials which attempted a revival of interest in the Indian classics and culture (Rajagopal 2001). Doordarshan, however, lost out to private channels when the skies opened up as a consequence of economic liberalisation in the early 1990s. Not only does it face competition from the private Hindi channels today, but it has come to be overshadowed by the regional channels in the non-Hindi belt.

With the sole aim of the private channels being to make a profit, there has emerged an entertainment fare that is best described as 'mega serials'. They mark a conscious shift from Doordarshan's fare. The 'mega serials', that can run up to seven years, revolve around a woman protagonist who makes a mark in the male-dominated society, without giving up any of the traditional values and attributes that have come to be known as the hallmark of a 'good' Indian woman. While it is not surprising that changes in the portrayal of women have been necessitated by globalisation, as it has provided more employment opportunities for women, what is significant is that the 'mega serials' ensure that the changes remain merely superficial. The 'good' woman in the TV serials is still defined by her contribution to her home and family and her adherence to the traditional values of obedience and patience in the face of undue provocation and adversities. Her success in a career is prompted by her desire to advance her family economically, which remains her primary concern. Ironically, in an age when women are said to be storming male bastions, the traits of ambition, enterprise and working towards a goal with unwavering commitment are associated with the 'bad' woman of the 'mega serials'. Of course, the 'bad' woman has other traits as well, such as coveting others' possessions and being inconsiderate of others and being in haste to achieve her ambitions at any cost, often through unbridled scheming.

The emergence of production houses like 'Balaji Telefilms' and 'Radaan', that dub the serials in different regional languages, have ensured that the formula is operative across India, irrespective of the linguistic and cultural differences. Thus, the 'K' series from the Balaji Telefilms stable includes portrayals of ideal women who are no different from the 'Sati Savithri' image glorified in the films and literature of yore. Although, this chapter restricts itself to Tamil TV serials for methodological reasons, the argument can well be extended to serials in other regional languages and those in Hindi.

In Tamil Nadu it was Kalanidhi Maran, grand nephew of Dravida Munnetra Kazhagam President and Chief Minister M. Karunanidhi, who began a daily programme called *Tamizh maalai* ('A garland of Tamil') through the cable TV circuit in the years that led to liberalisation. This turned into a completely privately-owned TV network, Sun TV, in 1993. Starting with just three hours of programming, it grew into a 24-hour channel by 1995. Sun TV, which set out as a purely entertainment channel, seems to have set the trend in programming that subsequent channels have followed, so much so that Kalaignar TV, a new channel, started following Karunanidhi's face-off with the Marans in 2007 faithfully copied the Sun TV programming format (Ranganathan 2007). The format consists of a mix of films, film-based programmes, political interviews, game shows and serials.

The TV serials that have committed viewership form the main source of revenue for TV channels. While initially TV serials were in 13-part episodes or ran for no more than a year and boasted some creative endeavours by famous Tamil film directors,[6] the commercial factor resulted in the emergence of a formula that could sustain a serial for up to six or seven years. This has come to be the 'mega serial' of today. The 'mega serials' have given rise to a new breed of producers, directors, actors and technicians who have replaced the film and theatre artistes who dominated the small screen in the initial stages of satellite TV.

The sociological impact of 'mega serials' has sparked debates, demonstrations and discussions in various fora. There are chat rooms devoted entirely to the discussion of particular serials, and online communities, which are formed to air viewers' disdain.[7] In the absence of an in-depth survey of audience reception and responses, it is indeed difficult to understand the reasons for the popularity of the 'mega serials' among women or to gauge effects of the portrayal of women, on viewers. The popularity is perhaps because the majority of viewers, who are most likely to be home-bound women, are able to take the positions that the text constructs and relate to the celebration of the 'mundane', the extension of hope and the allowing of a second-hand experience (Anger 1999: 19). Studying television serials in India is fraught with methodological problems. First, as in the West, most viewers, especially urban women, are reluctant to own up to being addicted to such serials.[8] Second, in view of their resale or re-telecast value, they are never sold to the public, even years after they are initially telecast. The spread of the Tamil diaspora that has necessitated the starting of local channels in different countries to cater to their needs has ensured a timeless and growing market for the serials. This renders even study of the potential of the TV serials to construct certain identities among the viewers, difficult and labourious. Third, the mega serials that run into several years contain parallel story lines, making concerted studies difficult and time-consuming. Fourth, the economies of production and the disorganised nature of the television industry often dictate changes and adaptations in storylines and prompt re-telecasts of old episodes, calling into question the desirability of focussing attention on so fickle a product.

Publishing the results of the 2006 survey of the Indian Science Monitor (ISM), *The Hindu* quoted its director T.K.V. Rajan to point out that the effect of bad portrayal of women in television serials was 'more harmful' than that of women in a two-and-half-hour flick, as these serials ran for at least more than a year. The study's consultant psychiatrist, Shalini, reportedly said that the evil characters could 'become role models for the less-educated or rural audience'. 'Also the "evil woman" was conceived by male writers' (Varma 2006). 'What we are seeing is a grotesque synthesis of two very different approaches to violence and reprisal' (Ibid.). Given the stranglehold that the 'mega serials' have on television viewers, especially women, and their growing popularity as can be seen from the Television Rating Points (TRPs), it becomes imperative to take cognisance of the identities they purvey.[9]

I place the analysis of how hegemony operates in the portrayal of women in the 'mega serials' in the context of two issues: first, the changes in the role of Indian women in the era of globalisation, the spread of education and the increase of their numbers in the workforce; and second, the way in which the more popular and powerful medium of Tamil cinema, the influence of which is indisputable on television, treats the subject of women.[10]

Indian women in the era of globalisation

I am aware that globalisation can be perceived in many different ways and the relationship between women's roles and globalisation is indeed complex. However, the most apparent effect of globalisation in the context of this chapter is the shifting of labour-intensive industries to developing countries, including India, which has meant an increase in employment opportunities for women. This is not to discount the ills of globalisation and privatisation that have affected all vulnerable groups, and more so women. Even if grappling with low wages in unskilled jobs, long hours of work and no job security, the increasing number of women in the work force is an indisputable presence, at least in urban areas, contributing to changes in the fabric of Indian society. The increased money power has led to changes in consumption patterns and the media has reflected the changes.[11]

This development has also been accompanied strangely by young, educated upper and middle class urban women opting for the traditional wife-and-mother role and allowing themselves to be recolonised (Ghadially 2007). Interestingly, these women are not devoid of the trappings of progress and they boast of exposure to the West and sport 'modern' clothes and accessories, with 'modern' to be read as synonymous with 'western'. As Channa (2004) argues, 'While colonial India suffered from the racist constructions of the colonial rulers, postcolonial India is reinventing such images by the "cultural blindness" of its Western educated elite.' It is in this context that media images of women in the era of globalisation need to be assessed.

Much like in mainstream Tamil films, globalisation is represented in television at a superficial level with the trappings occupying centre stage and the more complex issues remaining unrepresented or non-verbalised. Liberalisation and the consequent exposure to foreign images and culture have also contributed to changes in world view, particularly among urban women (Dutta 2000: 71–82). These have been supplemented by the growing commercialisation of the print and electronic media in India. What globalisation has meant to the media is a process of image-making, where even professional women are fitted within the framework of the 'traditional' Indian women (Ibid.: 78).

This simplification of image-making divesting it from the historical or social context is only too apparent in Tamil films (Ibid.: 82). The slowly changing world of cosmopolitan lifestyles, where men and women seemingly enjoy more freedom, has hardly caused any noticeable changes in the portrayal of women in Tamil films, even those posited in the urban milieu. The presentation of women in 'stark bad versus good, pure versus impure contrasts, through songs, dialogues and visualisation' has continued from the early 1940s to this day (Lakshmi 2008: 17). Much like in the 1970s, Tamil cinema presents the independent woman asserting her sexuality as a 'cultural freak' or as one who hurtles towards disaster or death. Heroines dominating the narrative space of the film are still rare.

If one randomly looks at the portrayal of urban women in a few recent films, it becomes clear that Tamil films continue to remain the forte of the masochistic male where women's roles do not extend beyond being a prop.[12] A classic case is Mani Ratnam's *Aayudha ezhuthu* (2003) about present day youth and their idealism, where the women companions of the three male protagonists played by the popular actresses of the day are 'largely presented as objects of pleasure' (Chinnaih 2008: 29–42). In Selvaraghavan's part-autobiographical *7G Rainbow Colony* (2004), touted as a realistic film, the heroine, whose feelings for the hero moves from disgust to annoyance to sympathy to love, uses her sexuality to propel him towards greater ambitions. And perhaps because of her initiation and justification of pre-marital sex, she is fatally run over by a lorry leaving the hero an emotional cripple. Female director V. Priya, in her debutante film *Kanda Naal Mudhal* (2005) portrays the heroine as a high-strung woman who sways between doing her duty for the family by marrying a man of their choice and her love for a childhood friend, of which she remains unaware till almost the end of the film. Radha Mohan's hit film *Mozhi* (2007) traces the path of the female protagonist's self-realisation while Gautam Vasudev Menon's *Varanam Aayiram* (2008) almost relegates the women to the background in this tale of a father-son relationship.

Women in television

Unlike the films where female actresses, despite the popularity that they enjoy with the masses, are relegated to a subordinate position both

213

within the film and without, television serials are clearly women's forte (Oza 2006: 60). Most serials sport the name of the female protagonist as titles, and unlike the 'pure' Tamil film heroines, the women characters in 'mega serials' seem more adventurous. They seem to make their own choices in careers, relationships and family. Sometimes, they brazenly have relationships outside wedlock, almost making one believe what popular author Shobha De' asserts, 'The star of Indian television today…is the woman…almost every serial you see is in one way or another projecting what is called the new Indian woman' (Ibid.: 61).[13] This aspect has indeed been identified as one of the reasons for the popularity of 'mega serials'.

It is undoubtedly true that the 'mega serials' have brought negative issues and emotions out of the closet, often blurring the distinction between the 'good' and the 'bad' women of Tamil cinema. For instance, Pooja in the popular serial *Kalki* (Jaya TV), now on a re-run, pursues her lover even after he ends up marrying his late brother's wife Kalki; the famous Abhi (short for Abhinaya) in the still-showing *Kolangal*—roughly translated as 'Rangoli'—(Sun TV), divorces her husband Bhaskar and seems to face life square; Shanthi of *Anandham*—'Happiness'—(Sun TV) marries her husband's friend after being widowed; Usha of *Kolangal* has pre-marital sex with the villainous Adi (short for Aditya); and Rekha in *Kasturi* (Sun TV) throws her husband Ram out of her house when she learns that he had earlier married and deserted Kasturi. Almost all these women are shown as heading business enterprises, striking up friendships to realise their ambitions, being as comfortable in the board rooms as in their kitchens and sporting designer saris or trendy Western wear. At first glance, it does seem as if the 'mega serials' are epitomising Bharatiyar's *pudhumai penn*.[14]

The operation of hegemony and the reiteration of the 'traditional' values become apparent only on closer analysis. With the sanctity of marriage, retribution for sin, rewards for fidelity, uncomplaining humility and inexhaustible patience being glorified, the 'mega serials' make no dent in the traditional image of women. Sensitive problematic issues are swept under the carpet or continue to be stereotyped as in the case of eunuchs in TV serials. This perhaps explains Derné's findings that globalisation has not led to 'changes in family and gender arrangements in India' (2005: 33–47). In the following sections, the construction of the woman protagonist in 'mega serials' is detailed to throw light on 'the use of complex cultural elements to maintain a power base' (Brown 1994: 40).

The women in the public space

If the portrayal of the economically independent woman in the 'mega serials' is taken as a starting point of the discussion, then it must be conceded that the 'mega serials' are filled with women occupying the public space. They are often journalists, doctors, entrepreneurs or police officials. In *Kolangal*, Abhi is seen in her office, on the streets travelling by auto-rickshaws, cars and taxis and attending meetings; Kalki and Pooja are crossing swords in the offices as much as in the house in *Kalki*; at least two of the four daughters in the hugely successful *Mettioli*—loosely translated as 'the sound of a toe ring'—(Sun TV) are employed; Shanthi and Abirami in *Anandham* rush in to help the men when they are grappling with business problems and Kasturi, for all her rural upbringing in *Kasturi*, proves to be more than a match for the city-bred and educated Rekha in business acquisitions; and in *Rekha IPS* (*Kalaignar* TV), Rekha, a dogged woman police officer, handles criminals with panache. Yet, what is surprising is that all of their lives are defined by the private space of home and revolve around personal relationships. Their 'outside role' is either to support the family in the case of the 'good' woman and to get even with the man or serve as a vehicle for vendetta in the case of the 'bad' woman.

Lamenting television serials' preoccupation with the homebound women, Chatterjee (2003) cites the findings of P:SNAP (Pathfinder's: Study of nation's attitudes and psychographics). After all, building a new media genre necessitates 'building of the loyalties of this audience' (Brown 1994: 40). Considering that only one in 10 married women work and they have no time to watch these serials, they cater mostly to the homebound women (Chatterjee 2003). It is hence not surprising that the serials reiterate the perceived 'values and beliefs of the homebound majority'. Thus, the journalists, doctors and police officials are not shown as professionals in the true sense of the term, but are essentially women employed in respectable vocations who are, swayed by personal emotions, just like the homebound women.

In almost all the 'mega serials' cited above, the transgression of the women from home to the world outside has been dictated either by economics or family responsibilities or personal circumstances. Abhi (*Kolangal*) almost single-handedly supports her large family of four women and two men; Kalki (*Kalki*) assumes responsibility to save the company, that her father-in-law founded, from falling into the hands of the wily Pooja; Shanthi (*Anandham*) battles along with the patriarch in her husband's family to save his life's achievements; Kasturi (*Kasturi*) is driven to ambition by a wayward husband; and being jilted by a police officer, leads Rekha (*Rekha IPS*) to the police academy. Little is known of their qualifications or training, with all the women seeming to be natural entrepreneurs. As the public space ends up becoming the 'home' where emotional conflicts are played out, none of the workplace 'women isssues', say of lower wages or sexual harassment in the workplace, are dealt with, leading one to believe that television leads to what Tuchman et al. termed 'social annihilation' (1978). This transgression into the public space usually takes women to places where the ordinary working woman in the real world seldom goes—police stations and prisons. Abhi of *Kolangal*, a building contractor, ends up in a women's prison at least twice.

Interestingly, their role in the public space is aided by men. Abhi leans on her friend Tholkapiyan; Kalki on her husband Dharani; Shanthi on her father-in-law and brother-in-law and Kasturi on her father-in-law, reiterating the many aspects of patriarchy. Ironically, the men themselves are often shown to be inadequate in handling situations of crisis forcing the women to take on their mantle. Although, the women show that they are more competent than the men, they willingly give up their roles in the public space once the crisis passes and the serial hurtles to an end. Patriarchy is perhaps best exemplified by *Mettioli* where the decisions of the daughters of the patriarch are shown to be dictated by the fear of their father losing his standing in society rather than by reason.

The archetypes of Sita, Kaikeyi and Surpanaka

The 'goodness' of the women is evident in their generosity and their manners and expressions. Soft-spoken and well-mannered to a fault in the most trying circumstances, they are the epitome of Indian woman-hood.

They are seldom shown raising their voices, unlike women in real-life situations, but like average women, are prone to tears often. However, they get over their feeling of helplessness soon and find ways of tackling the situation. Abhi, who ventures into building construction, an area of activity that is dominated by men in real life, faces adversities in business stoically but is moved to tears by the emotional conflicts at home. She rushes to the aid of her uncle, Tiruvengadam, who faces a financial setback even though he has constantly belittled her. When her divorced husband Bhaskar hits a low patch she more than happily accommodates him in her business venture. She continues to be favourably disposed towards her friend, Usha, who ends up marrying her business adversary, Adi. It is this generosity and gentleness of the mythological Sita that they follow, that sets them apart from the other women in the serial. The divorced Abhi, although desired by a number of males she comes in contact with, including a foreign-qualified psychiatrist, spurns all men. At times she even seems to be considering returning to her former husband Bhaskar, the man she was forced to divorce. In some ways the characterisation also seems to be influenced by the epitome of Tamil womanhood, Kannagi, who burnt Madurai in retribution for the injustice meted out to her wayward husband, Kovalan.

Needless to say, the 'bad' women are the antithesis of the 'good'. Given to loud and abusive language, their facial expressions—sly looks and wry smiles—are harsh, indicating their characteristics at the outset to the viewers. The villainous older women cast in the roles of mothers-in-law harass the daughters-in-law. The younger 'bad' women who attempt to steal men, thus, disrupting what should be an ideal family life that is the right of every 'good' woman, seem to draw characteristics from the demon 'Surpanaka'. Cast as the seductress, she does not hesitate to use her sexuality to lure married men, or break families up and is willing to go to any lengths to realise her dreams, as in the case of Madhu coveting a married Prasanna (*Rekha IPS*). The obsession for the man could even lead her to marry a much older man, rob the men who are objects of desire of their inheritance, bring about their downfall and even attempt to kill them, as did Pooja of *Kalki*-fame. For her sin of pursuing a married man, Pooja, like the mythological Surpanaka, is humbled.

The 'mega serials' uphold the one man, one woman dictum that is supposedly the essence of Tamil culture, but allows for remarriages. Kalki and Shanthi and a number of other women in the 'mega serials' are shown to be remarrying or considering remarriage after unhappy occurrences. For instance, Kalki, who almost flits from one man to another, ends up marrying her deceased husband's younger brother. However, realising the sanctity of the institution of marriage, she soon reconciles to becoming a dutiful and loyal wife, knowing fully well that the affections of the man she has married were till then engaged elsewhere. Shanthi remarries after she loses her husband in war, only because her daughter needs a father, and desists from granting her second husband conjugal rights. It is not difficult to see the influences of the mythological Sita and Savithri who fought for the lives of their husbands in such characterisations. Neo-liberalism simply does not permeate.

The male protagonist

Even if the women are cast in the mould of Sita, Kaikeyi or Surpanaka, the men are neither Rama, Lakshmana or even Ravana. The bad men are consumed by hatred and the good ones remain weak and ineffectual witnesses to atrocity and oppression. The good men are worthy of the women protagonists' affections and attentions merely because they adhere to the age-old values. The powerful women of the serials may battle with men and often emerge victorious, but they are bogged down more by the women. Even if the causes of their emotional trauma are men, they identify women to vent their frustrations on. When her lover Dharani ends up marrying Kalki in *Kalki*, a heartbroken Pooja turns her anger towards Kalki rather than Dharani, the reason ascribed being that Dharani spurns Pooja's advances due to the presence of a wife, who happens to be Kalki. Similarly, Abhi in *Kolangal* is able to forgive her husband Bhaskar who willingly obliges his villainous mother, but is unable to reconcile with her mother-in-law who uses the son as a pawn. While the general pattern is to fill the villain's slot with a woman, men occasionally occupy the position, as in *Kolangal*. And much like the 'bad' woman, the 'bad' man is shown to be beyond reason, nursing an illogical antipathy to the woman protagonist, often creating situations to showcase the woman's capacity for kindness and patience.

The other men in the 'mega serials', who are not as villainous, are also preoccupied with the women's concerns of family, love, loyalty and jealousy, reassuring the audiences that these are 'legitimate and fascinating' concerns (Mumford 1995a: 168). However, the men's roles do not imitate the women's in other areas. They are hardly seen sharing the women's work or even contributing to the domestic front with more than their presence. Tholkapiyan of *Kolangal* offers support to Abhi through his constant presence; Bharani of *Kalki* extends support to Kalki by being unswervingly loyal and Karthik of *Anandham* is the silent but faithful presence in Shanthi's life, who, if not in person, is always available on the phone, even when enlisted by the Indian army to fight terrorists in Kashmir.

Much like the dichotomy between the 'good' and the 'bad' woman, the difference between the 'good' and the 'bad' man is painted in stark colours. Adi, Abhi's *bête noire* in *Kolangal* is clearly a 'bad' man not only because he crosses swords with the patient, suffering and 'good' Abhi, but also because of his arrogance and singular obsession to see Abhi vanquished. More importantly though, Adi has no respect for traditional Indian values, except perhaps a blind love for his mother. He treats his father with disdain; has pre-marital sex and refuses to marry the woman he has an affair with; engages in a liaison with another woman despite being married; is rude and uncaring to his employees and gloats over his victories and is given to violent acts and words when defeated. In contrast, the 'good' Tholkapiyan unswervingly stands by the woman he loves; changes his romantic feelings to friendship and helps her in all her endeavours; saves her life and family honour by undertaking grave risks; offers refuge to a woman deserted by her husband and takes care of her child as his own and at all times treats her with the utmost respect. Individual characteristics notwithstanding, a 'good' man is one who implicitly believes in the traditional values of marriage, loyalty and morality. Thus, Abhi treats her father-in-law with affection even when he remains a mute spectator to his wife's and son's misdoings.

Underscoring traditional values

Almost all the 'mega serials' offer lessons for the women of today in balancing a lifestyle dictated by changing society with the traditional values that have all along defined a 'good' Indian woman. They, in no way, question the relevance of the age-old values, but reiterate that in such values can be found solutions to the problems that are faced in the domestic and public spaces today. Typically, a woman's worth is measured in terms of her success on the home front in keeping the family together. Thus Kalki, Abhi, Shanthi, Kasturi, along with scores of other protagonists, are first and foremost women who realise and never fail to fulfil their responsibilities for their families, even in the most trying circumstances—even when the family members are undeserving of any goodness. In simple terms, the 'good' woman is one who, in the age of nuclear families, keeps the family together, while the 'bad' woman is one, who is responsible for frictions in the family or who remains indifferent when the family splits.

Sex is still taboo and while 'mega serials' contain a generous dose of bigamy, pre-marital sex, extramarital sex and love affairs, there is always punishment awaiting those who stray from the straight and narrow path. The meek and righteous women who wait and watch are rewarded in the end, while the sinners are annihilated or reformed. Thus, in the final episodes of *Mettioli* when the patriarch passes away, the daughter vents all her pent up anger against her mother-in-law and husband and explains the reason for her silence. It was not weakness but strength that kept her quiet all the years, she explains—strength derived from being obedient to her father and sparing him grief.

Interestingly, clothes are used to convey characteristics of the women. The 'good' women are clothed mostly in the traditional sari, half-sari or the salwar-kameez, while western wear and outlandish clothes and accessories are reserved for the seductresses. At a time when the salwar-kameez of the north of India and the jeans and skirts of the West were threatening to overshadow the sari, the 'mega serials' helped bolster the sales of saris in Chennai, with the popular outlets sponsoring the clothing of one actress or the other. Incidentally, 'mega serials' have also led to one other business—opulent houses are built to be let out to television production houses and old run-down houses have found a second lease of life as shooting venues.

Conclusion

While there is no doubt that commercial considerations demand that all 'good' women retain the Indian traditional values despite the trappings of modernity that they carry on their bodies, not all 'mega serials' face the same success. Success here is not just a TRP measure but refers to a movement of the woman from the surreal to the hyper real. Some 'mega serial' protagonists, with the help of other media, have grown to become hyper real, thus extending their small screen personae to the public sphere. A case in point is that of Abhi of *Kolangal*, produced by *Vikatan Televistas*, who 'penned' an agony aunt column for some weeks in the popular Tamil weekly *Ananda Vikatan*, published by the Vikatan group. The protagonist needs to be shown to walk the tightrope between tradition and modernity to gain acceptance among the viewers (Ranganathan 2006: 16–17).

The woman protagonist even if not exactly home-bound is to be governed by personal emotions. She may storm male bastions and prove to be equal to men in many fields, but is never allowed to forget that she is foremost a woman and, hence, must accord family and relationships the most importance. Even a bold and courageous IPS officer is fazed by the emotional problems at home. Despite her capabilities, she does not settle for a strong and capable male, but for one who is perhaps inadequate in a few areas. Once united with a man in marriage, she does her all to preserve the sanctity of the marriage and remain a devoted wife, assuming shades of Kannagi. Her troubles in the public space come from unscrupulous men, and those in the private space of home, from wayward men and women. It is with the strength of righteousness and her traditional values that she faces these troubles and emerges victoriously. The attributes of passionate pursuance of ambition, adventure and liberal attitudes towards sexuality, which have all, by and large, come to be associated with globalisation, are reserved for the 'bad' woman who faces her nemesis in the end. Interestingly, the representation of women in Indian television serials in the era of globalisation can be best summed up in the words of Modleski who was writing about the western soap operas (1982: 113):

A soap-opera woman might very well be engaged in important work like law or medicine, but even on the job she is likely to be obsessed with her love-life or perhaps actually carrying on her love-life, simultaneously weeping over and operating on the weak outlets for women's dissatisfaction with male-female relationships, they never question the primacy of these relationships. Nor do they overtly question the myth of male superiority or the institutions of marriage and the family. Indeed, patriarchal myths and institutions are, on the manifest level, whole-heartedly embraced, although the anxieties and tensions they give rise to may be said to provoke the need for the texts in the first place.

In essence, the 'mega serials', which although at one level seem to deal with the women of today, have a strong tendency to cast women in the moulds of the mythological Sita, Kaikeyi and Surpanaka. Much like in Ramayana, Sita wins through patience and forbearance while Kaikeyi and Surpanaka are humbled for their evil thoughts and designs.

Endnotes

1. For instance, Tamil culture supposedly advocates 'oruthanuku oruthi', a one man-one woman schema. However, in practice it is common to find men living with two wives in Tamil Nadu. See for instance, *The Times of India*, 'In South India more the merrier', 2 May 2006, online. It can be argued that the promiscuity in Tamil TV serials is a distortion of true Tamil culture or, is a representation of the Tamil culture as it is today.

2. Personal observation of author while living abroad for more than six years.

3. I desist from making a distinction between the serial dramas aired in prime-time and soap operas during day-time in Tamil TV as the format of both is much the same and depending on the popularity of the serial it is pushed into or out of prime-time. In the West, however, soap operas refer to dramas aired during daytime, while serials are those that occupy prime-time slots.

4. See also Lopate 1976: 69–82; Modleski 1982.

5. However, no argument is made that Indian TV serials are clones of western soap operas. See Blumenthal 1997; Brunsdon 2000; Mumford 1995b and Nochimson 1992, for analyses of soap operas from the cultural feminist perspective. The cultural aspects of soap operas have been dealt with by Allen 1995; Ang 1982; Anger 1999; Cassata and Skill 1983 and Matelski 1988. The literary study perspective is taken by Modleski 1982.

6. Tamil film industry's famous director K. Balachander began his tryst with Tamil television with 'Rayil sneham' ('Friendship in the train') in Doordarshan. His hugely popular 'Kai alavu manasu' ('Heart the size of fist') was shown on Sun TV and later Raj TV and 'Sahana' was replayed recently in Jaya TV. His TV production company 'Minbimbangal' is in the forefront of producing serials

for Tamil TV channels. Tamil film director Balu Mahendra's 'Kadhai Neram' ('Story time') on Doordarshan was critically acclaimed and actress Suhasini directed a serial titled 'Penn' for Doordarshan in the early 1980s.

7. 'Hate Kolangal serial' is a community in Orkut with 265 members who critique the serial.

8. Brown (1994) traces the reluctance of women to own up to watching serials, to 'disapproving valuation of soap operas on an emotional level.'

9. For the problems in taking TRP as conclusive evidence of a programme's popularity, see Rao 2001.

10. The influence of Tamil cinema on television is significant. Directors, lyricists, music directors and actresses dabble in both the mediums. The format of the 'mega serial' borrows from the films in part. For instance, all serials have a signature song, complete with groups of men and women dancing.

11. Whether the media reflects change or functions as a catalyst of change is an ongoing argument. Some changes in apparel, for example the replacement of the 'thavani', the half-sari which has been the traditional apparel of adolescent women in Tamil Nadu, by the ubiquitous 'salwar kameez' of the North, has been attributed to Tamil films. But other changes, like an increase in divorce rates, have no simple explanations, although the portrayal of the ambitious and courageous women in media has been cited as a reason. For instance, in his weekly question and answer sessions in *Kumudam Jothidam*, an astrological Tamil magazine from the Kumudam group of publications, editor A.M. Rajagopalan often blames the 'overarching influence' of the 'irresponsible' media in the country for the 'disastrous' sociological changes. *Kumudam Jothidam* is available online at http://www.kumudam.com, on registration.

12. Portrayal of urban women in non-action oriented films has been chosen for cursory examination as rural women are usually taken to be meek and submissive and the genre of action movies demands heroism and masochism.

13. According to Shobha De', the new Indian woman had her own money and hence could redefine her position within the family.

14. *Pudhumai penn* refers to an imaginative construct of a liberated woman celebrated by Tamil poets Bharatiyar and Bharatidaasan.

References

Allen, R.C. 1995. *To be continued...* London and New York: Routledge.

Ang, I. 1982. *Watching Dallas: soap opera and the melodramatic imagination.* London and New York: Routledge.

Anger, D. 1999. *Other worlds: society seen through soap opera.* United Kingdom: Broadview Press.

Blumenthal, D. 1997. *Women and soap opera: A cultural feminist perspective.* Westport, Connecticut. London: Praeger.

Brown, M.A. 1994. *Soap opera and women's talk: The pleasure of resistance.* New Delhi: Sage Publications.

Brunsdon, C. 2000. *The feminist, the housewife and the soap opera.* Oxford: Oxford Television Series.

Cantor, G. Muriel and Suzanne Pingree. 1983. *The soap opera.* Beverley Hills, California: Sage Publications.

Cassata, M. and Thomas Skill. 1983. *Life on daytime television.* New Jersey: Ablex Publishing Corporation.

Channa, S.M. 2004, 'Globalization and modernity in India: A gendered critique', *Urban Anthropology*, 3 (1): pp. 37–72.

Chatterjee, P. 2003. 'TV serials still show traits of home bound women'. *The Hindu-Business Line*, 5 September. Available online http://www.thehindubusinessline. com/2003/09/06/stories/2003090600650600.htm (downloaded on 31.12.2008).

Chennai Television. 2007. 'Chennai Television: why Tamil serials are popular?' 27 October. Available online http://www.chennaitvnews.com/2007/10/why-tamil-serials-are-popu... (downloaded on 22.12.2008).

Chelliah, M. 'Petition against the portrayal of women in Tamil TV-serials'. Available online at http://www.petitiononline.com/TVWAR001/petition.html (downloaded on 22.12. 2008).

Chinnaih, S. 2008. 'The Tamil film heroine', in Selvaraj Velayutham (ed.), *Tamil cinema: the cultural politics of India's other film industry,* pp. 29–42. London: Routledge.

Derné, S. 2005. 'The (limited) effect of cultural globalization in India: Implications for culture theory', *Poetics* 33: 33–47. Also available at http://www.uoregon. edu/~aweiss/indianfilmclass/Steve%20Derne.pdf (downloaded on 11.02.2010.)

Dutta, S. 2000. 'Globalisation and representations of women in Indian cinema', *Social Scientist*, 28 (3/4) (March–April): 71–82.

Ghadially, R. 2007. *Urban women in contemporary India.* New Delhi: Sage Publications.

Lakshmi, C.S. 2008. 'A good woman, a very good woman', in Selvaraj Velayutham (ed.), *Tamil Cinema: the cultural politics of India's other film industry,* pp. 16–28. London: Routledge.

Lopate, C. 1976. 'Daytime television: You'll never want to leave home', *Feminist Studies*, 3 (4): 69–82.

Matelski,1988. *The soap opera evolution.* Jefferson, North Carolina and London: McFarland and Co.

Modleski, T. 1982. *Loving with a vengeance: mass-produced fantasies for women.* Hamden, Connecticut: Archon Books.

Mumford, L.S. 1995a. 'Plotting paternity: looking for dad in the daytime soaps', in Robert C. Allen (ed.), *To be continued...soap operas around the world,* pp. 164–180. London, New York: Routledge.

Mumford, L.S. 1995b. *Love and ideology in the afternoon*. Bloomington and Indianapolis: Indiana University Press.

Nochimson, M. 1992. *No end to her*. Berkeley: University of California Press.

Oza, R. 2006. *The making of neoliberal India: nationalism, gender and the paradoxes of globalization*. New York: Routledge.

Rao, B.N. 2001. 'Tripping over the TRP trap'. *Indiantelevision.com*, 13 September. Available online at http://www.indiantelevision.com/headlines/y2k1/sep/sep31.htm (downloaded on 5.1.2009).

Rajagopal, A. 2001. *Politics after television: Hindu nationalism and reshaping of the public in India*. Cambridge: Cambridge University Press.

Ranganathan, M. 2006. 'A tale of two women: political economy and hyper-reality in Indian soaps', *Biblio* XI (9–10).

———. 2007. 'Kalaignar TV makes its debut'. Available online at http://www.thehoot.org/web/home/searchdetail.php?sid=2679&bg=1 (downloaded on 29.12.2008).

Rogers, D. 1992. 'The afternoons of our lives', in S. Frentz (ed.), *Staying tuned: contemporary soap opera criticism*, pp. 54–56. Bowling Green, Ohio: Bowling Green State University Popular Press.

The Times of India. 2006. 'In South India more the merrier', 2 May 2006. Available online at http://timesofindia.indiatimes.com/articleshow/msid-1513322,prtpage-1.cms (downloaded on 29.12.2008).

Tuchman, G., A. K. Daniels and J. Benet. 1978. *Hearth and home: images of women in the mass media*. New York: Oxford University Press.

Varma, D.M. 2006. 'Tamil serials give women bad image: Study', *The Hindu*, 12 January. Available online at http:/www.hindu.com/2006/01/12/stories/2006011207340100.htm (downloaded on 22.12.2008).

Media Policy

Chapter 11

Freedom in Indian Blogosphere

Maya Ranganathan

The era of globalisation is also the era of convergence where communication technologies come together in pocket-sized gadgets. The phenomenal advances in technology have no doubt made communication much easier, leading to the evolution of ever newer forms of expression that seem to be bound neither by rules nor convention, blurring boundaries between the producers and the consumers, and even the different forms of communication. The opening up of new vistas of expression has led to new debates about the ways in which communication technologies are evaluated. Computer-aided technologies offering a range of platforms for expression, call for a fresh evaluation of issues such as freedom of expression, libel and language. This chapter looks at one such increasingly popular platform–the blogs. As communication technologies allow any person with an internet access to self-publish, blogs have proved extremely useful in situations where the more organised and dominant media have not been able to respond swiftly. Looked at in isolation, blogs seem to typify 'free media'. However, recent instances reveal that bloggers are increasingly battling restrictions. This chapter deals with the issue of freedom of expression as it applies to the blogosphere in India, calling for a rethink on the laws that are applicable, in tune with the technological features that govern the use of the platform of blogs.

The rise of the blogosphere

One of the many platforms that the internet offers, 'weblog', a term coined by John Barger in 1997, abbreviated to 'blog' by Peter Merholz in 1999, is part of the social network with 'special qualities' termed 'blogosphere' (Tremayne 2007a: x). Tremayne lists the features of the blog as, primarily being in text form; in most cases being archived; linked to other blogs and a rapidly evolving network (2007a: xi). Yet only the first two features seem common to all blogs and not many blogs incorporate links to other blogs (Baron 2008: 11). The early blogs were just headlines with links to the actual stories (Ibid.: 108). Blogging received a boost after 9/11 when most people took to blogs to write about the events of the day and subsequently about US President Bush's 'war on terrorism' (Tremayne 2007a: xiii). Typically, war and politics provide fodder to the bloggers. Blogs have helped galvanise public interest leading the platform to be called 'the fifth estate' (Cooper 2006). The tsunami in 2004 and terrorist bombings in London in 2005 spurred the growth of the blogosphere (Ibid.). For blog readers, some of the blogs provided a one-stop shop for information on any current topic of interest. Bloggers not only provided news but also views, which were even more valuable when the bloggers were, themselves, an eye-witness to any event, such as the tsunami. Recent examples of the contribution of bloggers in crisis situations, be it in bringing to light the authoritarian acts of governments in the Middle East or the human rights violations in Sri Lanka or the destruction caused by terrorist acts in Mumbai, have been many and significant. They have supplemented the dominant media and often helped by surmounting the odds that stifle the dominant media such as the economies of operation. The ease with which blogs can be created and sustained, and the potential reach of the platform itself have contributed to the popularity of blogging as an activity, and also made them worthy of attention. While some bloggers aim to reach the 'largest possible audience and have the largest possible impact', others are amateurs who write for other reasons (Knobel 2005: 53).

The reasons for blogging according to the Pew Internet and American Life Project are to 'express themselves creatively; to document their personal experiences or share them with others; to stay in touch with friends and family; and share practical knowledge or skills with others' (Lenhart and Fox 2006). The fact that blogs are, at the same time, entertaining and educational and offer companionship, have provided an impetus to free expression and have led to the rise of blogs that deal with issues far removed from 'news' or 'politics' (Baron 2008: 113). For some, like academic intellectuals, blogging offers a way to bypass the 'superficiality or the hostility of their reception in their media' (Mills 2005: 5). The rise of blogging, indeed, seems to have diluted the powers of editorial page editors who had 'sovereignty over that region of public dialogue'

(Rosen 2005: 30). However, the sheer variety of blogs, in terms of form and content, renders clear classification problematic.

Baron cites Herring, who distinguishes three genres of blogs–topical blogs, which are news-based; personal journals or diaries that include travel blogs and knowledge blogs where people share their expertise (Baron 2008: 110). Of particular interest to this chapter is the class of blogs that are termed 'personal blogs', described as 'that most notorious aspect of the blogosphere' (Barlow 2008: x). Recent studies have examined blogs as a form of self-expression and social connectivity (Papacharissi 2007: 22). Replete with opinionated views, personal blogs offer a forum for individuals to air their views and also for others—most often a small circle of friends and acquaintances—to respond and to react. The ease and the freedom of expression that the platform offers, have, in some instances, made it a popular vehicle of mass communication and also an entertaining form that often veers towards the 'trashy, frivolous and studiously non-serious', a 'never-ending stream of confessions' that attempt to interpret events beyond the known categories (Lovink 2007: 3, 17). Yet, the very same features have also made blogging rife with legal complications.

It is perhaps to be expected that authoritarian and totalitarian regimes will clamp down on bloggers who use the platform to either highlight their commissions and omissions or lobby for more freedom. And there have been quite a few of these examples in recent times. Prosecution, under various laws of the land, of citizens who have ruffled the governments to Egypt, Malaysia, Singapore and Myanmar, have made it to the headlines. While this is indeed of concern, what is of greater interest to this chapter is the concept of personal blogging and its legal implications. The issue of personal bloggers' rights came into prominence in 2004 when a picture in uniform and comments that Delta Airlines flight attendant Ellen Simonetti posted on her blog, were termed inappropriate by the employer. While no case can be made in support of bloggers who breach contracts of employment, the consequences of blogging were unforeseen and perhaps disastrous. Erik Ringmar, a senior lecturer at the London School of Economics, was ordered by the convenor of his department to destroy his blog in 2006, for discussing the quality of education in the institution and Catherine Sanderson, alias Petite Anglaise, lost her job in Paris at a British accountancy firm because of blogging. Blogs indeed have changed the world we live in, but the issue here is how to interpret them (Lovink 2007: 1).

The issues facing blogosphere in India

In India, the blogosphere that contains more than a million blogs, has shot into the limelight recently for all the wrong reasons (*The Hindu* 2006). The initial euphoria about the phenomenal potential of the medium, which was realised when blogs helped trace and track people during the tsunami in December 2004, the Bihar floods in August 2008 and the Mumbai terror attacks in November 2008, has now given way to one of fear and caution. The Information and Technology Act 2000, in India, under the purview of which fall all activities that involve electronic data exchange, focuses more on 'electronic commerce'. The incidents of employment of the technologies to disrupt law and order, particularly terrorist activities, necessitated some amendments to the Act in 2006. Meant to tackle cyber crime including fraud, phishing and cyber terrorism, 45 amendments were suggested (Mediavidea 2009). The Bill was passed by the Parliament in December 2008 and renamed the Information Technology (Amendment) Act 2008. The Act seeks to give teeth to existing laws on information technology and cyberspace. As per the draft, in the name of national security and safe internet use, the government can intercept email, block websites and web content without giving the owners a right to be heard, monitor and collect traffic data relating to a website in order to foil cyber fraud and to set up an Indian Computer Emergency Response Team (CERT-In) that can demand data from the internet service provider (Ninan 2009). The threat to blogosphere, however, does not come merely from the IT Act. Much as in other countries, in India too, the 'gravest dangers' to bloggers are the legal challenges in the form of libel, prior restraint and copyright (Carroll and Frank 2007: 205).

Gaurav Mishra laments, ironically in a blog, about how traditional institutions are trying to limit the internet's freedom, when he points out the case of Ajith, who has been charged with criminal intimidation and hurting religious sentiments (Gauravonomics blog 2009). Ajith, a 19-year-old computer science student was instrumental in setting up an anti-Shiv Sena Orkut community, in which an anonymous commentator had posted a death threat against the Sena leader Bal Thackeray. The Supreme Court has refused to throw out the case, causing bloggers to fear a total clamp on freedom of expression. While such extreme reactions are, perhaps, uncalled for, considering that the judgement of the Maharashtra High Court where the Shiv Sena has filed the case was still awaited at the time of going to press in June 2009, the incident focuses attention on two issues. The first of course is the larger issue of freedom of expression in India, particularly media freedom, under which blogs and social community sites are classified, and the other, is the more academic debate on the space blogs occupy–the 'public' or the 'private' or somewhere in between. Barlow, in his exposition on how bloggers see their relationships to the wider communities around them, argues that bloggers merely see themselves as employing a new set of tools and that 'their expressionism' is merely a new way of speaking to the same type of people they would be speaking to in the 'real' world, perhaps to more numbers of them (2008: xi).

The case against Ajith is not the first. The Shiv Sena itself had taken exception to a community on Orkut, which was anti-Sivaji, the Maratha warrior, in November 2006. Following cases of violence, the police had instructed cyber kiosk owners to block the site. A Public Interest Litigation (PIL) had been filed, seeking a ban on Orkut, a popular social networking site, in which the community had found a place. Again in January 2007, the Maharashtra Government had sought the help of the Computer Emergency Response Team (CERT-In), a regulatory body under the Ministry of Information and Technology, to remove the content. Following representations to Google and the Mumbai Police, the Sena managed to highlight the need for policing the internet for hate campaigns. There are also incidents of an Information Technology (IT) professional being arrested for obscene comments about Congress leader Sonia Gandhi in the Orkut community, 'I hate Sonia Gandhi' (Pramod 2009). However, community groups that profess hatred to particular programmes on television, to actors, to politicians and even historical figures continue to sprout.

While perhaps recourse to legal action can be taken on the grounds that such acts could lead to 'disruption of public order' or 'incitement to an offence', the leeway that the law offers also seems to encourage fanatic elements, as has been proven by the Shiv Sena, time and again.

The fear of violence has often led authorities to take extreme measures, totally disproportionate to the act. In the case of the comments about Sonia Gandhi, while it was held by the authorities that action was taken against the language used, it was generally believed to be a consequence of the political clout of the person denigrated. This, of course, leads to the much larger issue of media freedom in India. The classification of blogs under 'media' seems to be made on the premise that the platform allows for self-publication. It is common knowledge that the Constitution of India makes no specific mention of freedom of the press, but the freedom of the press is incorporated in the general freedom of expression contained in Article 19 (1) (a) and is subject to the restrictions provided in Article 19 (2) of the Constitution. Article 19 says, 'Everyone has the right to freedom of opinion and expression, this right includes freedom to hold opinions without interference and to seek, receive and impart information and ideas through any media and regardless of frontiers.' While there are many instances where the judiciary has upheld the freedom of the media, there are also instances of the legislature having succeeded in curbing it. Perhaps in the larger context of the freedom of the media, the limitations placed on expression of online media are small. However, it is significant in the context of the online media enjoying the potential of being relatively the most free and unhindered media.

'Free' platform

Indian bloggers have been repeatedly made to bow down for taking on other media, the most recent case being that of Holland-based blogger Chyetanya Kunte's criticism of Barkha Dutt's coverage of the Mumbai attacks on NDTV (Thehoot.org 2009). On 27 November 2008, the blogger, in a piece headlined 'Shoddy journalism', listed the acts of omissions and commissions by NDTV reporter Barkha Dutt, who covered the Mumbai attacks, implying that the coverage could have worsened the situation rather than saving lives. The blogger had made references to reports in newspapers and also the entry in Wikipedia about the journalist having given away confidential information in her reportage of the Kargil conflict. In a response on 4 December 2008, Ms Dutt wrote on the NDTV.com website dismissing criticism of her coverage as 'offensive, malicious and entirely untrue' and citing instances where the coverage had been lauded by notable personalities. She explained that what was done was well within the line of her duty and responsibility; that she only interviewed those people who consented to go on air and also clarified the Kargil allegations. While the Wikipedia entry continues to remain online, Kunte was forced to unconditionally withdraw the blog posting on 26 January 2009. One can only guess that Kunte must have received a legal notice from NDTV to have forced him to retract his charges and make an educated guess on what the terms were. What is interesting in the context of this chapter is that Kunte was not the lone critic of Ms Dutt's coverage and that mainstream media (Chakrabarti 2008) also had reservations about it. Surprisingly, however, the whole issue was only fought in blogosphere. When Kunte's post was re-posted on the social community website 'Facebook', Ms Dutt reacted by pointing out that a legal notice had been served by NDTV for libel for the 'utter and total rubbish' peddled in the post. The mainstream media that is quick to act in unison on issues relating to freedom of expression remained largely indifferent to the issue (Karunakaran 2009; Vantagepoint). What perhaps irks the mainstream media is that blogs seem to question the hierarchical and top-down approach of the media organisations (Barlow 2008: xii).

The Kunte incident had an echo in the fate of 'Mediaah', the media criticism blog and in the instances where Indian Institute of Planning and Management (IIPM) issued legal notices to Gaurav Sabnis, Varna Sriraman and Rashmi Bansal for their posts on the management institute. To borrow the term from Axel Bruns, the role of these blogs was 'gate-watching'—to monitor—even if it was not fellow-bloggers or new media gatekeepers themselves (2005: 23). In March 2005, Pradyuman Maheshwari, who is now the editor-in-chief for 'Exchange4Media', shut down his blog called 'Mediaah' as he was unable to face legal action threatened by the powerful Bennet, Coleman and Co., the publisher of the multi-city daily 'The Times and India', for 'singling out' the newspaper for criticism (Glaser 2005). In 19 posts he questioned some of the issues concerning the newspaper, including the much-discussed blurring between editorial and advertising content, challenging indeed the 'information monopoly' of the dominant media (Hewitt 2005: 108). Interestingly, the 19 posts that 'Mediaah' was asked to delete, resurfaced soon enough in another blog called 'Mediaha' (http://mediaha.blogspot.com). Yet in this instance, the dominant media remained a silent spectator calling into focus the issue of media criticism in India.[1] However, Maheshwari was not without detractors. In her column condemning the threat against Maheshwari, Ninan pointed out nevertheless that his remarks were 'gossipy' and 'irreverent' and the 'media editor' of dancewithshadows.com (2005) held that 'Mediaah' had none but itself to blame for the fate that befell it.

In October 2005, business school IIPM was criticised by bloggers for the claims made in its advertisements regarding infrastructural facilities available at the Institute. One of the bloggers, Gaurav Sabnis, had to quit his job at IBM in order to subvert any damage to the image of the organisation he was employed with. Interestingly, Businessworld, of which Rashmi Bansal was a consulting editor (Wikipedia), 'Outlook' magazine and the Chennai-based eveninger 'News Today' picked up the issue but the rest of the mainstream media ignored it, perhaps unwilling to forego the huge advertisements issued by the institute. The Monopolies and Restrictive Trade Practices Commission (MRTPC), an arm of the Indian Government in charge of overseeing fair trade practices, is currently investigating the claims made by the institute in its advertisements (Wikipedia).

In all the above cases the charges laid related to libel, defamation and incitement to an offence and the bloggers have been made to apologise and retract their posts or have been forced to stop blogging altogether. Some of the moral and ethical issues, besides technological issues, are still being discussed at length in blogosphere (Gauravonomics.com). The main criticism against bloggers has been the lack of factual evidence, the 'malicious' and 'unsavoury' language—terms open to interpretation.

Blogging = Journalism?

The above cases lead us to visit the symbiotic relationship that blogs share with the news industry (Lovink 2007: 6). Studies exploring the relationship between the mainstream media and blogs in the US have shown that top 10 blogs accounted for 54 per cent of citations in the mainstream press (Meraz 2007: 64). Studies elsewhere have not confirmed that the blogs pose a threat to mainstream media or that they are even regarded as 'credible' sources (Tremayne 2007b: 264). The issue is further confounded by the fact that the personal diary format of many of the blogs, especially those that belong to the younger generation of bloggers, have sparked off theories on blogging as a 'technology of the self' (Ibid.). As Lovink points out, blogging often straddles the two worlds of publishing and dairy keeping (Tremayne 2007b: 7). What needs to be borne in mind is that while perhaps blogs that deal with particular issues are more like newspapers—reporting events and carrying well-justified opinions—a large number of blogs are purely vehicles of personal opinion, conveyed by people who are neither trained in the science of journalism nor in the craft of writing. Proof is not far to seek, for a definite indication lies in the names that people give their blogs. It is the personal voice that makes blogs interesting and refreshing, and has caused many publications to incorporate blogs as part of their online publication. Indeed, citizen journalism thrives on the very fact that the citizen functions as a journalist without any formal training that is likely to affect perception.[2] Amit Varma, a blogger at indiauncut.com 'went to write for MINT business newspaper', picking up the Bastiat prize for reporting and a contract to a write a novel 'My friend Sancho' (Singh 2008b).

Blog entries are often 'hastily written personal musings, sculptured around a link or an event' (Lovink 2007: 8). Tracing 'blogging' to a 'nihilist impulse', Lovink argues that blogs express 'personal fear, insecurity and disillusion' (2007: 17). In such a scenario, can bloggers be treated as media commentators? Can they be expected to substantiate stories or even discern the difference between prejudices and agendas (dancewith shadows.com 2005)? One blogger responding to the stand-off between Barkha Dutt and blogger Kunte wrote:

> However being a journalist myself I can say that we have been trained not to do any name-calling as it can result in a libel suit for the publication we write for. In fact even while quoting from sources, one has to use terms like 'allegedly' or 'accused of' because otherwise the publication can be sued. The only time one can actually say that a person has done something wrong is if the person has been tried and convicted in a court of law. These are the rules which any responsible journalist will live by. From what I know, bloggers who write in a public domain also can be sued. Now whether B. Dutt (*sic*) should have come down so heavily on a blogger or not is not something I want to go into…all I want to say is that clearly the blogger did break the

law. And if he hadn't, NDTV would never have been able to sue him. It is possible to say a lot of things about people in a clever way, ensuring that the message is spread, but no one can sue. If one wants to that is. Personally I prefer to be on the right side of the law. (Chandani 2009)

Indeed the 'truth' in blogging is at best a 'question mark' that is not an 'absolute value sanctioned by higher authorities' but an 'amateur project' (Lovink 2007: 13). Going by the dominant media's response or more particularly the lack of it, to instances where bloggers have faced the flak for irresponsible comments, it seems clear that the journalist fraternity does not treat bloggers as part of their ilk.[3] In fact, bloggers have invited scorn for exposing their 'unremarkable opinions, sententious drivel, and unedifying private lives' (Kline and Burstein 2005: 249). Conversely, not having been schooled in journalism, bloggers cannot claim the rights extended to journalists. In an interesting chapter, Hendrickson explores the argument if blogs are a new form of press and if, in the context of the First Amendment in the US, they deserve special protection (2007: 187).

Second, the converging technologies enable blogging on the go. Two features that distinguish a blog from the hosts of others are the 'personal voice' and 'a rapid response time' (Lovink 2007: 3). Mobile phones that incorporate the internet and the digital camera, make transmitting of information at the touch of a button possible, unlike more traditional media, which is often, if not always, subject to editing and review. Reliance Mobile, the second largest mobile service provider in India, offers mobile blogging to cater to users who want to exchange news and snippets. Websites like smsgupshup.com and Vakow.com are becoming increasingly popular (Singh 2008a). Email and text messages, unlike blog diaries, cannot be 'revoked or revised through an editing process that keeps them from being seen until "ready"' (Barlow 2008: 15). The advantages of such instantaneous communication are many, especially in instances of natural disasters and man-made disasters. In times of distress, the technology comes in handy, not requiring as it does, heavy equipment, space and energy. While it cannot be denied that this feature is open to abuse, it does not however take away the argument that technology needs to be considered when charges are made against bloggers for not writing 'wisely'. There is always the danger that the technologically-savvy may move towards encrypted, untraceable networks to prevent being tracked down. It must also be noted that the evolution of online language, which is perhaps best characterised by the language of short messaging service (SMS), redefines many of the established notions of propriety and decency. The 'subtle' and 'invidious' transformations that email and 'its descendants' have had on language, are calling for a rethink on assumptions about interpersonal communication and 'conventional notions' about spoken and written language worldwide (Baron 2008: 5). The rules governing use of language have been a casualty in a platform that is itself not governed by any rules and is leading to what Baron interestingly terms 'linguistic whateverism' (Ibid.: 169). It was her racy and revealing posts that fetched Meenakshi Reddy Madhavan, blogging at 'Compulsive confessor', a book deal with Penguin India (Singh 2008b). The evolution of language needs to take into account much more than the creeping in of acronyms into the written language. Much like morality, 'decency' and 'obscenity' varies from time to time and place to place. With biting commentary and rude reviewing slowly seeping into media language, 'decency' needs to be defined legally, if not re-defined.

Indeed, pertinent in the context of the chapter is the Supreme Court's contention that, as a computer student, Ajith must be aware of how many people access internet portals. In a developing country where infrastructure cannot be taken for granted, the figure of 42 million (of a total of 1.2 billion) which constitutes a mere 3.7 percent (Worldstats), the internet-enabled communication remains a medium that has a very limited reach, perhaps among small sections of the society. 'But their influence on the Web matters' (Sruthijith 2005). This brings us to the third issue of whether the content of a personal blog that is theoretically meant for a small community, does indeed constitute defamation. The point to be borne in mind while discussing the power of blogosphere is that while there is indeed no barrier to entry 'to a world offering a nearly limitless audience', the truth is that the entry does not automatically 'guarantee' a vast audience (Hewitt 2005: 105). If indeed a correlation can be made to the 'real' world, would not a blog catering to a group of friends, be a private space even if it had a presence in the virtual world? If the analogy could be extended further, utterances in a blog are perhaps akin to making pronouncements in the living room of one's home with windows open for a passer-by to hear what is said.

Even if the blogger indeed has expressed 'great ideas' unless 'disseminated or syndicated' to a large audience, the ideas reach very few people (Beecher 2005: 72). Not only does blogosphere remain insular, but also is extremely transient. Many bloggers tire and abandon the effort in course of time (Hewitt 2005: 106). The internet, although it has the potential, does not hold everything forever and ever (Lovink 2007: 33). The mainstream media, especially the press, scores in the 'relationship of trust established between the reader and a "newspaper of record"' (Rundle 2005: 96). Most often, it is the threat of legal action that draws attention to comments contained in blogs and online communities, with large sections of the population generally being indifferent to it. Blogs not only create their secluded networks but are also at the same time 'public' and 'private', 'characterised by a culture of desired affiliation' (Lovink 2007: 2). As Barlow points out, what the blogs do is, 'carry debate to a new venue, but there is nothing revolutionary in what the blogs are doing' (2008: 5).

In this context, yet another significant issue is how culpable are those online publications that allow readers to vent their ire in their columns. For instance, every time *The New Indian Express* carried any report on the ethnic issue in Sri Lanka, the comments online spewed venom against one or the other party involved in the conflict, or still worse on those who participated in the online discussions. While much of this goes on under fictitious names, it is not clear who, if any, should be held responsible for defamation and hurting the sentiments of readers at large.

In almost all the cases, lone bloggers have been targets of legal proceedings by business houses or powerful organisations, leaving no option but for most bloggers to compromise. The predicament is best summed up by 'Mediaah' blogger Maheshwari, when he stated in his last post, 'As a solo performer, I don't have the time, energies and monies to fight a biggie'. As Sevanti Ninan wrote, the price of free speech is 'at the very least' lawyer's fees (2005). Similarly, rationalising the decision of blogger Kunte to retract his comments on Barkha Dutt, one blogger wrote:

> I think he has taken the right decision to take down the blog post because he wanted to make a point and he made it and now he is getting ample coverage. Had he been sued by Barkha Dutt and company (*sic*) he would

have had to bear the cost unnecessarily, unless of course there were people to help him out or if he himself had enough resources. 'Big-shot journalists' like Ms Barkha Dutt wouldn't have to spend from her own pocket because the TV channel would take care of the entire hassle while she carried on with her routine job. (Writing Cave 2009)

Conclusion

While the tightening of measures to protect copyright and prevent online frauds have been lauded, bloggers have expressed dismay over the lack of discussion over the provisions of the IT Act. Interestingly, the mainstream media has remained indifferent to the issue and most bloggers who have commented have based their comments on the information made available by online groups and communities. The power granted by the Act to the police, to intercept emails, mobile text messages and conversations in order to investigate any offence, even non-cognisable offences and block any website in the name of the national interest, has raised concerns regarding privacy and seems at best to reflect the State's 'bewilderment' and 'fear' of a technology that is new (Baron 2008: 3). In light of some past incidents when the Chief Executive Officer of Bazee. com was arrested in 2004 for putting on sale a video clipping involving students of the Delhi Public School and Blogspot blogs being blocked in 2006 as some blogs contained 'inflammatory' material, such concerns cannot be dismissed. Indeed, one suggestion has been the setting up of the 'National Netizen's Rights Commission' which could be developed on the lines of the National Human Rights Commission (Naavi's portal on Indian cyber law).

The plethora of discussion on cyber crime, electronic frauds and the legal and executive efforts to control and pre-empt these crimes are no doubt necessary, but what is of concern to those who use information technology as a tool of communication, is that law makers and upholders in India seem to have little grasp of the technological features of the medium. If indeed 'medium is the message', information technologies that spawn newer and newer forms of communication, call for an understanding of the platforms and cannot always be treated in the context of earlier media. A solution to the problem may perhaps lie in the users of information technologies evolving their own codes of ethics that

241

allow them to use the technologies as a refreshing source of information and communication, while at the same time staying on the right side of the law of the land. The issue assumes significance when considered in the light of the phenomenal advancement of technologies that empower more and more of the young in the era of globalisation.

Endnotes

1. See Glaser (2005) for a discussion on how media criticism is yet to take root in the sub-continent.
2. Bentley et al. define 'citizen journalism' as a 'form of media that involves moderated reader participation. Citizen-based media generally starts as web-based publications, but one of the long-term strategies is to develop a "best of" print edition that ultimately serves as the publication's revenue source.' (2007: 240).
3. But interestingly, as the IIPM issue dominated blogosphere, hitherto unknown information about the institute came to light or as Sruthijit claims, 'Bloggers have discovered in a week more than what a mainstream reporter may have in a month.' It was reportedly revealed that IIPM's office address in Toronto was fictitious and the qualifications of IIPM founder Malay Chaudhri were under suspect (Sruthijith 2005).

References

Baron, N.S. 2008. *Always on*. London: Oxford University Press.

Barlow, A. 2008. *Blogging America: The new public sphere*. London: Praeger.

Beecher, E. 2005. 'The end of serious journalism?', in Jonathan Mills (ed.), *Barons to bloggers: confronting media power*, pp. 65–74. Melbourne: The Miegunyah Press.

Bentley, C., Brian Hamman, Jeremy Littau, Hans Meyer, Brendan Watson and Beth Walsh. 2007. 'Citizen journalism: a case study', in Mark Tremayne (ed.), *Blogging, citizenship and future of the media*, pp. 239–259. New York: Routledge.

Bruns, A. 2005. *Gatewatching: Collaborative online news production*. New York: Peter Lang.

Carroll, B. and Bob Frank. 2007. 'Blogs without borders: international legal jurisdiction issues facing bloggers', in Mark Tremayne (ed.), *Blogging, citizenship and future of the media*, pp. 205–223. New York: Routledge.

Chandni. 2009. 'You disappoint me Barkha Dutt', *Bohemian Rhapsody*. Available online at http://chandni.wordpress.com/2009/01/31/you-disappoint-me-barkha-dutt/ (downloaded on 28.04.2009)

Freedom in Indian Blogosphere

Chakrabarti, S. 2008. *Indian Express*. 'We the pupil'. Available online at http://www.indianexpress.com/news/We-the-pupil/394940 (downloaded on 27.04.2009).

Cooper, S.D. 2006. *Watching the Watchdog: Bloggers as the Fifth Estate*. Spokane, Washington: Marquette Books.

Dancewithshadows.com. 2005. 'Mediaah shuts shop – again'. Available online at http://www.dancewithshadows.com/media/mediaah-to-shut-down.asp (downloaded on 12.02.2010).

Gauravonomics blog. 2009. 'Shiv Sena's Orkut campaign: The limits to freedom of expression in an intolerant India'. Available online at http://www.gauravonomics.com/blog/shiv-senas-orkut-campaign-the-limits-to-freedom-of-expression-in-an-intolerant-india/ (downloaded on 12.02.2010).

Gauravonomics.com. Available online at http://www.gauravonomics.com/blog/

Glaser, Mark. 2005. 'Indian media blog shuts down after legal threat from Times of India', *Online Journalism Review*, 15 March. Available online at http://ojr.org/ojr/stories/050315glaser/print.htm (downloaded on 06.01.09).

Hendrickson, L. 2007. 'Press protection in the Blogosphere: applying a functional definition of "press" to news web logs', in Mark Tremayne (ed.), *Blogging, citizenship and future of the media*, pp. 187–203. New York: Routledge.

Hewitt, H. 2005. *Blog: understanding the information reformation that's changing your world*. Tennessee: Nelson books.

The Hindu. 2006. 'Blogs in India set for a new landmark'. 14 November. Available online at http://www.hindu.com/2006/11/14/stories/2006111403801902.htm (downloaded on 25.06.2009).

Thehoot.org. 2009. 'Barkha versus blogger'. Available online at http://www.thehoot.org/web/home/story.php?storyid=3629&mod=1&pg=1&sectionId=6 (downloaded on 12.02.2010).

Karunakaran, B. 2009. 'Why Barkha Dutt should walk the talk?', *Countercurrents.org*, 30 January. Available online at http://www.countercurrents.org/print.html (downloaded on 28.04.2009).

Kline, D. and Dan Burstein. 2005. *Blog: how the newest media revolution is changing politics, business and culture*. New York: CDS books.

Knobel, L. 2005. 'Nullius in verba: navigating through the new media democracy', in Jonathan Mills (ed.), *Barons to bloggers: confronting media power*, pp. 37–63. Melbourne: The Miegunyah Press.

Lenhart, A. and Susannah Fox. 2006. 'Bloggers: a portrait of the internet's new storytellers'. *Pew Internet and American Life Project*, 19 July. Available online at http://www.pewinternet.org/pdfs/PIP%20Bloggers%20Report%20July%2019%202006.pdf (downloaded on 20.08.2006).

Lovink, G. 2007. *Zero comments: Blogging and critical internet culture*. Routledge: London.

Media editor. 2005. 'Mediaah shuts shop – again', *dancewithshadows.com*. Available online at http://www.dancewithshadows.com/media/mediaah-to-shut-down. asp (downloaded on 06.01.2009).

Mediavidea. 2009. 'A simple guide to Internet and cyberlaws in India'. Available online at http://mediavidea.blogspot.com/2009/01/simpleguide-to-internet-an... (downloaded on 29.04. 2009).

Meraz, S. 2007. 'Analyzing political conversation on the Howard Dean candidate blog', in Mark Tremayne (ed.), *Blogging, citizenship and future of the media*, pp. 59–81. New York: Routledge.

Mills, J. 2005. 'Preface', in Jonathan Mills (ed.), *Barons to bloggers: confronting media power*, pp. 1–6. Melbourne: The Miegunyah Press.

Naavi's portal on Indian cyberlaw. 'Information Technology Act 2000 amendment details unveiled'. Available online at http://www.naavi.org/cl_editorial_08/ edit_dec_30_itaa_analysis_6_privacy_2.htm (downloaded on 24.05.2009).

Ninan, S. 2005. 'Stand up for free speech', *Savemediaah.blogspot.com*, 14 March. Available online at http://savemediaah.blogspot.com/2005/03/sevanti-ninan-writes-abo... (downloaded on 06.01.2009).

———. 2009. 'Giving in to prior restraint', *Thehoot.org*, 8 June. Available online at http://www.thehoot.org/web/home/story.php?storyid=3895&mod=1... (downloaded on 09.06.2009).

Online Journalism Review. Available online at http://www.ojr.org/ojr/stories/ 050315glaser/ (downloaded on 27.04.2009).

Papacharissi, Z. 2007. 'Audiences as media producers: content analysis of 260 blogs', in Mark Tremayne (ed.), *Blogging, citizenship and the future of the media*, pp. 21–37. New York: Routledge.

Pramod, H. 2009. 'Freedom of expression under threat', *IT Examiner.com*. Available at http://www.itexaminer.com/freedom-of-expression-under-threat.aspx (downloaded on 12.02.2010).

Rosen, J. 2005. 'Each nation its own press', in Jonathan Mills (ed.), *Barons to bloggers: confronting media power*, pp. 21–35. Melbourne: the Miegunyah Press.

Rundle, G. 2005. 'Frontier tales: the hype and the reality of the online transformation of news', in Jonathan Mills (ed.), *Barons to bloggers: confronting media power*, pp. 88–101. Melbourne: The Miegunyah Press.

Singh, P. 2008a. 'A simple guide to biggest moments in Indian blogging history', Mediavidea.com. Available online at http://mediavidea.blogspot.com/2008_ 12_21_archive.html (downloaded on 12.02.2010).

———. 2008b. 'Online journalism India: moblogging is citizen journalism in India.' Available online at http://blogs.journalism.co.uk/editors/2008/02/27/ online-journalism-i... (downloaded on 24.04.2009).

Sruthijith, K.K. 2005. 'Can bloggers take on the role of public regulators?' *DNA*, Mumbai, 17 October. Available online at http://dnaindia.com/report. asp?NewsID=6136&CatID=5 (downloaded on 06.01.2009).

Tremayne, M. 2007a. 'Introduction: Examining the blog-media relationship', in Mark Tremayne (ed.), *Blogging, citizenship and future of the media*, pp. vii–xiii. New York: Routledge.

Tremayne, M. 2007b. 'Harnessing the active audience', in Mark Tremayne (ed.), *Blogging, citizenship and future of the media*, pp. 261–271. New York: Routledge.

Vantage point. 'What does NDTV's silence mean?', *Gauravsabnis.blogspot.com*. Available online at http://gauravsabnis.blogspot.com/2009/01/what-does-ndtvs-silence... (downloaded on 27.04.2009).

Wikipedia. Available online at http://en.wikipedia.org/wiki/The_Indian_Institute_of_Planning_and_Management (downloaded on 23.01.2009).

Worldstats. 'India: Internet usage stats and telecommunications market report'. Available online at http://www.internetworldstats.com/asia/in.htm (downloaded on 25.04.2009).

Writing Cave. 2009. 'Barkha Dutt forces a blogger to take down blog post and apologise'. Available online at http://www.writingcave.com/barkha-dutt-forces-a-blogger-to-take-down-blog-post-and-apologize/ (downloaded on 12.02.2010).

Chapter 12

Television Policy in India

An Unfulfilled Agenda

Usha M. Rodrigues

Introduction

On 26 November 2008, when India's commercial capital, Mumbai, was taken hostage by terrorists, viewers from all over the world watched the drama unfold on their television sets and/or on their personal computers via live feeds provided by a number of 24×7 Indian news channels. Scores of reporters took turns to provide a blow-by-blow account of what was happening at the three main spots of attack in Mumbai—Taj Mahal Hotel, Trident Oberoi Hotel and the Jewish Centre. In the aftermath of the coverage, some criticised the 24-hour coverage for being sensational and excessive, but it was the coverage that kept people informed and, to some extent, secure in the knowledge that they knew everything that was happening in Mumbai, which was made possible by the coverage of the Indian television channels' reporters. Compared to the 1984 coverage of the assassination of then Prime Minister, Indira Gandhi, by her own security guards, when the Indian population depended on UK's BBC radio feeds to confirm the rumours of the prime minister's murder, Indian television has come a long way. In fact, some might say it has reached the other end of the spectrum where now Indian citizens are bombarded with images of what is happening on the ground, sometimes resulting in creating chaos and maniac panic in the minds of those watching.

Whether live coverage of bloody events is good or bad is a moot point. The fact, however, remains that Indian viewers now, more than ever, have access to a number of television channels including a number of 24×7 news channels vying for their eye balls. The numbers cannot be more of a contrast than this—when in 1991, most Indians with a television set could access one or two channels (one national and one regional) broadcast by the monopolistic public service broadcaster, Doordarshan. Today, according to an estimate, there are nearly 450 television channels available to a cable and satellite television subscriber in India (Indiantelevision.com 2009a), catering to around 500 million[1] viewers in India (Indiantelevision.com 2008a). The number of cable and satellite homes in India is around 67 per cent[2] of the total number of homes with access to television (Indiantelevision.com 2008b). Doordarshan no longer has a monopoly in the Indian television market, albeit it remains a significant player with an extensive network of channels and nearly 90 per cent reach in the country. However, it is the private and foreign-owned channels which have achieved significant popularity, particularly with urban viewers. As a result, the Indian television software industry too has grown and is estimated to be around Rs 30 billion (AU$ 1 billion) in 2009–10 (Indiantelevision.com 2008c).

With the multiplication of television channels and their content in the past two decades, it has became significant to realise that television, in India, has a dual role in disseminating information to all segments of the population, particularly the poor and the disadvantaged, while entertaining others, particularly the middle class. The expansion of private and foreign television in India can be seen as a move towards democracy and a choice for the individual rather than abandoning the support for the 'state' controlled public service broadcaster—Doordarshan—in the 1990s. Similarly, the subsequent autonomy granted to Doordarshan along with All India Radio under the aegis of Broadcasting Corporation of India (Prasar Bharati) in 1997 also points to a positive impact of globalisation and privatisation of Indian television (Rodrigues 1998 and 2005). However, questions remain whether the Government of India has done enough to guide this prosperous and popular industry, including the public service broadcaster, to meet the development goals of the television as envisaged in 1959, when television was launched in India. The criticism of Indian television industry being hijacked by the middle class for their own needs still resonates among some critics.

In this discussion about the Indian government's television policy post 1991, it is essential to look at historical events which shaped the mindset of policy makers in the past two decades. It is also important to understand why it took so long for the government to lay down some parameters and provide an appropriate legal framework for the burgeoning cable and satellite industry and allow private and foreign sectors to operate in India without official sanction. The Indian government has been criticised for making ad-hoc decisions and appointing committee after committee to make recommendations, only to shelve their reports without much action. This chapter argues that this openness to cultural invasion from the skies was part of the larger economic policy of 'liberalisation' adopted by the Indian government since 1991. Although, at the time of writing this chapter, India still did not have a comprehensive television policy or a law governing all aspects of the broadcast industry, this discussion critically examines the 'catalyst' role television can still play in this developing nation. This is significant considering the commercial imperative for the Indian public service broadcaster and the severe competitive conditions in the television industry vis-à-vis the entry of private and foreign media, which, some contend, has skewed television programming towards entertainment.

Historical events that shaped Indian television policy

After attaining independence from British colonial rule in 1947, the Indian government had a massive task ahead of uplifting the lives of half its population out of a subsistence existence (The World Bank 1997). The policy makers under the stewardship of then Prime Minister, Jawaharlal Nehru, were convinced that the task of wealth generation via industrialisation could not be left to the private sector, which might spend resources on the production of consumer goods rather than build infrastructure required in the country. Therefore, the government at that time adopted the principle of a mixed national economy and a top down model (McDowell 1997; Parekh 1995). As a result, television, when launched in 1959, was kept within the aegis of the nationalised All India Radio network and the private sector was not allowed in the broadcast media.

The Indian government at the time was influenced by the arguments presented by scholars such as Wilbur Schramm, Daniel Lerner and Everett Rogers from the last century to point out that yet another opportunity was being lost to assist the economically disadvantaged groups in India. Schramm's (1964) argument, in *Mass Media and National Development*, also influenced many governments in developing countries. According to Schramm, a Third World nation could facilitate development by expanding the mass media, at least to the extent that information was a vital ingredient in moving a nation towards development (in Singhal and Rogers 1989).

> If sufficient information is available, then it contributes to a spiral of development activity. It helps farmers to improve methods and produce more. It also helps some of the excess manpower on the farms to transfer to other more productive jobs. More productivity leads to improved income, to widening consuming habits, to increased economic activity within the village (such as shops and restaurants), to new appetites for consumer goods, to a seeking after new opportunities, and so on in a chain of related development. (Schramm 1964: 49)

Subsequently, Rogers (1969) developed the 'diffusion model' to explain the communication process where he argued that mass media's influence manifested in a two-step flow—higher status members of a group, who were more exposed to media messages and spread those messages to others. 'Mass media communication is more important in changing cognitions (i.e., in increasing knowledge of ideas), whereas interpersonal communication is more likely to cause attitude change' (Rogers 1969: 14). However, modernisation theory has been criticised for generating inequality and underdevelopment by accelerating 'the westernised elite structures or urbanisation' (Servaes and Malikhao 2003: 4).

As a result, during the 1950s and 1960s, the broadcast media in India was seen as a catalyst and vehicle for social change and development. The government wanted to use the broadcast media to further development through health, agricultural and educational programming. Over the years, television expanded from Delhi (India's capital) to other cities and to some rural communities as part of the educational and development experiment. However, critics say that the government's monopoly in broadcast media was either underutilised (NAMEDIA 1986; Singhal and Rogers 2001) or abused (Ninan 1998; Verghese 1978). The unease with the ruling party's control of the broadcast media between 1960 and 1990, and the resultant unmet responsibility caused many to criticise the government over its broadcasting policies. As early as 1966, a government appointed committee noted that 'suspicion of official information has deepened in India because of an incorrect, even improper, use of media for personalised publicity and an undue accent on achievements' (Ninan 1998: 4). The concern over misuse of broadcast media by the ruling party during the state of Emergency in 1975 was so great that a 'White paper on the Misuse of the Mass Media during the Emergency' in 1978 foreshadowed a role for commercialisation in attaining autonomy for the broadcast media. In 1985, the P.C. Joshi report titled *An Indian Personality for Television*, examined the role of Doordarshan as a public service broadcaster and concluded that 'more creative approaches were necessary to genuinely fulfil the potential of television in an illiterate, information-starved country like India' (Gupta 1998: 36). The report warned against the middle class monopolising this medium, and recommended the use of low-cost production equipment to address specific local needs in local languages (Johnson 2000). 'It (the report) reiterated the need for community viewing so that larger numbers of people could be reached via socially conscious programming' (Gupta 1998: 36).

Meanwhile, on the economic front, many analysts were dissatisfied with the pace of industrialisation between 1960 and 1990, blaming the two wars with Pakistan and China in the 1960s and a complex system of restrictions on private enterprise growth (Crook 1997; Naik 1999). India's gross domestic product (GDP), which came to be known as 'Hindu rate of growth' of a little under 4 per cent a year, was much less than other Asian countries (Crook 1997). As a result, in 1991, there was a break away from a sheltered economy to embrace the principles of a liberal economy when the government announced the New Economic Policy (McDowell 1997). Bardhan (in McDowell) argues that the development policies did not succeed as much as expected because 'resources were siphoned off from the central investment projects in which the developmental state should have been engaged and used to provide benefits to these (a coalition of dominant proprietary classes) groups' (McDowell 1997: 69). The trigger for the launch of New Economic Policy in 1991, which included the New Industrial Policy, was a serious foreign debt crisis which led to India borrowing substantial amounts of money from the International Monetary Fund (IMF) to satisfy the loan conditions by opening up Indian markets to foreign competition and foreign investment. Those in favour of liberalisation policies argued that the India economy was shackled by a complex set of government controls, whereas, critics said a greater role for market processes would intensify existing socio-economic inequalities and make the Indian economy more dependent on foreign capital (Ghosh 1998: 324–26). Consequently, as part of this new policy of economic openness, the government looked the other way, when in the early 1990s, satellite channels started beaming their programmes into the country from foreign soil. The Indian government ignored the sprawling of cable networks broadcasting foreign, in effect illegal, television signals to Indian viewers (Rodrigues 1998). The non-enforcement of the policy of maintaining Doordarshan's monopoly in the country and allowing unfettered growth of private and foreign television media was part of the new economic policy of liberalisation.

At first, the expansion of cable networks was in the form of cable operators connecting neighbourhood television sets to a VCR so that they could watch three-to-four movies a day at a fractional cost via cable subscription. This cable expansion received a huge impetus when satellite channels came on to the horizon in 1990–91. The Gulf War and subsequent events at international level sparked sufficient interest among Indian viewers to prompt CNN, BBC and STAR TV to start beaming their channels into the country as part of their Asian footprints. Within a decade and a half, the penetration of cable and satellite television had reached unimaginable levels. The mood of liberalisation in the country in the early 1990s meant that no action was taken to regulate or direct the expansion of cable and satellite television in India. In legal terms, the Indian Telegraph Act, 1885, governed the cable operation where there was no prohibition on receiving a television signal, but laying cables in public property was prohibited, and distribution of broadcast signals was the government's monopoly. The Act required the cable operator to apply for a licence with which most of them did not comply (Rahim 1994:15).

Supreme Court of India criticises government for lack of policy

Doordarshan, in the face of serious competition from private and foreign television channels, began localising its programmes to lure increasing number of Indian viewers and its purse-string holder—the Information and Broadcasting Ministry—decided to defend the public service broadcaster's advertising revenue by aggressively competing for sports and entertainment events, resulting in a significant court case. In a landmark judgement in the Union of India versus the Cricket Association of Bengal case in February 1995, the Supreme Court of India held that 'the airwaves are public property and a monopoly over broadcasting whether by the government or anybody else was inconsistent with the citizen's right to free speech' (IPAN Online 1997). The highest court in the land recommended that an autonomous corporation be established to oversee the workings of All India Radio and Doordarshan. The court ordered the government to chart out an appropriate television policy for the country and severely criticised the outdated 1885 Act, which it said was completely inadequate to deal with important media like TV and radio. '... this is the result of law in this country not keeping pace with technological advance,' the Supreme Court pointed out (Ibid.).

In the wake of the court order, the government appointed two committees to draw up the broadcasting policy and passed the Cable Television Networks (Regulation) Act 1995,[3] making it mandatory for a cable operator to be registered with the post office for a small fee. In 1997, the Indian Broadcasting Bill was introduced in Parliament. The Broadcasting Bill 1997, which envisaged the creation of an independent authority to be known as The Broadcast Authority of India, raised people's expectations about the government facilitating and regulating broadcasting services in India (Broadcasting Bill 1997). However, the Bill never became an Act, as political consensus on the far reaching consequences of the Bill could not be reached (Gupta 1998; Indiantelevision.com 1998 and 1999).

As per the Supreme Court of India's orders, the government finally set up an independent board to oversee the functioning of the two public service broadcasters. The granting of autonomy to Doordarshan and All India Radio, which had gone through a long history of no-shows since its first call in 1977, finally became a reality when the Prasar Bharati Act 1990 was ratified in 1997, creating the Broadcasting Corporation. Meanwhile, the Indian government gradually eased legal restrictions on private and foreign broadcasters, allowing them to uplink their channels from Indian shores. At first, in June 1998, the Indian government passed a legislation allowing Indian broadcasters to uplink live from Indian shores, using the overseas communications carrier VSNL, capping foreign investment in Indian broadcast companies at 20 per cent (*Asia Pulse* 1998; Indiantelevision.com 1998). Then, on 25 July 2000, the government issued guidelines to further liberalise its uplinking policies and permit Indian private companies to set up uplinking hub/ teleports for hiring out to others. The new policy allowed uplinking of any television channel from India, including those with 49 per cent foreign equity, to both Indian and foreign satellites (Indiantelevision. com 2000). Meanwhile, in August 2001, the government made another attempt to regulate the television industry by introducing another Bill which sought 'to provide a combined regulatory structure for the information technology, telecom and broadcasting sectors' (*Business Line* 2001). The Convergence Bill 2001, which would pave the way for the establishment of the Communications Commission of India (CCI), was envisaged as a 'super regulator' and licence granter in the telephone, information technology and broadcasting industries, including all aspects of convergence in these services (*Business Line* 2001). However, industry players expressed concerns about the proposed Ministry. They feared the law would become a maze of super bureaucracy (*The Tribune* 2001).

In 2002, the Indian government made another attempt to control the burgeoning cable and satellite industry by mandating that all cable channels be received via a set-top box in all subscribing homes under the Conditional Access System (CAS). This was expected to create a transparent system and compel people to pay for what they watched. The system was never fully implemented and by March 2004, the experiment with CAS was abandoned (Sinclair 2005). In 2006, the government again tried to build a consensus on regulating the broadcasting industry by introducing a revised Broadcast Bill (from 1997). But, the bill ran into controversies because it contained clauses which would have allowed the government to take over the management of any broadcasting company in specific circumstances (Indiantelevision.com 2006b).

Competition and commercialisation

By 2008–09, India had nearly 450 channels vying for the eyeballs of Indian viewers. It is by far one of the most competitive environments for a television industry in the world, but it still has room to grow further because of the sheer size of the Indian population. As a result of the intensification of competition among commercial and, for that matter, the public service broadcaster network (Doordarshan), the channels are trying a number of formulas to maintain and increase their audience numbers. Some of the strategies include, launching specialised programmes for niche audiences, one long-story-a-day format when covering significant events, generating conflict on screen to entertain the audience during serious public interest debates, editorialising news coverage and promoting a handful of journalists as stars/icons on a channel. Nupur Basu (2009), former journalist from NDTV and other media critics believe these strategies have resulted in 'trivialisation' and 'sensationalisation' of news, whereby media today is facing 'credibility crisis because people don't believe in the media anymore'. Basu blames the 24-hour news format for the fall in standards, where channels are busy filling on-air time, rather than focusing on the substances of stories. Also, 'media and boardroom decisions have been taken that they will have 2–3 stars...which is following the American model instead of the British model—Fox way—promo them, show them, while the rest can be show horses' (Ibid.).

Serious concerns have been raised about television channels and their presenters who went over-board when covering the Mumbai terror attacks, calling for immediate retribution and revenge on a neighbouring country for their alleged involvement in the attack, almost sending the country to war. 'A responsible journalist presents the news and analyses the news, presents all sides... not provoke or make the audience angry' (Basu 2009). Sevanti Ninan (2009), media commentator, agrees, 'what they are trying to do is to take news away from traditional definition of news into reality show... it is broadening the news market by bringing new less educated audiences into the market.'

However, Arindam Sengupta, Executive Editor of *The Times of India*, says that television industry had learnt a number of valuable lessons from their mistakes during their coverage of Mumbai terror attacks. He said:

> ...any medium requires time to mature, to learn to nuance things, to get the right pitch, tone of coverage as time goes by. Right now there is frantic

competition, the sector hasn't evolved its own codes of ethics, of journalistic propriety, and instances like this can actually become opportunities for evolving all of those... Second, 26/11—60 hours of coverage is a very very long time—how do you do it? The problem I felt about television was it didn't rise to the occasion. There would be about one hour of live coverage where something would happen, say an explosion or somebody comes out of a hotel, and that was played again and again and again...whilst television to some extend irritated a lot of people, it also brought world attention on this heinous crime. It brought recognition of the fact that India was actually a target of these kinds of terrorist attacks, and helped in bringing national opinion together. (Sengupta 2009)

Although the success formula for television seems to be to offer viewers 'short, sharp and sensational' news coverage in the belief that otherwise viewers will switch to another channel, according to Karan Thapar, a veteran television show host, comments that:

...I personally think that the Indian channels are wrong, that in fact viewers are intelligent, but they don't miss what they don't have...Were you to give them good sensible BBC style informed, illuminating channel with good programs, you'll find that people will be quite happy to watch for longer and concentrate more. (Thapar 2009)

Thapar blames lack of education and hard work on the part of journalists and provision of resources on the part of employers, for the slipping standards.

Research takes time, it costs money. Making phone calls, meeting people, travelling, digging up documents, understanding them and labouring over them, then working out the story...it takes time and money. The net result is this populist dumbing down 'kichidi' (mix) that you throw at people, and the explanation of this laziness is that Indian audiences do not have a concentration span. (Thapar 2009)

Meanwhile, following an outcry over media's live coverage of November 2008 Mumbai terror attacks, the Indian government is considering amending the Cable Television Network Regulation (Amendment) Act, to make it mandatory for television channels to carry authorised video footage released by the government alone, during a designated emergency situation (Dhawan 2008). However, the industry peak body News Broadcasters' Association is keen to adopt a self-regulatory emergency protocol for coverage of a conflict situation (Joshua 2008).

Critics see governments' reaction to the Mumbai terror attack coverage as knee-jerk reaction, which does not take into consideration its own failings on the security front where governments and security forces at various levels failed to coordinate its own efforts and provide media with a one-stop shop where they were briefed by one person. The local authorities also failed to cordon-off sensitive and dangerous areas from television crew.

> Government wants to add amendments to the Cable Act so that 400 magistrates from each district will decide what a cable broadcaster can broadcast or not, not only the terrorist acts, but also religious and gender issues, social issues of rape…if you look at the Cable Act, if you look at the program code, the Act works in tandem with the program code…in essence, all amendments are in the program code, so really no change is required. What really is needed that the government regulates itself, issues directions to the media, they could have cordoned off the area, they could have told the media where to go, this is our briefing person, you will take developments from him, you will use that information, and not anything else. (Ninan 2009)

Media experts agree that the government needs to provide a regulatory framework for the burgeoning television industry, by setting up a body similar to the 'Press Council of India' (for print media) to hear viewers' complaints against miscreants. Ninan (2009) says there is need for basic regulation of content on television including times when children's programmes can be broadcast, after-hours time slots, advertisements of products. Most of the draconian suggestions made by the government, however, amount to censorship, instead of sensible recommendations.

Indian population's needs

India is the second largest country in the world, with a diverse, multi-religious and multi-lingual population. Historian E.P. Thompson (in Sen 1997) describes the Indian diversity as: 'All the convergent influences of the world run through this society. Hindu, Muslim, Christian, secular, Stalinist, Gandhian. There is not a thought that is being thought in the West or East that is not active in some Indian mind.'

Similarly some philosophers see India as 'two Indias'—divided between two distinct segments of populations with varying socio-economic realities. Indian political scientist Kothari (1988 and 1993) identifies these 'two Indias' as the ever growing middle class and the poor, those who have not yet benefited from the country's recent prosperity. The former Indian President K.R. Narayanan (2000) alludes to this socio-economic divide in India:

> We have one of the world's largest reservoirs of technical personnel, but also the world's largest number of illiterates; the world's largest middle class; but also the largest number of people below the poverty line; and the largest number of children suffering from malnutrition. Our giant factories rise from out of squalor; our satellite (antennas) shoot up from the midst of the hovels of the poor. Not surprisingly, there is sullen resentment among the masses against their condition erupting often in violent forms in several parts of the country. It has been accompanied by great regional and social inequalities.

To this extent if it is assumed that media and, in this discussion television, with its tele-visual capacity, can be utilised as the bearer of news and information so that it contributes, in Schramm's (1964: 49) words, 'to a spiral of development activity', assisting people in improving methods and productivity, transferring excess manpower to 'other more productive jobs', 'to increased economic activity' and to seek 'new opportunities'. The Indian government's broadcast policy in 1959 had assumed this 'catalyst' role for television during its inception in 1959. In 2008, with its exponential growth and pre-dominance of a for-profit agenda, the questions remain: Is television meeting its original aim of assisting all Indians? Is it playing the role of a 'catalyst' for the disadvantaged groups in the country? This is significant considering there are about 300–350 million people (of the more than one billion population in 2001), who have remained untouched by the recent economic growth in the country (Asian Development Bank 2002). The government has to protect the interests of these 'two Indias'[4] when formulating its broadcast media policy, making sure that the country has a vibrant broadcasting industry to meet the needs of the latter group.

Policy agenda

The Indian government's television policy to date can be summarised as:

- a monopoly for public service broadcasters between 1960–1990s to protect the population from private sector's commercial imperative;
- expansion of hardware around the country, building an extensive terrestrial broadcast network;
- neglect of quality programming fuelled by lack of competition in the television market;
- bureaucratic and ministerial control of the public service broadcaster, rendering it as a 'boring' and a 'government channel' in the eyes of the population;
- 'no action' strategy on the expansion of private and foreign television expansion in India since the 1990s;
- ad-hoc decisions since the 1990s, controlling the entry of global and local media players in the private section, but a lack of coherent policy on ownership of television networks, cable and satellite television's sprawl and the content broadcast by nearly 450 channels; and
- the development oriented agenda of television seems to be paid lip service by the public service broadcaster, but is lost in the commercial and entertainment world of television.

In 1995, the Supreme Court of India in a landmark judgement, directed the government of India to formulate a coherent policy on all aspects of the television industry. The mid-to-late 1990s saw a succession of activities in the form of changes in the Cable Act, granting of autonomy to All India Radio and Doordarshan and later (1998–2000–2003) allowing Indian and foreign television networks to uplink their services from Indian soil. However, on several fronts, the government did not convert its intentions to reality. Doubts remain about Prasar Bharati Board's independence and ability to function as an autonomous body since its constitution in 1997 (Bera 1999). The Broadcasting Bill tabled in Parliament in 1997 still needs to see the light of day, while the Convergence Bill 2001 (which incorporates regulation of the broadcasting industry) may never come to fruition.

Although many analysts have reservations about the commercialisation of public service broadcasting in India, the alternative to a government funded public sector is also seen as unpalatable. Under the new economic policy of liberalisation, the government has been determined to reduce the burden on the exchequer by reducing funding of non-essential activities. Whether public service broadcasting is an essential or non-essential activity is a moot point. Some analysts fear that liberalisation of broadcast policies in India will follow the American path 'where a handful of powerful media conglomerates dominate the entertainment software and hardware markets, while the Public Broadcasting Service languishes despite carrying some of the best programming' (Gupta 1998: 60). There are others who are critical of the need to raise commercial revenue by both Doordarshan and the private sector, sidelining the original aim of television as an education and development tool (Ibid.). According to Gupta, autonomy for Doordashan is not enough for formulation of telecasting policies in the country. She says that other policy guidelines are required to ensure that the flow of information, education and entertainment is really free, so that all citizens of India—the haves and have-nots—are empowered with knowledge, which in turn can ensure a true consensus culture which captures and represents the 'throbbing drama of Indian life today' (Ibid.: 60). To that end, the public service broadcasting has to meet the needs of the 'two Indias', if it is to distinguish itself from private and foreign competitors and remain relevant in the crowded multi-channel market. The Prasar Bharati Board, as the Public Service Broadcasting Review of 1999 suggests, also needs to concern itself with 'developing taste', by encouraging creativity and production of quality programming, thereby 'correcting market deficiencies' (Narayanamurthy 2000: 2).

As for private television channels, the government needs to put a balanced legal framework of regulation in place in the Indian market, where the broadcasting industry, along with its convergence with information technology and telecommunication, can grow for the benefit of its citizens. Whether it goes down the path of finally implementing The Broadcasting Bill of 1997 or The Convergence Bill of 2001, the bureaucracy it creates should not be an impediment to the growth of this significant industry and others. The government must provide a level playing field to all players, be it public service broadcasters or private television networks. As noted by several committees in India, there is a real need for plurality of voices and decentralisation in the broadcast industry, with a role for non-commercial and more community-based players such as universities, local governments, cooperative institutions or non-government organisations (Paswan 1996; Varadan 1991; Verghese 1978).

It is not that the Indian government does not have the power or control to regulate the private sector. It seems more a case of not wanting to, due to the dual-level need of the population from the broadcast media—education and entertainment. The dichotomy between the broadcast media meeting the needs of the underprivileged class and the middle class continues, making the government, in part, impotent. Similarly, the Prasar Bharati Review committee emphasises that All India Radio and Doordarshan must meet their charter as the public service broadcasters in India for all sections of the society; and yet reiterates the message that public broadcasting needs to be self-sufficient. 'Once the vision and framework of Prasar Bharati are clearly defined, then, within these, revenue maximisation should be a goal' (Narayanamurthy 2000: 3). Correspondingly, public service programmes focused on education and development messages do not have to be 'boring' and produced by the public service broadcasters alone. The burgeoning private sector can be co-opted into introducing competition in this genre of television programming. In Europe and elsewhere, commercial media has raised issues with providing public funding to public service broadcasters alone, even though they may be more inefficient than private media, in utilising these funds (Cox 2003), it is important to consider the role of the private sector in public service broadcasting. Jacka quotes Hartley in saying that, in this post-modern era, public service broadcasting has no claim to a special role in relation to education and democracy (Jacka 2003: 184).

> If, however, we see democracy as pluralized, as marked by new kinds of communities of identity, as a system in which the traditional public-private divide does not apply, and as a system in which there are no universal visions of the 'common good' but, rather, pragmatic and negotiated exchanges about ethical behaviour and ethically inspired courses of action, and modes in which such a diverse set of exchanges will occur. [Then] we will be open to the notion that ethical discourse can be present in many different kinds

and genres of media texts and in many different forms of media organisation. Jacka (2003: 183)

In this multi-channel digital environment, the broadcasting policy needs to take into account the pluralisation of society, pluralisation of spaces for citizen discourses and dismantling of traditional hierarchies of values and knowledge (Hartley in Jacka 2003: 187).

As for the role of television in the development of India, a return to the discussion of the modernisation theory is warranted, where Daniel Lerner (1958 in Singh 2003: 193), among others, has argued that modernity is 'primarily a state of mind—expectation of progress, propensity of growth, readiness to change'. In this case, popularity of television as a means of mass communication in India, then, can be used as a 'means of swift mobilization' (Rajagopal 2001: 11). Rajagopal uses the phenomenon of the spread of Hindu nationalism via the telecast of mythological soap operas on television to demonstrate television's power, as a means to mobilise the masses in India in late 1980s. However, he notes that the media alone cannot be credited for the rise of the Hindu nationalism movement. According to Rajagopal (2001: 32):

> ...the media neither cause nor reflect events, they participate in them. To an important extent, television, like the media in general, exteriorise and consolidate the social foundations of communication and representation, leading to a quicker, more efficient network of signs and messages, and in turn changing the context for social communication in general.

However, it can be asserted that television with its tele-visual capacity can be utilised to provide the message of modernisation and relevant information necessary for 'a spiral of development activity' (Schramm 1964: 49) to under-developed population of India. Of course, this public service broadcasting needs to go hand-in-hand with the grass roots reform of the social, economic and political systems prevailing in India. Johnson in 2000 noted that television is influencing the economic, social and political landscape and relationships of village life in India. 'Whether it is the messages portrayed or the mere presence of television, villagers' relationships, economic decisions, political awareness, participation, and worldview are being influenced by television' (Johnson 2000: 227).

There is a note of caution that must be added to this assertion. Johnson found that although the villagers' vocabulary had changed, their actions were still influenced by the age-old traditions of rural culture. As referred to earlier, a change at the grassroots in economic and political systems are necessary to change people's behaviour. Acknowledging the unproved power of the media, Stevenson notes that Schramm's words about the benefits of development or modernity: 'it is better to be well fed than be (sic) hungry, better to be a participant in one's country than isolated from it, and better to be educated than illiterate' (Stevenson 2003: 12). Emphasising that underdeveloped countries have underdeveloped communication systems, Schramm (1964: 249) notes that 'the band of economic scarcity around the world is also the band where literacy is lowest, where newspapers, radios, television receivers, and cinemas are least widely available, where newsprint is scarcest, where electrification and telecommunications lag, where children are least likely to be in school.'

Here, it is envisaged that the accessibility to television broadcast will be assisted by the accessibility to television production process, where local population is co-opted as participants and communicators in the process of development. Instead of top-down flow of ideas and information, the communication will be a two-way process where information is shared between communities via mass media. Hitherto, the question remains, will the Indian government regulate the television industry so that it benefits all of its potential audiences–be it the wealthy, the middle class, the poor or the marginalised? Or will it, once again, stifle the television industry with censorship, as was the case pre 1991 when the Indian government controlled the lone network of Doordarshan?

Endnotes

1. According to the Indian Readership Survey report released in November 2008, about 352.83 million viewers watch television at home, while 105.786 million watch television at their friends and neighbours' houses and 49 million watch on community sets (Indiantelevision.com 2008b).
2. According to the Indian Readership Survey report released in November 2008, there are about 100.38 million homes with television, of these 66.54 subscribe to one or more cable and satellite service (Indiantelevision.com 2008c).
3. See Cable Television Networks (Regulation) Act (1995).

4. The concept of 'two Indias' was first discussed by Kothari. According to Kothari, the 'two Indias' are: one that comprises the urban and rural elite, the big farmers, the industrialists, the bureaucrats, the executives and professionals and the intelligentsia; and the other, which is impoverished, malnourished, toiling day and night for survival including the poor, the untouchables, the tribals, the backward classes, the lower castes, and also a large section of the religious minorities and women (1988; 1993). According to Asian Development Bank (2002), 300–350 million people in India have not been touched by the 1990s rapid economic growth in the country.

References

Asian Development Bank. 2002. 'Monthly reports', March 2002. Available online at http://www.abdindia.org/janeco-02.htm (downloaded on 18.01.2005).

Asia Pulse. 1998. 'Indian government clears private satellite uplinking facility', Press Trust of India, 25 June. Available online at http://www.asiapulse.com. (downloaded on 13.01.2005).

Bera, A. 1999. 'Prasar Bharati: a victim of witch-hunting', *Ganashakti.com*, 6 June. Available online at http://www.ganashakti.com/old/1999/991206/nation.htm (downloaded on 19.02.2005).

Broadcasting Bill. 1997. 'The Broadcasting Bill 1997'. Available online at http://www.indiantelevision.com/indianbroadcast/legalreso/broadcast.htm (downloaded on 10.01.2005).

Business Line. 2001. 'Convergence Bill Tabled in Lok Sabha'. Available online at http://www.blonnet.com/businessline/2001/09/01/stories/14016840.htm (downloaded on 03.04.2005).

Cable Television Networks (Regulation) Act. 1995. 'The cable television networks rules, 1994', *Ministry of Information and Broadcasting, Government of India*, pp. 1–20. New Delhi: M/s Akashdeep Printers.

Cox, B. 2003. 'Four lectures on TV in the digital age', *Guardian*, media supplement 28 January; 4 February; 11 February; 28 February. Available online at http://www.guardian.com (downloaded on 11.09.2003).

Crook, C. 1997. 'India is changing fast, but not fast enough', *The Economist*, 2 February.

Dhawan, Himanshi. 2008. 'Law likely to regulate coverage', *The Times of India*, Chennai. 21 December, Front Page, p. 3. Available online at http://epaper.timesofindia.com/Repository/ml.asp?Ref=VE9JQ0gvMjAwOC8xMi8yMSMN BcjAwMzA1&Mode=HTML&Locale=english-skin-custom (downloaded on 22.12.2008).

Ghosh, J. 1998. 'Liberalization debates', in T.J. Byres (ed.), *The Indian economy: major debates since independence*, pp. 295–334. New Delhi: Oxford University Press.

Gupta, N. 1998. *Switching channels: ideologies of television in India.* New Delhi: Oxford University Press.

Indiantelevision.com. 1998. 'Swaraj and after'. Available online at http://www.indian television.com/newsletter/121098/briefs121098.htm (downloaded 12.01.2005).

———. 1999. 'Moves on broadcasting bill again'. Available online at http://www.indian television.com/newsletter/081199/bill081199.htm (downloaded 05.01.2005).

———. 2000. 'Guidelines for uplinking from India'. Available online at http://www.indiantelevision.com/indianbroadcast/legalreso/uplink.htm (downloaded 07.03.2005).

———. 2002. 'EnterMedia 2001 moots broadcaster-MSO promoted regulatory body', Special report. Available online at http://www.indiantelevison.com/special/y2k2/spenter.htm (downloaded on 04.04.2006).

———. 2003. 'News Channel uplinking guidelines issued'. Available online at http://indiantelevision.com/headlines/y2k3/mar/mar131.htm (downloaded on 27.03.2003).

———. 2005a. 'C&S penetration grows 53% to 61 million homes in 3 years: NRS 2005'. Available online at http://indiantelevision.com/mam/headlines/y2k5/june/junemam49.htm (downloaded on 09.06.2005).

———. 2005b. 'Indian TV ad spend to grow @ 14%: Pwc. frames 2005'. Available online at http://indiantelevision.com/headlines/y2k5/apr/apr34.htm (downloaded on 21.04.2005).

———. 2006a. '179 channels being uplinked from India: Dasmunsi'. Available online at http://www.indiantelevision.com/headlines/y2k6/mar/mar121 (downloaded on 04.04.2006).

———. 2006b. 'Draft broadcast bill: big brother wants to do more than just watch'. Available online at http://indiantelevision.com/special/y2k6/broadcast_bill-comment.htm (downloaded on 04.05.2006).

———. 2006c. '51.2 million C&S homes in India: IRS 2006'. Available online at http://www.indiantelevision.com/special/y2k6/nrs-report06.htm (downloaded on 16.07.2007).

———. 2008a. 'IRS 2008 R2: The lowdown on TV viewership', 5 November. Available online at http://www.indiantelevision.com/headlines/y2k8/nov/nov63.php (downloaded 15.12.2008).

———. 2008b. '66.54 million C&S homes in India: IRS', 8 November. Available online at http://www.indiantelevision.com/headlines/y2k8/nov/nov94.php (downloaded 15.12.2008).

———. 2008c. 'Going global is a key part of our TV content scale up plan', 8 September. Available online at http://www.indiantelevision.com/interviews/y2k8/executives/ajit_thakur.php (downloaded on 15.12.2008).

———. 2009a. '180 TV channels await government clearance', 26 February. Available online at http://www.indiantelevision.com/headlines/y2k9/feb/feb245.php (downloaded on 28.05.2009).

IPAN Online. 1997. 'Overview: Indian Broadcast Bill on the anvil'. Available online at http://www.ipan.com/reviews/archives/brd0397.htm (downloaded on 10.01.2005).

Jacka, E. 2003. 'Democracy as defeat: the impotence of arguments for public-service broadcasting', *Television and New Media*, 4(2):177–91.

Johnson, K. 2000. *Television and social change in rural India.* New Delhi: Sage Publications.

Joshua, Anita. 2008. 'Emergency protocol for news channels', *The Hindu.* 19 December. Available online at http://www.hinduonnet.com/mag/2008/12/21/stories/2008122150060100.htm. (downloaded on 22.12.2008).

Kothari, R. 1988. 'Class and communalism in India', *Economic and Political Weekly*, 23 (49): 2589–92.

———. 1993. *Human consciousness and the amnesia of development.* London: Zed Books Ltd.

McDonald, H. 1994. *An Australian correspondent abroad: two lectures on India and Asia in transition*, School of Politics. Victoria: La Trobe University.

Naik, S.D. 1999. 'India: the country goes global', *Businessline, The Hindu,* 21 December.

NAMEDIA. 1986. *A vision for Indian television.* New Delhi: Media Foundation of the Non-aligned.

Narayanamurthy, N.R. 2000. *Prasar Bharati review committee,* Ministry of Information and Broadcasting, National Informatics Centre. Available online at http://mib.nic.in/informationb/AUTONOMOUS/nicpart/pbintro.html (downloaded on 06.01.2005).

Narayanan, K.R. 2000. 'Address to the nation by the president on the eve of Republic Day'. *M2 Presswire Coventry,* 26 January. Available online at http://www.indianembassy.org/special/cabinet/president/RDspeech2000.htm. (downloaded on 10.01.2005).

Ninan, Sevanthi. 1998. 'History of Indian broadcasting reform', in M.E. Price and S.G. Verhulst (eds), *Broadcasting reform in India*, pp. 1–21. New Delhi: Oxford University Press.

Parekh, B. 1995. 'Jawaharlal Nehru and the crisis of modernisation', in U. Baxi and B. Parekh (eds), *Crisis and change in contemporary India*, pp. 21–56. New Delhi: Sage Publications.

Paswan, R.V. 1996. *Working paper on national media policy (Paswan Committee).* Available online at http://www.indiantelevision.com/indianbrodcast/legalreso/Ramvilaspaswan.htm (downloaded on 14.11.2004).

Rahim, A. 1994. 'Impact of cable TV on Television and video viewing in Hyderabad: a survey', *Media Asia*, 21(1): 15–20.

Rajagopal, A. 2001. *Politics after television.* United Kingdom: Cambridge University Press.

(Rodrigues) Manchanda, Usha. 1998. 'Invasion from the skies', *Australian studies in journalism,* 7: 136–63.

(Rodrigues) Manchanda, Usha. 2005. 'Commercial influence on Indian public-service broadcasting', *Australian studies in journalism*, 15: 219–47.

Rogers, E.M. 1969. *Modernization among peasants: the impact of communication.* New York: Holt, Rinehart and Winston Inc.

Schramm, Wilbur. 1964. *Mass media and national development.* Stanford, California: Stanford University Press.

Sen, A. 1997. 'How India Has Fared'. *Frontline,* 14: (16), 9 August. Chennai: *The Hindu.* Available online at http://www.frontlineonnet.com/fl1516/14160350. htm (downloaded on 21.01.2005).

Servaes, J. and P. Malikhao. 2003. 'Development communication approaches in an international perspective', in J. Servaes (ed.), *Approaches to development: studies on communication for development,* pp. 1–38. Paris: UNESCO.

Sinclair, John. 2005. 'Globalisation and grassroots: local cable television operators and their household subscribers in India', *Media Asia,* 32 (2): 69–77.

Singh, J.P. 2003. 'Communication technology and development', in B. Mody (ed.), *International and development communication,* pp. 189–207. London: Sage Publications.

Singhal, A. and E.M. Rogers. 1989. *India's information revolution.* New Delhi: Sage Publications.

———. 2001. *India's communication revolution: from bullock carts to cyber marts.* London: Sage Publications.

Stevenson, R.L. 2003. 'National development and communications', *Encyclopedia of international media and communications,* 3 (0324): 1–13.

The World Bank. 1997. 'India—achievements and challenges in reducing poverty', povertynet library, The World Bank Group. Available online at http://poverty. worldbank.org/library/view/8680 (downloaded on 09.02.2005).

The Tribune. 2001. 'Welcome merger'. Available online at http://www.tribuneindia. com/2001/20011001/edit.htm (downloaded on 01.03.2005).

Varadan, K.A. 1991. 'Introducing competition in the electronic media'. Available on-line at http://www.indiantelevision.com/indianbroadcast/legalreso/kavaradan. htm (downloaded on 14.11.2004).

Verghese, B.G. 1978. 'Excerpts from 'major recommendations' of the working group on autonomy for Akashwani and Doordarshan'. Available online at http://www.indiantelevision.com/indianbroadcast/legalreso/verghesereport. htm (downloaded on 14.11.2004).

Interviews

Basu, Nupur. 2009. Former senior journalist, *NDTV.* Interviewed by author, Bangalore, 28 January 2009.

Mitra, Chandan. 2009. Editor, *The Pioneer.* Interviewed by author, New Delhi, 9 January 2009.

Mudgal, Vipul. 2009. Research Editor, *Hindustan Times*. Interviewed by author, New Delhi, 10 March 2009.

Ninan, Sevanti. 2009. Editor, *thehoot.org* and media commentator. Interviewed by author, New Delhi, 12 January 2009.

Sengupta, Arindam. 2009. Executive Editor, *The Times of India*. Interviewed by author, New Delhi, 12 January 2009.

Thapar, Karan. 2009. Host, Devil's Advocate, CNN-IBN. Interviewed by author, New Delhi, 12 March 2009.

Index

and process of localisation, 59–60
quality of journalism, fall in,
61–64
threat from internet, 65–66
public service broadcasting, 181–182
features of, 182
funding for, 183–185
geographic availability of, 182
in India, 257
autonomy for, 189–190
commercialisation of, 185–188,
193
as development communication
tool, 192
future of, 194–200
government control on,
192–194
Prasar Bharati Board and,
190–191
principle of, 191–192
role of, 182
public sphere, concept of, 108–109

Radio Audience Measurement
(RAM), 73
radio disc jockeying, 75–76
reverse migration, 158

Satellite Instructional Television
Experiment (SITE), 186
satellite television, 3, 14–15, 17, 187,
207, 247, 251
self-respect movement, 89
serials, portrayal of women in, 208
Shillong Accord, 129
STAR TV network, and localisation
policy, 16
Sun TV, 210

Swades, case study of, 161
domicile in India, 166–168
and Dual Citizenship Act,
167–168
invocation of tradition, 161–165
narrative of, 170–173
use of symbolism, 165–166
Swadeshi, concept of, xiii, 28

Tamil film industry and Sri Lankan
Tamils, nexus between, 92–94
Telecom Regulatory Authority of
India (TRAI), 70, 74
television in India, 21, 246–247,
261
competition and glocalisation of
programmes, 15–16
cultural imperialism, concept of,
6–7
de facto deregulation of, impact of,
19–21
economic reforms and satellite
television, 12–14, 29, 250–251
globalisation and, 8, 11–12
launching of, 4, 248
local cultures in global
environment, mixing of, 18
needs of Indian society and,
16–17
role of, 20, 247
and theory of development and
modernity, 4–6
transformation in, 3
television policy in India, 246–248.
See also television in India
commercialisation, and need
of regulatory framework,
253–256
historical events and, 248–251

About the Authors

Maya Ranganathan is currently a post doctoral research fellow at the National Centre for Australian Studies, School of Humanities, Communication and Social Sciences, Monash University, Australia. Her PhD with the issue of online nationalism continues to be part of her post doctoral research project. Since being awarded a PhD, her research interests have extended to media and identities, particularly in the context of Indian media. She has published widely on the subject, while working as faculty at the Manipal Institute of Communication, Karnataka, India between 2005–2007, in such reputed academic journals as *Nationalism and Ethnic Politics*, in newspapers and online journals. Prior to her PhD, she worked for 12 years with *The New Indian Express*, Chennai, in the newsroom as well as with their news bureau.

Usha M. Rodrigues is currently a senior lecturer of Journalism in Faculty of Arts and Social Sciences, University of the Sunshine Coast, Australia. Her PhD research project was based on the 'impact of private and foreign television on Indian news and news audiences'. The study was significant as it shed light on the burgeoning issue of how global competition can affect local content and public service broadcasting roles. She has published widely in the area of globalisation of media and its local impact, media policy, public service broadcasting, and journalism theory and practice. She has co-edited a book titled *Youth, Media and Culture in the Asia Pacific Region* (2008) and is currently undertaking research on community media. She has nearly 24 years of experience in journalism practice and journalism education, working and teaching across multimedia platforms—print, online and television. Her research interests are: Journalism theory and practice; global media; multimedia journalism and Asian media. Usha continues to freelance on media related issues for the Indian and Australian media.